ARCTIC APPRENTICE

by

Rob Ellis

Highgate of Beverley

Highgate Publications (Beverley) Limited
2007

Acknowledgements
Cover picture: Hull Trwlers leaving St. Andrew's Dock 1946 by Geoff Woolston (courtesy of
Jull Daily Mail).
Criterion by kinf permission of Paul Gibson.

British Library Cataloguing in Publication Data.
A catalogue record for this book is available from the British Library.

ISBN 9781 902645 49 0

Published by
Highgate of Beverley

Highgate Publications (Beverley) Limited
24 Wylies Road, Beverley, HU17 7AP. Telephone (01482) 866826

Produced by Highgate Print Limited
24 Wylies Road, Beverley, HU17 7AP. Telephone (01482) 866826

PREFACE

In the years 1946 to 1948, after the Second World War, the men and ships of the Humber ports returned to resume their trade of fishing the deep-sea banks of the Arctic waters, where six years' respite had allowed fish stocks to grow to huge proportions. The large fishing trawlers of Hull and Grimsby that returned from the war were better able to exploit these distant grounds than those of most other fishing ports, and the two quickly established themselves among the largest fishing ports in the world. Indeed, during the 50s and 60s, they constantly competed against each other for the title of the world's largest fishing port, one using the criteria of money earned from fish landed, the other claiming the title for quantity landed.

The trawler fleets of the two ports grew rapidly in size, power, sophistication and numbers, so that the ships and men soon became a source of pride and prestige to the local communities. Skippers and crews competed ever more recklessly to lead the field for recognition as the world's greatest fishers.

I came of age in this period and, coming from a seafaring family, it was inevitable that I should also harbour thoughts of going to sea, but not as a fisherman. I dreamt of entering the merchant navy as an officer cadet, as my elder brother had before me. I hoped to attend one of the nautical schools and eventually take my place as an officer and a gentleman, sailing the seven seas to exotic ports in the east and the south, attended by stewards while I practiced the art of navigation and ship handling.

Then the war intervened. Brought up mainly by my mother and my educated sisters, I was sheltered from most of the rough side of life. I also missed my chance to attend any of the nautical schools because we had to move away from Hull when our house was bombed. When we returned after the war my schooling years were soon finished. This left me, practically, with only one opportunity to go to sea, and that was to follow my father, a successful trawler skipper of some twenty-five years, into fishing. This was something that none of the family wanted me to do, aware as they were of the hardship and the fatalities endured in the profession.

To succeed at fishing I had to adjust to the severe conditions, and the rough ways of the fishermen, in order to be accepted. Yet I had to make these changes without conflicting with a rather genteel family.

Thrown in at the deep end – so to speak – this is the story of how I managed to lead this double life, and triumph. At the same time, the book strives to rekindle an era that is still dear to the memories of Hull people, before the rapid demise of a massive industry and community. I also hope the layman will find it informative of the complexities of deep-sea trawling.

THE AUTHOR

Dedication

To my friend Tony Jessop who inspired me in the first place to write this book and to my dear wife Patricia who has supported me to the end.

The Fishermen of England

Around the shores of England, that stretch towards the sea,
There dwelt an ancient people and they laboured mightily,
In Havens unfrequented that a busy life forgets,
The Fishermen of England are working at their nets.

In tiny vessels they defy the perils of the deep,
And scan the waters dreary waste with eyes that never sleep.
And when at night you safely lie in blankets snug and warm,
The Fishermen of England are riding out the storm.

And when the foes of England assail in fury blind,
The children of the storm arise and leave their nets behind,
With merry oath and laughter and a smile upon their lips,
The Fishermen of England go out to war in ships.

[from *The Rebel Maid* by Montague F. Phillips and Gerald Donson]

CONTENTS

Chapter 1

FIRST TRIP – ONE RUNG UP ALREADY

It was 1.45 in the morning, on 5 January 1950, as the taxi sped through the silent, well-lit streets of Kingston upon Hull. Other taxis cruised across and by us, as they rushed down the side streets collecting other fishermen to catch the tide.

Beside me in the back of the car sat the skipper of the ship I was to join, my father. He sat in characteristic pose, his elbow on the armrest, his chin propped up by the palm of his right hand, the little finger dragging down the corner of his right eyelid as he stared unseeingly out of the window, silently wrestling with his own thoughts as I was grappling with mine.

As the cab turned off the main Hessle Road into West Dock Avenue on its approach to the docks, I watched as the gaunt, grey, crowded buildings of my last school passed by. Only two or three weeks before, I had kicked a rugby ball around its narrow, paved playgrounds. Now, here I was on my way to my first job, where I knew the hours would be long and the conditions very hard in the distant Arctic Ocean.

I felt that my father didn't want this situation. It was my decision to make my career in fishing instead of the Merchant Navy, which would have been my first choice if circumstances had allowed. Against the wishes of my family, I had asked him to take me with him for my first trip, but he had refused to do so because, as he put it, he already had a good galley boy and he wasn't going to sack him for me. However, his gaffer had got wind of my request and had pressurised him to take me on as decky learner, thinking, I suppose, that like father, like son, I would eventually make a successful skipper. I had sailed twice before with my father, at the age of eleven and twelve, on pleasure trips during the summer holidays, just observing so to speak, and I had no training and little knowledge of deck work. But now the die was cast.

There was more activity now, the hollow clip-clop of bobbers' clogs could be heard as they strode singly and in pairs towards the dock to discharge the fish from the trawlers just arriving. I watched in awe as a young decky stood saying his last goodbyes to his girlfriend in the small porch of one of the back-to-back houses that lined the street. His forearm rested on the wall above her head, his other arm around her waist and one knee pressing between her reluctant thighs. Her silver dance-shoes glinted in the street-light as we passed. The crossing and passing of taxis at road junctions was much more frequent now. They were like bees buzzing to the hive as they rushed towards the tunnel under the railway lines that led to the dock, carrying their load in and streaming out empty from that dark orifice; except that bees don't work through the night.

The butterflies flapped wildly in my stomach, as our motor echoed hollowly through the dimly lit tunnel and climbed the cobbled road on the other side. It was like coming into another world. Here there was much more activity; the cars and taxis were crowded together now, queuing and squeezing past parked vehicles. Many men were milling around; there were steam-raisers and fitters in their boiler suits and elderly ship watchmen, with their belongings in sailcloth bags, waiting to board vessels not yet docked. The bobbers and fish porters clip-clopped their way round to the north or wet side of the dock, and a sizeable crowd of men milled around the fishermen's clothing store, where most of the taxis were endeavouring to set their passengers down and wait. Most of the group was made up of fishermen collecting their personal stores before joining their ships, but among them were scattered ship's runners and runner's mates ticking off the crew members as they arrived, some of them with friends who had come to hovel them, as they called it, while seeing them off.

Our car edged forward in the queue until my father saw Jack (Gibby) Gibson, the company ship's runner, and alongside him the bulky figure of Benny Cargill, his assistant. 'You'd better get out here and get some gear from the store,' said my father, turning to me. Struggling into his back pocket, he produced a £20 note. 'You'd better not run up a bill on your first trip. Take this, you can pay me back sometime when you can afford it.' He wound down the window and shouted, 'Hey, Benny!'

Both runners stepped forward and crouched down squinting into the darkened cab.

'Oh! Good morning, Skipper. Most of the crew are here. Only three or four more to come and I've sent taxis for a couple of 'em.'

'Good,' grunted Father. 'Here, Benny. Take young Bob into the store and make sure he gets all the gear he needs, and don't forget he'll want a bed.'

'Aye, aye!' grinned Benny. 'I'll see to it. Come on, young fella, let's get you fixed up.'

I stepped out into the crush of bodies and pushed my way into the store, followed by Benny as the car moved on taking my father directly to the ship.

Inside was my idea of a store, rather than a shop. A wide, polished counter, with only a couple of showcases at one end, stretched the full width of a very large room. Large, boxed-off shelves covered the whole of the wall behind the counter and a doorway led into another storeroom. In front of the counter, another crowd of men stood jostling and shuffling about on the bare wooden boards. There was quite a bit of laughter and banter from some of them, but a fair proportion were quiet and subdued at the thought of leaving their loved ones for three long weeks in the Arctic. All were trying to form into four unruly queues in front of the four brown-coated storemen, who were dashing about the various shelves, and slapping boots, oilskins and other waterproof clothes and accessories on the counter to be ticked off on the bill pads in front of them. I noticed some of the crewmen were swilling from bottles of beer and quite a few had half-drunk bottles of spirits dragging down their coat-pockets.

Benny gently nudged me towards the nearest queue. 'Get in there, kid, or you'll get pushed out and we haven't a lot of time to spare.'

I closed up behind a small, stubbly-faced man, who was swaying slightly as he stared down, concentrating on the cigarette he was rolling between rough, gnarled fingers, the tobacco pouch flap trapped neatly between the last two fingers of his right hand. When he finished, he turned uncomprehending, bloodshot eyes towards me and without a word extended his pouch, still dangling from his little finger, in my direction.

'No thanks, I don't smoke.' I smiled awkwardly, a little taken aback at the spontaneous generosity of a complete stranger.

'Doan shmoke?' He looked around at the grinning faces for confirmation that this was unusual.

'This your first trip, son?' An amused face grinned at me from the next queue.

'Yes,' I admitted.

'What are yer, galley boy?'

'No, decky learner.'

'A snacker on your first trip, this time o' year?'

'Well, I've done a couple of trips pleasuring.'

'Oh! You're an old hand then.' He guffawed at the lads around him. 'Well, I don't think you'll get much pleasure out of this one.' He roared again.

I felt very conspicuous among them, even though I had tried to dress similarly with a jersey under my old blazer. I vowed to get a white guernsey like most were wearing under their suits.

Benny, sensing my discomfort at finding myself the centre of attention, stepped forward with some news about an exceptional trip that was due that morning. This was always a good topic for discussion and I was left to my own doubtful thoughts.

I arrived at the counter surprisingly quickly and gave my name and ship. The storekeepers were certainly bursting a blood vessel to get these men away. The brown-overalled figure leaned expectantly over the counter, pencil poised, and stared pointedly at me. Benny closed up alongside me to assist in the ordering. I paused, trying to think what waterproofing I would need to stave off the ice-laden Arctic seas and sub-zero temperatures.

'Look sharp, sunshine, or we'll miss the tide,' blurted the impatient storeman. 'You don't want to join 'er in the river, do you?'

'Better give him an oilskin frock for a start,' chipped in Benny.

'What size?' snapped back brown-coat, scribbling on the pad.

I stared back at him helplessly.

'Stand up straight,' he said resignedly. 'By, you're bloody tall, even if you are skinny. Better give you a size seven, anything bigger and your shoulders 'll slip through the neck-piece,' he chortled.

To the oilskin smock, which all refer to as a frock because of its length, were added various other items, including a pair of thigh boots, a pair of white-wool fearnought trousers, a flat cap, three heavy-duty, fold-up gutting knives (three because Benny said I would probably throw the first two over the side when learning to gut fast), two pairs of woolly mitts and six pairs of thin cotton gutting gloves. The list completed, the storeman finished it off with a flourish and spun the pad round for me to sign.

'Wait a minute' said Benny. 'He'll need a bed.'

The storekeeper reversed the pad again with a groan. 'Flock bed or donkey's breakfast?' he said, pencil poised again.

'Donkey's breakfast?' I queried.

'A palliasse of straw, 7s. 6d.,' he responded.

'Better give him a proper mattress, if he's to get a decent sleep,' muttered Benny.

'After a couple of days' heavy fishing, he'll sleep where he stands.' The storeman grimaced and once again offered me the pad to sign.

'He's not signing, he's paying cash,' Benny interrupted.

I flashed the £20 note.

'Cash?' the assistant raised his eyebrows.

Once again the man from the next queue, seeing the note I flourished, chimed in: 'Fucking hell! If I had that much money, I wouldn't be going to sea at this time in the morning,' and he laughed out loud at his feeble joke.

I was beginning to feel that this excessive mirth was just false hilarity to hide their true feelings.

Once outside the store, my heart began to pound again at the sight of all the trawlers laying silently in a continuous line, sometimes two or three abreast along the dockside. Some had their deck lights on and belched a little smoke or steam from their funnels from time to time. These were the ships that would be sailing this tide.

I walked along in silence, my arms laden with clothing. Benny walked beside me, wheeling his bike, which supported my rolled-up bed on the seat, and keeping up a continuous chatter of advice, his words flowing out in puffs of steam in the bitingly cold night air. We walked on over the dew-varnished cobblestones which had been polished by the passing traffic. From across the darkened dock came the crash of wooden fish kits being set out for the ten-stone parcels of fish about to be landed from the newly arrived trawlers on that side. Finally Benny indicated with his outstretched arm a path between the bobbins and cables and trawl doors littering the quay. 'She's laid over there, alongside No.2 ice chute,' he said.

The *St Apollo* was different from the ships around her. She was newer, being only one year old, and the rake of her stem was greater, with a beautifully flared bow. She looked more streamlined compared with the bluff, squat shape of the other, older, vessels. Although her fo'c'sle still housed the deck crew forward, it was on deck level rather than down below. I admired the gentle curve of the wheelhouse front and the way it sloped back slightly to reduce wind resistance; also the housing beneath and the engine room casing behind were all nicely painted in mock-wood graining.

The skipper, mate and wireless operator were all that slept amidships; the galley staff, engine room staff and bosun slept aft, and the rest of the twenty-man crew, including myself, lived forward.

There was the gentle hum of machinery from somewhere down below as I stepped over the lowest part of the ship's rail amidships and stumbled on the twenty-inch steel bobbins that ran nearly the full length of the bulwarks. I dumped my newly acquired possessions on a dry part of the deck and turned to retrieve my bed from Benny.

'Here you are, Bob, you can manage now,' he said. 'I've got to get back to chase up the rest but I'll see you again before you go.'

I thanked him as he turned away. Someone staggered out of a doorway aft and began to urinate in the scuppers there. I started forward and bumped into the old watchman.

'You the old man's lad?'

I confirmed it was so.

'Well, he give me your kitbag to put in the fo'c'sle. I've lit a nice fire in there, so it's nice and warm for you all.' He gave me a gap-toothed grin.

'Thank you very much,' I beamed, and gave him a two-shilling piece from my change.

'Ta, mate.' He grinned again and tapped his cap peak as I moved on towards the forecastle. I swaggered a little to complete the impression of a seasoned deck-hand (galley boys lived aft).

I pushed my rolled-up bed through the narrow doorway and stepped over the high step into the hoodway, then into the accommodation. Two tiers of bunks lined the walls or bulkheads on either side of the room, nearly meeting to a point at the fore-end; a coal fire burned in the stove nearly in the centre; kitbags and oilskin bundles littered the floor and surrounding bunks, but only three men sat around the wooden forms adjoining the lower bunks. One I recognised from my pleasuring days as Arthur Medlam, a regular with my father for more than twenty years. Arthur was a short, squat fellow with hooded eyes and a mouth that sloped down at the corners. Showing a bottom set of brown, almost pointed, teeth, not unlike those of a cod, he sat with elbows on knees, staring into the fire.

The man sitting opposite, in contrast, was tall and angular with a lantern jaw and short-cropped greying hair. He spoke as I staggered in.

'Naa then! What have we got here? A new snacker by the look of it.'

Arthur looked up from the fire. 'Oh! It's young Bob, the skipper's lad.'

'Ugh! A spy in the camp then,' continued the tall one.

'Now Bill, none o' that,' said Arthur hastily. He turned to me again, 'So you've decided to join us then, in spite of my advice. You'll be sorry. Why didn't you get a nice, cosy job in the office?'

'No, I didn't fancy it,' I smiled. 'My dad wanted me to go on the market as a barrow boy and learn the job on the wet side. If I could learn all about buying and selling fish, he might have bought me a stand.'

'Fuck me,' blurted out the third man. 'You stupid cunt, you could have made a packet there, instead of swilling your arse at this lark. You ought to have your 'ead examined.'

'Yis, one t-trip out here in the winter and you'll soon change your mind,' added Bill, who was inclined to stutter at times. 'You better tell your old man you're thinking about it.' He swilled rum from the dram glass he was holding. 'Anyway, you'd better pick yourself a bunk and get changed. There'll be plenty of work for you to do when we get started.'

I looked around at the bunks either side of the fire. All of them seemed to have gear on them. Big Bill read my thoughts.

'They're all taken,' he said, 'there's only the thwartship ones left.'

These were either side of the door. I looked in the one nearest to me, it had old papers and magazines in the bottom of it. 'I can clear those out later,'

I thought, and thrust my bed into it. Right now I wanted to get out into the fresh air, away from the tobacco smoke and that strange mixture of smells I couldn't describe.

Once out on deck again, the night seemed colder still. A light breeze had sprung up and was whipping over the port rail and cutting across my face. I looked around the large fore-deck at the clutter of hides, cables, bobbins and other heavy gear waiting to be stowed as soon as we left. There was only one other occupant strolling around and kicking his heels, and looking as much out of place as I felt. He was young too, and a good bit smaller than I, but the blue around his unshaven mouth and chin suggested he was older.

'Hello!' I greeted him. 'You one of the crew?'

Hands in pockets, he glanced up at me without lifting his head.

'You decky learner?' he asked.

'Yes.'

'Well, I'm the other one,' he replied.

'Oh good,' I said. 'Well, you'll be able to show me the ropes. It's my first trip.'

'I shouldn't think so,' he muttered. 'It's my first trip too.'

'Oh well, I'm pleased to meet you. My name's Bob Grant. What's yours?'

'Charlie.'

'Charlie who?'

'Just Charlie,' he said.

'But what's your second name,' I pressed.

'Why?'

'Well, if ever I meet any of your mates, I'll need to know who they're talking about. There are loads of Charlies at sea, I expect.' I stopped abruptly. There was a pause.

'Chaplin.'

'Chaplin,' I blurted. 'Charlie Chaplin?'

'That's right,' he glowered.

'OK. Charlie. Let's go and see if there's any tea aft,' I moved in that direction thinking it had better be just Charlie from now on. If the rest of the blokes got hold of that name they'd be merciless.

As Charlie and I sauntered aft, we passed the old watchman helping a latecomer on board with his gear. I heard him say, 'I've lit a fire in the fo'c'sle. It's nice and warm for you all in there . . .' I should think lighting that fire would have been pretty rewarding for him.

We sampled some of the stewed tea in the large tin kettle on the corner of the galley stove. It didn't go down well with either of us. Most of the crew were in the mess-deck adjoining the galley, and it sounded like some of them were in the large cabin down below, where the officers messed. There was plenty of banter as they swapped stories of their wild escapades during their brief forty-eight hours ashore. Few of them took any notice of us. Then the mate's voice blasted down from the hooded companionway that led to the boat-deck, and he told us all to 'STAND BY, Third Hand on the bridge.' Everyone started to move out, still chattering, on to the deck; the third hand passed us with a wink and clambered up the steel rungs of the hoodway to the boat-deck, the shortest way to the bridge.

I made my way behind half of the crew to the fo'c'sle head; I wanted to see everything around the dock as we left. Charlie stayed aft with the bosun's gang to stand by the stern ropes.

There were other ships on the move now, with plenty of toots on the whistle as two little dock tugs fussed about, nosing each in turn towards the lock entrance.

At a command from the bridge, Benny threw our ropes off and we joined the throng. Everybody seemed to be on the move at the same time. It was just about high water; soon the tide would ebb and the lock gates would close. No one wanted to have to pen out or risk missing the tide.

Pretty soon we were passing through the lock, tight behind another ship. The men on the fo'c'sle head were kicking their heels and stamping their feet in an effort to keep out the cold. They looked down, quiet and subdued, at the few souls gathered on the dock entrance, just an occasional call as friends spotted each other: 'Morning, Sid . . . ', 'Cheers, Harry . . .', 'All the best . . .', 'Have a good trip . . .'.

The faces slipped by remarkably quickly as the ship cut quietly through the calm waters and out into the black river, the lights of the dock receding rapidly astern. Now I could feel a vibration under foot as the engines were increased to full speed, and a lifting feeling as the bow met the slight swell that was running up the river to meet us, occasionally nudging the bigger wave hard enough to make one stagger. The hiss and swish of the bow wave could also be heard as the St Apollo built up her full speed of twelve and a half knots. I was startled by the harsh voice of the mate as he turned from his stance in the eyes of the ship and strode quickly aft towards the whaleback ladder, barking orders right and left. 'Put these mooring ropes down below. Don't try and secure them up here this time o' year; they'll gather too much ice. And you better cement that anchor cap; it'll be long enough before we need it again.'

The crew seemed reluctant to acknowledge the mate or accept that the trip had indeed begun and this was the man who would be giving them most of their orders throughout. They chose instead to talk past him at each other, but obeying his commands nonetheless.

'Where are we gunna put these ropes, then?' asked Jim, a Grimsby fisherman who had found his way across the river. 'Does he want 'em down the 'old?'

'Naw, they'd be on top of everything,' said big-nosed Jackie Brown. 'They go in the outside shithouse.'

'Oh, typical. If anyone wants to crap in there then they've had it.'

'Don't worry, you won't want to crap in there when we get up north. As soon as you drop your keggs in there you'll freeze your bollocks off.'

Both men were pulling back bights of rope to pass the end down on deck. I had stepped forward unsteadily to help, when Charlie's head appeared at the top of the fo'c'sle ladder.

'Come on, Bob,' he shouted. 'Bosun sez we've to grease the brasswork.'

'Grease it?'

'Yeah, come on. It'll take us long enough in this ship, by what I've seen.'

Tide Time.

St. Andrew's (North Sea) Dock.

I followed Charlie aft along the deck.

'Look at all these portholes,' he said. 'There must be about thirty of 'em altogether. And have you seen all the brass handrails on the monkey island on the bridge top and those massive engine-room banjos (vents). The bosun says we've to use bollard grease and we'll get it off the engineers. I've seen a box of cotton waste in the liver house. I'll get some of that. You go down the engine room.'

I looked down the long engine-room ladder before starting down; it passed through a platform grating. The tremendous thump from the massive triple-expansion steam engine was quite deafening as the great piston conrods whipped round at 120 revs a minute. I stared in fascination at the flashing highlights of the oil-varnished metal and the terrific movement that suggested such frightening power as I descended into the cacophony of sound and heat.

Only the fireman was apparent as he came into the engine room from the stokehold, wiping his hands on some cotton waste, the inevitable sweat rag around his neck. He canted his head and offered an ear as I shouted what I wanted and what I wanted it for.

'BOLLARD GREASE?' he repeated. I nodded. He tossed his head and pursed his lips in an exaggerated flinch. Grinning, he pointed to some fourteen-pound kegs wedged behind a generator platform.

'Take the first one,' he bellowed.

Returning to the comparative quiet at the top of the engine room, I found Charlie in the galley, holding two great bundles of waste in each hand.

'Better get a spike or knife or something to open the tin.'

When we did get the lid off, we found a very thick oil that more resembled tar than grease.

'Well, one thing's for certain. I'm getting changed before I handle that,' said Charlie, 'and you'd better do the same.'

Ten minutes later and we were both clumping back on deck, sporting our lovely, new, white-woollen fearnought trousers.

'We'd better start at the top and work down,' Chas suggested.

I agreed, so we climbed the ladder to the bridge veranda and from there on up to the top of the wheelhouse, dragging the fourteen-pound tin with us. The trouble was once up there we could see nothing. It was still only four in the morning and in January you don't get much light at that time. What you do get is plenty of cold, especially when you are steaming down a river towards the open sea.

What little light reflected up from the deck where the men were working was barely enough to show us outlines, but even so the effect the cold was having on the toffee we were trying to spread was soon apparent. The waste, made up of cotton fluff and threads, soon began to break up in our hands and stick to the glue-like substance we were trying to smear on the brass. I was thinking that come daylight it would provide a pretty sight of white, fleecy handrails and vents, which might not be appreciated by the bosun, but Charlie was pressing on and I had to do the same. The ship was rushing on towards the sea, and the increased movement in the vessel as she met the larger swell was already making it difficult to stand on these higher reaches.

We had to make several visits to the galley to heat the tin on the stove and make the grease workable, but eventually the job was done, although we were the last to finish and scurried forward thankfully into the nodding fo'c'sle to prepare our beds.

I had barely an hour's rest before one of the watch clumped in to announce it was 7 o'clock and time for breakfast.

There was much more movement in the ship now, and the bow was diving and thumping regularly into the larger oncoming seas. I was tired and weary but I was also hungry. I knew that there was only half an hour to eat before the day's work started and so I forced myself to roll out over the jolting bunk board to dress.

Daylight had not yet broken as I looked out over the dripping fore-deck; occasional sprays whipped over the starboard bow and swept across the fore-end of the ship, as she dipped her head into the larger of the rolling seas. I timed my run with one of the other deck-hands and scampered aft, hooking my arm over the man-rope, which now stretched from fo'c'sle to winch, trying to reach the lee of the bridge housing before the next spray caught me, and leaping up on to the raised deck in the waist of the ship to reach blessed shelter from the whipping spume.

I ran on. The vessel dipped its head into the next trough and lurched to port. The scupper ports scooped up a dollop of water from the racing wave tops and shot it across the deck, hitting my clumping boots and nearly knocking my feet from under me. Only the support of the handrail on the casing side prevented me from going down while I kept going to the comparative safety of the slightly higher after-end. As I slowed to a walk approaching the alleyway leading to the after accommodation, I came upon two or three of the men who had preceded me, now urinating into the scuppers.

How uncouth and unnecessary, I thought, particularly as we had just left one toilet forward and the other one was just inside the companionway. I stepped into this small compartment on to a wooden grating and tried to concentrate on hitting the pan as the ship continued to butt its way into the oncoming rollers. But with the powerful engines beneath me still pulsing at maximum speed and causing her to lurch and buck, throwing my left shoulder against one bulkhead and then my right against the other, I was beginning to see the wisdom of my shipmates' choice of ablutions.

The crew's mess-deck took up most of the accommodation on deck level aft, situated aft of the galley, with a connecting serving hatch. It was just a large, square cabin, completely filled by a large table surrounded by polished lath benches along the bulkheads, with a fold-down bench at the galley end, allowing you to walk past the serving hatch. When I arrived there after stumbling in my cumbersome thigh boots over every high-stepped doorway, it was already occupied by the other two 'daymen' (I was the third), the relieving deck watch and the relief fireman. The smell of bacon, sausage and tomato already had the saliva welling in my mouth, and the others were already tucking into their breakfast, with only an occasional word of banter so early in the morning.

I climbed over the back of the fireman to the first empty seat and turned over my soup plate (soup plates only were used on trawlers to stop the gravy or juices from running off the plates in a constantly moving ship). I reached over and pulled the nearest oval tin platter towards me, but the bacon had been well picked over; only the fattiest pieces were left and they were awash in grease. The sausages too had been baked in the oven and were floating in an inch of fat. But I filled my plate anyway and spooned some tinned tomatoes from an enamel jug.

Of course, stuttering Bill Steech had to have his say, 'Yuh-you didn't need to get so m-much. By the look of this weather, you'll be eating it twice, once going down and once c-coming back up.' He leered from across the table. I chose to ignore him, took a slice of bread from the nearest package and stood up to scrape some butter from the metal dish in the middle of the table. As I withdrew to my seat the decky next to me slashed his knife across mine, neatly took the butter off and began to spread it on his own bread – to the merriment of all.

'You're bigger than me, kid,' he chortled. 'You can reach better.'

I repeated the process with the same result, in spite of my attempt to dodge him; but he had sufficient now and my third attempt was not challenged.

The food was not particularly to my liking, but it was good enough and my hunger carried it down, in spite of the strong tobacco that some of the men were now smoking. But I had not been taught to eat quickly and my plate was nowhere near empty when Bill Steech stood up. Pointing at the clock, which showed 7.30, he sneered, 'Come on, you've had your time, let's have you for'ard and do some work.' He snatched his cap and, stuffing his pouch into his doeskin trouser-pocket, moved off with his straddled walk and exaggerated dip at the knee, Charlie in tow and me scampering after them.

Out on deck, the bow was plunging deeper now in the strengthening wind, throwing out a great lace collar of white water with every thump into the incessant rollers. Ahead of us Big Bill indicated with a glance over his shoulder and a flap of his hand that Charlie and I should keep close to the engine room casing as we moved along the lee deck. When we approached the winch in front of the bridge there was only the open fore-deck before us and Bill paused to brief us, shouting above the hiss of the sprays thrown up by the tossing ship's head and whipping periodically across the deck. In order to avoid getting wet, the idea was to time your run when the last of the spray was drifting over the lee rail and before the bow dived into the next watery hill. With speed one could reach the shelter of the fo'c'sle hoodway on the ascendancy, while the scooped-up sea still hung on the fo'c'sle head.

Bill, his head cocked over into the wind to shield his face, edged to one side and put his hand in the small of Charlie's back. 'Now,' he shouted, and with a thrust sent Charlie dodging round the winch barrel on to the fore-deck. Another thrust sent me right behind him. Charlie's boots clumped splay-footed up the slimy deck, water flying from the dripping man-rope as his hand slid along it to steady him. My legs pistoned in pursuit, my eyes squinting and flinching from the gusting wind. Our knees nearly buckled as the ship raised itself for the next head-butt into an oncoming trough; then the deck disappeared beneath us as that wicked ship took an extra deep dive just to taunt us. One minute we were running in air, then the deck came up like a big dipper and we crumpled in a heap, just short of our haven. The water poured down on us from the fo'c'sle head as we scrambled over the doorstep. We hung on gasping and spluttering in the shelter of the hoodway, as the violent motion of the ship steadied down and the water cleared from the deck. A minute later, Bill shot through the door, comparatively dry, but with a look of disgust on his face.

'You pair of cunts. What a time to doss down when you're going for'ard. You better look sharp and get dried off. The bosun'll be coming soon and he won't stand you frolicking with your aqua sports.'

He pushed past us to the inner hatch and descended the ladder to the net-hold. Soon after, while we were changing, the bosun came forward with one watchkeeper. Pausing only long enough to poke his head in the fo'c'sle, he gave us a toothless cackle and then a sharp, 'Play smart, you loafers, let's have you down below,' before disappearing into the hold.

It's hard to describe the misery of that morning down the hold; so many things contributed. It was not just the fact that the men were intent on ridicule, taking the mick and making me feel inadequate, as indeed I was. I should have got my sea legs as a galley boy, and I was under age anyway, but it was the sheer squalor of the conditions. I had been to sea pleasuring twice before and was sick on both occasions, but I got over it after a couple of days. So, while not obsessed with sea-sickness, I was wary of it.

Wooden boards divided up the hold into net-pounds, which were full to overflowing, leaving space down the centre where we were supposed to work. But that too was cluttered with bundles of new net and large coils of rope, wires and shackles, which the shore gang had just dropped down the hatch, so we spent the first half hour clearing a space to work in. All the time, the ship kept rising and dropping eight or ten feet at a time, sometimes coming down so quickly that your stomach was still going up when the rest of your body was on its way down, lifting that greasy breakfast I'd eaten right up to the base of my throat.

Each dive ended with a tremendous thump as the next sea struck the outside of the bare plates at head height either side of us. With no panelling or insulation to muffle the sound, it resonated so loud it was like working inside a contorting big bass drum. At every dip, shackles slid along the stowage bars where they were hung, steel bobbins clashed together, iron crowbars and other ironware tipped, collapsed and clattered, and the eight inches of foul-smelling water at the after-end of the hold rushed and swished from side to side, all adding to the misery. I was finding it difficult to stand without support, as with each drop the ship would kick to one side or the other. I could ride the cakewalk at Hull Fair, showing off to the girls, with both hands in my pockets, but this was something else. I wouldn't want them to see me now. The mixture of smells that fouled my nostrils in this floating dungeon came from many sources: from the sisal and manila of the nets and ropes, the aroma of hemp and tarred twine, numerous oily smells, and the stench from old net infested with dried seaweed and particles of rotting fish.

We were to fix some net for the new trawls, but that needed vast amounts of space and we only had room (or so the bosun decided) to lace some rope down the bellies, the middle or tunnel part of the trawl. Charlie and I filled some needles with twine, while the men hung up the net and spliced eyes in the rope. The twine, dry and rough, soon chafed my soft-skinned fingers and made them raw. As a result, the needles I filled were slack and quickly brought a stream of abuse from the bosun.

'What the fuck do you call this, you dozy knucklehead?' He held up the offending article. 'What do you think you're doing? Winding wool for your mother's knitting?'

I sniggered timidly; he mimicked me exaggeratedly.

'It's nothing to laugh at,' he bellowed. 'I've a good mind to ram this up your arse and stuff some sense into yer. Now pull the bastards tight.'

Bill Steech chipped in. 'W-what do you expect, with someone who's never been away from his mother's apron strings. I s-s-should think this is the f-first time he's had his hands out of his pockets.'

'Or out of his dad's pockets more like,' chortled big-nosed Brown.

The ship gave an extra big lurch throwing me off balance. My outstretched hand found only a bundle of soft net, which gave no support, and I fell, striking my face on some jockey irons which were hung on the dividing boards, chipping a tooth and bruising my cheek. As the violent motion continued, the weakness in my stomach erupted and I dashed, retching, for the hold ladder. My feet stumbled up the iron rungs to the accompaniment of jeers from below. As the saliva welled up in my mouth, I rushed tight-lipped for the toilet, not wanting to put my head out of the hoodway door in full view of the bridge.

Wrenching the toilet door open, I stooped and grasped both sides of the metal toilet bowl, and my half-digested breakfast gushed forth, my hands hanging on to support my trembling knees. The sight and smell of the tomato and half-digested sausage caused me to empty all, until there was nothing left but yellow bile; and still the ship performed trying to shake me from this degrading sanctuary. Oh, God! Was there nowhere on this ship that was still, where I could rest my aching limbs and calm my stomach? I was feeling a little better now, with nothing left in my tummy to erupt. The sickness was subsiding and I just remained there, kneeling over the pan, panting and slavering; my skin was cold and clammy but my strength was gradually returning.

Still feeling far from well, I made my way sheepishly back down the hold, to be totally ignored as I returned to my duties. I could see that Charlie was far from comfortable; probably the difference in years was enabling him to grit his teeth and hang on to his self-respect.

Suddenly the bosun straightened up from his task with an exasperated sigh, rove the rest of the twine from the needle in his hand and, cursing, began to refill it.

'Hey, Green Gills!' he spat out at me. 'You'd better pack that in. These fucking things that you're filling are useless, like you. And, anyway, we don't need two snackers filling needles. You can grease the new shackles. Get a tin of barrel grease off the shelf, and you'll find a crocodile spanner behind the ladder to loosen them with. Make sure you do every one and hang 'em on that bar above your 'ead.'

The morning watch dragged on, the continuous motion sapping my depleted strength, and when the men lit up their strong, hand-rolled cigs, even Charlie moved quickly towards the ladder with a strangled remark about going for a piss. At last, dinner was called and the gang scrambled out of the hold and made their way aft to get their victuals, but I couldn't face the dash along the deck, and the smell of cabbage water and greasy roast potatoes I knew would greet me, I turned instead towards the fo'c'sle and, kicking my rubber boots off, scrambled gratefully into my bunk for half an hour's desperate rest. But in my weakened state the lack of sleep from the night before overwhelmed me and I fell into a deep, exhausted sleep. In my dreams, I was vaguely aware of someone shaking me and remonstrating, but with the rolling of the ship it all swirled round in my head like smoke, and blackness descended again.

Suddenly I was awake, my limbs were stiff but the ship was comparatively steady, the water now only tinkling and lapping on the hull, accompanied occasionally by the creak of the timbers within. The fo'c'sle was in darkness, apart from the glow from the fire in the stove. I lifted myself up on one elbow and looked around the dimly lit fo'c'sle. All was quiet, makeshift curtains drawn across most of the bunks, where men were in slumber. I rested my cheek on the high bunk sideboard; there was a stab of pain, and suddenly yesterday's events came back to me with a shock. I was still wearing my watch. It showed 1.40 a.m. I had been in my bunk since lunchtime; I had not completed my work. I had disgraced myself and my father. What must the men think of me? What would they say when I faced them in the morning?

I tumbled out of my bed onto the seat locker and searched in the semi-darkness for my boots. I was, of course, still dressed and my mouth was foul. I needed a drink and a wash, but my main concern was to see if those remaining shackles still needed greasing or if the job had been done by someone else. The lights were still on in the hold and things had been moved around, but the bundles of shackles were still being lapped by the pool of water on the after-end of the hold floor. For an hour I worked away, happy to be making up some of my deficiencies, though some of the shackles had been corroded with the water and needed belting.

I was startled by a voice from the ladder. 'NOW THEN! What are you up to, trying to get in a bit of overtime or what?' It was Jackie Brown; the bosun's watch was obviously back on.

'No,' I blurted, 'I just thought I'd better finish this job as I didn't get it done yesterday.'

Jackie gave me a wry smile. 'Well I'm just going to call the 3 o'clock watch, so you'd better get yourself turned in or you'll be knackered again tomorrow.' With that he disappeared up the ladder. In a while, I heard the next watch turn out. Soon after I finished; I had a drink of water from the bathroom, which was foul, then stripped off my clothes and turned in for three blissful hours.

At breakfast the next morning, my appetite had returned, but this time I was more selective with what I ate. Nevertheless Bill Steech couldn't resist pointing out that I hadn't yet earned what I was eating. Jackie Brown had turned out for his breakfast and he stood up for me, pointing out that I had tried to make up for my failings through the night.

'And s-s-so he s- should,' snarled Bill. 'I reckon it was shame did that and ash-shamed he should be, leaving his work to other people. But he'll earn his keep today down the fishroom, I'll see to that.'

Bill was as good as his word. We worked all day down the fishroom, stacking boards on the shelves, shipping up the fish-pounds and sweeping them out, and cracking ice to lay on the bottoms. As dayman, Bill was also fishroom man. The ultimate responsibility for stowing the fish belonged to the mate, but in his absence Bill was in full charge down the fishroom and he exercised that right to the full. At the end of the day, once again, my bunk was the big attraction.

On the third day steaming we entered the Arctic Circle. Being January it had been cold all the time, but now the frost bit really hard, pinching at the nose and cheeks and paralysing the fingers. We were working on the deck, lacing the new trawl to the ground bobbins. The biting wind was so cold I could not hold the needles, so I took to filling needles with mittens on, which amused most but annoyed some. However, I coped better than I would have done without, at least most of the time. Even the men were feeling the cold, and the skin on *their* hands was like leather. They soon showed me how to buff my hands to make the blood flow and restore the feeling.

As time went on, Charlie and I came in for plenty of verbal abuse from the men because when lacing they tended to use the needles faster than we could fill them, especially as we were expected to fetch and carry whatever they needed as well. The men were stretched along the deck, so we had to split up. I worked more towards the fore-end while Charlie, as he had done when we first sailed, worked aft, the bosun's domain. I observed Charlie working in the confines of the narrow after-deck, harassed and confused, as I was, by the strange orders barked at him by various individuals. Although in his twenties, he looked like a young boy, dressed in a large rollneck guernsey and smock, with his thick, woollen fearnought trousers, two sizes too big for his slim body, stuck out at the back. As I watched him, the bosun, pointing his finger down the deck, snapped at him, 'Hey, slack arse! Pass me the end of that rope.'

Charlie, his feet hampered by net, wires, basket and bobbins, grabbed the nearest bight of the rope indicated and dragged it towards the bosun. Not good enough. 'THE END, I said. THE END,' screamed the bosun. 'The place where there's fuck all past!'

Even the abuse was tinged with humour, although it was somewhat degenerate.

It was another long and tiring day, but after tea (everyone turned out for the evening meal) I stayed back to listen to the stories and take stock of my shipmates.

The seats around the mess-deck table were pretty full. The officers ate separately down below in the cabin, but all the deckies were there from the third hand down, with the exception of the two who had just gone on watch. Having finished the day's work and fed well, all were in a happy mood, enjoying their favourite pastime, swapping stories of their exploits ashore and of previous trips shared with some of the characters that adorn the fishing fraternity in Hull.

To survey them you could see that these men were a hard lot, committed to a hard dangerous job. They would give no quarter if they were not inclined, and yet it was well known that they were very generous to their fellow men and fun loving, having to indulge in pranks and chiding to amuse themselves. It was noticeable that most were heavy-shouldered, with forearms that Popeye might have envied, proof of the heavy lifting and pulling on ropes and nets that the job required. The swollen veins on the back of the hands of the older men showed how long they had been at it. Tattoos were predominant, even on the arms of young Freddie Nottsworth, a previous decky learner in the ship, who had been promoted to spare hand and was popular with the crew because he knew his job, worked hard and was always cheerful, though often cheeky.

Jim Mullett, the kindly third hand, was telling a story about one of the well-known characters he had sailed with in another ship, a decky called Bunny. A distorted little figure of a man with long arms, a hump on his back and a cast in his eye, Bunny was also credited with being well endowed sexually. Apparently the incident took place when trams were still running in the city. Bunny was riding a tram that ran the length of Hessle Road from Dairycoates to Osborne Street, where the tram had to slow down to take a right-angled turn. Bunn rang the bell for the stop just before the turn and moved up front to stand on the platform alongside the driver. The tram slowed down approaching the curve, then once around it accelerated away again.

Bunny glared at the driver. 'Hey up, there! What's the game? I wanted to be off at that stop,' he snapped.

The driver, startled, glowered in return. 'Well, you should have jumped off, when I slowed down.'

'Jumped off! Jumped off !' repeated Bunny, jerking his thumb over his shoulder. 'This in't a fucking parachute, you know.'

Bunny it was, who also featured in the next story. Hounded on deck one day by a bucko mate, being overworked and spot-balled, Bunny had a pee in a corner of the deck, omitted to return his tackle to his trousers and worked the next few minutes with it swinging about, until spotted by the mate.

'What the hell are you larking at?' he remonstrated.

'Well, if you're going to work me like a fucking horse, I might as well look like one,' retorted Bunny.

The stories got spicier as the night wore on and, having led a rather sheltered life, I sat in awe at the abandoned lewdness of the tales. The growing movement of the ship indicated that the weather was deteriorating again and the older men recommended that we younger ones should get for'ard before it got any worse.

It was pitch black on deck, but the watch put the floodlights on for us. Even so the journey forward was precarious because the deck was glassy and slush ice was forming everywhere. Once in the fo'c'sle, the increased rise and fall of that swing boat had my tummy feeling queasy again, and I was thankful to climb into that blessed bunk once more. The night was a restless one for me. The ship was doing more rolling this time, rather than pitching, and mine was the thwartship bunk. I was continually sliding up and down, first on my head, then on my heels, until my side ached and the wind outside increased to a howl. In the early hours I was suddenly startled as the fo'c'sle door burst open. There was a scrape of oilskins past my bunk and the fo'c'sle light switched on. Then came the dreaded words from the watchkeeper, 'Down Trawl'.

Chapter 2

BAPTISM OF ICE

Everyone stirred at once groaning and grumbling. As I swung down onto the seat locker, I was suddenly aware that the ship had slowed down for the first time since we had left Hull. The powerful throb of the engines was missing and the movement of the ship was slower; the rush of the bow wave too had eased to an occasional hiss.

'You want your woollies on this morning, lads,' said the watchkeeper, who was now stoking the stove. 'She's like a Christmas cake out there. It's been freezing hard all night. I reckon we'll be chopping for a while before we get the gear down.'

Men were hurrying past me now, wrapping their mufflers around their necks and dragging their best frocks and oilskins with them. I too was picking out my heaviest clothes, including a sou'wester; I knew I would need something to keep my ears warm and the wind off my face. I hurried out with the rest of them, intending to get myself a drink of hot, sweet tea before turning to.

The sight that greeted me was staggering. How could so much ice have formed in such a short time? All the lights were on, including floodlights, and against the inky blackness of the Arctic night the deck and superstructure stood out brilliant white. The bridge front was caked several inches thick in the stuff; only the black holes of the windows, where the heat from within and constant attention from the watch had prevented ice from forming, spoiled the continuity of the white cocoon. I was fascinated by the grotesque shapes that were formed by the frozen mass on the deck fittings; even the electric cables that ran from the floodlights we had suspended above the deck earlier were swollen to a diameter of six or seven inches. Great ice baubles hung from the rigging, formed by a single sitting of twine or strand of yarn. All this I took in very quickly as I hurried aft, sliding my feet over the glassy deck.

In the mess, the men sat hunched around the table, most of them in silence, cuddling their pots of tea and puffing occasionally on their tobacco rolls, staring blankly into space, each envisioning the cruel task ahead.

Bill Steech glanced up when I walked in. 'God, look at death warmed up. Those eyes are like piss holes in the snow. What have you been doing? Playing with yuhself all night?'

Jim Mullett, the third hand, chipped in quickly, in his sympathetic way. 'Find yourself a mug, lad, and get some tea out of the kettle. It'll be some time before you get another chance.'

Suddenly, I didn't want to be a part of this. It didn't seem to be the right conditions for catching fish, and it seemed unreasonable to me to even try with the ship frozen over as it was. I thought of the deck and the winch and the running gear, an unrecognisable frozen mass; even the trawl net lashed along the bulwark rail was hardly visible, encased in the cement-hard icing.

Typical icing conditions.

A Christmas cake indeed, but there would be nothing sweet about it. Chopping that lot away and shovelling it over the side was going to be a mammoth job in the biting cold, probably taking all hands several hours. No, I didn't fancy this at all!

I thought of my father on the bridge, whose decision it was to do all of this, and I began to wonder why he should choose to shoot at this time. But then common sense took over and I realised he could hardly steam around until winter was over. The owners and the markets expected fish and this is where it was, so he too was a victim of the system. Just then old Arthur Medlam stepped into the mess-deck; being slower and more deliberate in his movements he was the last to arrive, trailing his oilskin over his arm. In one hand he carried a drooping mug that slopped tea out of it, in the other was his sou'wester and mittens. His bleary eyes were watering, probably from the icy wind.

Arthur was only small and his once broad shoulders were rounded now after forty-three years at sea, but he seemed quite unconcerned about what was to come. All this was normal to him and he started chiding Bill Steech. 'I suppose that's your third pot of tea, Steechy? Only dregs and tea leaves for the rest of us. Trust you to be first in at the back there.'

Bill started stuttering and spluttering as he always did when he tried to rush his words. 'W-well, w-we can't all f-f-ff- hang around for doddering old b-bastards like you to s-stagger along, else we'd never get 'ere, you moaning old bugger.'

'No, but you'll hang around for an old bastard like me, when it's time to go on deck,' retorted Arthur. He stifled a smirk and his face was expressionless, but there was a twinkle in those watery eyes as he threw his gear on to a bench and concentrated on sipping his tea.

Arthur's casual approach to the situation had made me feel guilty. This old man should surely find it more difficult than I to combat the cold and arduous conditions, even though I was only fifteen and my body had not yet fully developed. I was long and lanky, standing five feet eleven inches, but my limbs were painfully thin in comparison to the rest of the men and my hands were still soft and tender. My skin was not weather hardened, but still my lungs were big and fresh and I was agile; I should be able to fight off the cold.

No more time now for reflections, the mate and bosun came in to the mess and stood side by side. The bosun carried two large ice axes in his hands, the mate a large new crocodile spanner. 'Right let's have yer, then,' said the mate. 'Let's get rid of this ice as quickly as we can so we can earn some money. Young Freddie, you whip down to the chief and tell him to start the donkey pump and give us plenty of hot water on deck. The rest of yer get for'ard and get some more croc' spanners or hatch battens or anything heavy to knock this ice off with.'

'Tell you what, Les,' piped up Grimmie, coming out of a doze. 'I reckon the quickest way to get rid of this ice is to steam south. Couldn't you have a word with the old man?'

'What's de matter, Grimmie? Can't you handle a bit of ice? You should have been born in it as I vas.' This last came from Falk Amunsen, a half Swede who was grinning through the galley hatch.

'All right, cut the cackle and move.' Les raised his voice at the end. Without any more complaint we moved.

Back forward again, with my sou'wester pulled well down over my ears and my woollen mittens on over thin cloth gutting gloves, I found a heavy crowbar in the corner of the iron foundry locker and trooped on to the deck, where the ice was already flying from the attentions of the many figures there. I moved over to the starboard rail, which seemed to be getting no attention. With a hefty swing, I took an almighty thwack at the ice encrusted there and was delighted to see it shatter and fly. I repeated this process all the way down the rail, the ice breaking away easily from the solid smooth bulwark.

Next I tried the same on the net that was lashed alongside it, but that was not so obliging. The base was not so solid and the crowbar only cracked the ice slightly and bounced off, so I soon lost interest in that target and looked around for another solid steel base. I spotted the gallows bar above my head and took a wallop at that, but the ice shattered down into my face, cutting my nose and nearly blinding me. I began to pick out odd shapes that stuck out from the mast and rigging and enjoyed cracking them to find out the cause, but my little game and aimless meandering was spotted by the mate.

'Now then, young Dasher. What are you playing at? We're not trying to make the ship look pretty you know, we're trying to get the gear down. If you can't find anything better to do you'd best get a shovel from the fishroom and clear some of this broken ice off the deck so we can stand. Either throw it over the side or push it through the scuppers.'

Young Dasher! It was the first time anyone had called me by my father's nickname. I soon acquired a shovel from the fishroom and set about the task of clearing the now heaped-up ice from the deck, but this was less enjoyable work. It was more difficult to keep your feet on a slippery, moving deck when you are bent over with a full shovel, and the cold was getting to me now. My new oilskin frock crackled in the brittle air and stood out from me like an iron casing. It was difficult to put my arms down by my sides. I felt like a cross between the Tin Man from the Wizard of Oz and the Michelin man. To make matters worse, the decky hosing down the winch with the hot-water hose (you couldn't use axes or battens on that) managed to dowse me with it, soaking my mitts. This was nice enough initially, but when the heat went out of the water it let the cold in more intensely. First the muscles of my hands became paralysed so that I could hardly hold the shovel, and then the pain began to bite.

I became aware that my whole body was succumbing to the blistering cold. I tried to buff my arms around my shoulders as I'd been shown, but the stiff oilskin prevented it. The frost was pinching at my face and I couldn't feel my nose. I remembered reading how some Antarctic explorers had lost their noses through frost bite for not massaging them, so I rubbed mine on the back of my mitten but that made matters worse. If only I could get off the deck for a few minutes to warm up. I suddenly thought of the fo'c'sle fire; it was the decky learner's job to look after it when all hands were on deck. Making my way forward towards the accommodation, I passed Steechy on the way.

'Where do you think you're going?' he growled.

'I'm just going to stoke up the fire, Bill,' I replied.

'Don't bother, kid,' he snapped. 'The other snacker's just done it.'

Damn! Trust Charlie to be one jump ahead in this situation.

I took off my mittens, wrung the water out of them and blew vigorously into my painful frost-crippled hands.

'Work a bit harder, kid, if you want to keep warm,' were Bill's only comforting words. I slouched back across the deck to my shovel.

The skipper shouted from the bridge and instructed the mate to work a tea break. Les looked up in surprise. This was unusual with the gear still laid on deck; maybe my father had spotted my distress and this was his way of easing the situation without favouring me.

'Right, Bogey,' shouted the mate. 'Take half of them and get a ten-minute drink.'

The bosun, I suppose naturally, took the half of the crew that had worked aft with him on our departure, which included Charlie and did not include me. The rest of us bent to our tasks. A few minutes later there was a banging from the winch. They had got the steam through to it and it was turning over. They began to heave things about the deck, prising some of the gear out of the ice. I noticed one of the men working at the winch slide his mittened hands over the steam cylinder; they sizzled from the heat within. I decided to work nearer the winch.

Just then a yelp, followed by a curse, came from the other side of the deck. It was Bill Steech

Jackie Brown was at the port winch barrel, heaving a coil of cable aft on the Gilson wire, when the hook hung up on a bollard rail and came up standing, causing the mast to shake and bringing down the ice from above, which rained great lumps on to the deck. Bill Steech was uncoiling the Derrick Gilson wire from the rigging, when one large sliver of ice hit him on the head and shattered. 'Hey, up there. W-what the fuck we doing?' bellowed Bill, glaring at Jack and rubbing his head. 'Why the hell don't you warn people when you're heaving on something?'

'Sorry, Bill,' grinned Jack.' 'Still, if it was your head, there'll be no harm done.' And he laughed out loud.

Bill was clearly furious. As fishroom man it was his job to use the wires on the port side and Jack had jumped in while he was busy.

Meanwhile I had just thought of an excuse to work alongside the starboard winch cylinder when I spotted the bosun's gang straggling back on deck. They didn't seem too happy but none of them spoke when they passed me. On the mate's order the rest of us trooped aft to get our drink.

By now my fingers were so painful that to touch anything sent a shock up my arm, so I stumbled aft with my hands hanging loose inside my soggy mitts, avoiding gripping anything and just steadying myself with elbows and forearms. Once inside the alleyway and sheltered from the wind, I shook my mittens off into a corner and plucked clumsily at the thin gutting gloves which seemed almost frozen to my fingers, before crowding into the warmth of the little galley in search of a mug. I glanced through the serving hatch at the clock in the mess-deck, nearly half past six. It should be breakfast in half an hour, thank God, though little seemed to be ready. The cook was in the galley, standing to one side, patiently waiting for the crush of bodies to subside. Others had noticed the time too.

'Now then, cookie,' sung out Jimmy, the Grimmie. 'What's for breakfast then. I can't smell anything cooking.'

'We aren't having breakfast yet,' said Tom, the cook, face expressionless and staring at nothing. 'The old man says we're to have it when the gear is down.'

'What! But that'll be another couple of hours yet, at least,' bleated Jimmy. There were moans and groans and curses all round. No wonder he sent us all aft for a drink – ten minutes off the deck instead of half an hour – to get the gear down that much quicker.

Jimmy rounded on me. 'You tell your old man from me, he's a fucking evil old bastard.'

'Tell him yourself,' I retorted. 'You'll see him just as soon as I, no doubt.' I stormed out of the galley into the mess-deck, incensed at such a cowardly remark.

In the mess, I took a seat and gulped at my tea, glancing again at the clock, only five or six minutes left now before returning on deck. The rest of the men filed into the mess still mumbling and grumbling to rest their legs and catch a quick smoke. I was feeling quite hungry now, knowing that the original breakfast time was so close. I had never had any desire to smoke but I envied the satisfaction the men seemed to get from their cigarettes.

Just inside the door, Bill Steech remained standing, to gain easier access to the bacca pouch in his pocket, and proceeded to roll a cigarette. Jackie Brown, a latecomer, strode into the mess and caught Bill's arm in passing, knocking the tobacco from the paper.

'Hey! Watch what you're d-doing, ya CUNT,' stormed Bill.

Jack turned quickly and took a step back towards Bill.

'Who're you calling a cunt?' he snarled and thrust his chin forward aggressively.

'I'm calling YOU a cunt,' snapped Bill, spittle flying.

They were two big men and the rest of us sat transfixed in silence.

'Can you MAKE me a cunt,' roared Jack, thunder on his face.

'YES,' Bill spat it out and thrust his face close to Jack's, evil burning in his eyes.

There was a pregnant pause, while each man stood glaring at each other, then slowly Jackie raised his hand to shoulder height in front of Bill and made a circle with thumb and forefinger.

'Then make me one about this size in time for my watch below, will ya?' He cackled in merriment as he turned away.

The rest of us chortled along with him, glad that a nasty moment had passed.

Shortly after, a bellow from the alleyway told us that the mate had arrived to chase us and with some groans we trudged back onto the freezing deck.

The shooting of a deep-sea bottom trawl is a very dangerous and complicated manoeuvre, which is probably why I was ordered about and pushed out of the way so much on our initial exercise.

The trawl measures about 120 feet across its mouth and weighs – including bobbins, floats, cables, shackles and otter boards etc. – several tons. It has to be lifted outboard in sections by Gilson wires running through blocks near the masthead and derrick ends. This has to be timed and synchronised since the weight transfers from wires to cables and ropes, and creates a danger to as many as a dozen men who may be working amongst it all on the deck. The mate controls the operation, mainly from the waist of the ship or the fore-deck, assisted by the bosun or the third hand, who mainly watch the after-end of the deck.

I do not intend to explain the details or complications of shooting a trawl at this stage of my story, except to tell you the order in which the trawl is placed in the water.

First over the side goes the cod end or tail of the trawl, followed by the belly or funnel part of the net. Then the bobbins and floats which surround the mouth of the trawl are hove outboard and lowered into the water, well below the surface, on cables varying in length up to fifty fathoms. At this point, the otter boards, or doors, are clipped to the cables in order to kite open the mouth of the trawl. The ship steams round in a circle until the trawl is flowing astern, and then the skipper sets course and steams away from this gigantic bag of water, streaming wire warps astern to a length approximately three times the depth of water.

+ + + +

Putting the net and its ironware over the side required plenty of heaving and pushing by the men, and you had to step lively to prevent the net or ropes catching your boots and taking you over with it. Things seemed to be happening all over the deck at once as the fore- and after-end went over the side at the same time.

I was not fully conversant with the routine and didn't know what was happening next. I was ordered out of the way one moment and then, when weight was required, told to get in there. The cold conditions were a problem. Apart from making it more difficult to hold your feet and making our hands less flexible, the Gilson wires would not grip on the ice-glazed winch barrels, and the Gilson men had to take extra turns and hang on grimly to prevent them slipping and trapping hands, which was difficult as the screeching and cursing of the mate did testify.

Eventually all ropes were cast off and the trawl floated freely in the water. The mate stood at the rail in the waist of the ship, casting his eye up and down the length of the net, making sure that nothing was foul, as did the skipper from the bridge window, before giving the mate the order to lower away, at which the winch-cable brakes were opened and the trawl slid away from sight. Even though the gear was off the deck, there was still plenty for the rest of us to do while the winchmen were slacking the warps away. We had to drag the deck-pound boards out of the hold and ship them up into stanchions to divide the fore-deck into sections, thus preventing the fish from sliding all over the deck when it came aboard. The ship was on the move again now and the motion became sharper as we picked up speed; the warps whipped off the cable drums and zipped around us, before slipping through the gallows blocks and over the side. At last the 300 to 400 fathoms of warp was paid away, the wires were hove aft into the towing block, and for the first of many times the bosun informed the skipper that the gear was towing even, as he shouted 'ALL SQUARE AFT.' We trooped towards the mess-deck for the last bacon and sausage we would get for a while; from now on our staple diet would be fish.

The watch that had been on the bridge when we stopped told us that we had shot our gear for the first tow on Cape Bank, which was about twenty to thirty miles north of the North Cape of Norway, but the ground was vast so there was plenty of scope.

Two hours after the gear was shot, the telegraph rang to warn the engineers that it was time to haul and there may be numerous engine movements, and we were still working on deck. It was mid-morning now, but the first daylight was only just showing on the horizon. In these latitudes, during the winter, there are only three or four hours of daylight. Snow was falling and, as usual with the snow, the wind increased and the swell was getting up. The ship swung and stopped on the weather tack; that is to say the side where we were hauling the gear was facing the wind and waves, so that the ship was blown away from the net lying in the water and prevented from drifting over the top of it, which would make it difficult to haul aboard. It was uncomfortable and more dangerous for the crew. But, alas, with a side-trawler this always has to be so.

Once the doors and Dan Lenos were up, and the bobbins inboard, my place was alongside the mate in the waist of the ship, at the lowest part of the bulwark rail, taking in the poke-line, while the rest of the men pulled back with net hooks on the net. There was just enough room for me to jam my feet between the bobbins and the bulwark plates, and with the top of the rail running across my groin I was able to brace my knees against the ship's side and sway backwards as it rolled heavily broadside to the oncoming seas and the rail dropped, until the water came up to, and sometimes over, the top to run down the front of my oilskin frock. I watched timorously as wave after wave built up in front of me, sometimes high above my head, and then broke into a line of white horses which came galloping down on to us, only to fade away in a hiss and disappear beneath us as the vessel lifted and rolled away.

I was glancing sideways at the mate, who was urging the men to keep in time, when I heard my first cry of 'WATER!' As the men scampered away from the side, the next wave shot over the rail and engulfed me, knocking me on my back and slopping me, gasping and spluttering, against the winch, until the back of my sou'wester struck the cylinder casing. I was swilling around in three feet of angry water among ropes, floats and net, my face awash, until the mate stepped quickly forward and grabbed my oilskin by the shoulder, dragging me to my feet with a frightened snarl, clearly shaken by my inexperienced vulnerability.

'Watch what y're fucking doing, you lanky drip, and keep yer bastard eyes on the water. What'll you do when it starts blowing?' Then, turning away, he made a grab for the net, which was quickly paying away again.

As the rest of the men followed his example with net hooks and mittened hands, a young voice not unlike Freddie Nott's chirped, 'You have now been baptised, Young Dasher, or should that be Young Splasher,' which was followed by a giggle and chuckles from the rest.

Soon the huge bag of fish was slung amidships and hauled forward along the rail by the heavy tackle, until it swung inboard with a crunch, arrested by the bag ropes. As the water drained out, the mate dashed under it to release the cod-line, and the fish poured out, jumping and writhing into the pound, looking like a huge box of giant maggots. The for'ard men scrambled into it, followed by me, to grab the bottom of the cod end and pull it out as the sling was lowered down so that the mate could tie up the cod-line again.

As I staggered among the fish, my feet squelching in my boots, which were full of water since my ducking, I felt as if I was walking on stilts, for I could not feel anything below my ankles. But I could feel the frozen snow, which was more like hail, whipping into my eyes and face, and my hands and wrists were tender again with cold in my sodden mitts. Yet I knew I couldn't leave the deck to change anything while the gear was inboard; getting the net over the side and on the bottom where it was catching fish was the most imperative thing now to the skipper and crew.

I was feeling very low again, not only because of my wretched condition but also because I felt so stupid and inadequate; everyone around me was cursing and ridiculing me because I could not anticipate what was required next. Fortunately for me, my greatest torment, Bill Steech, was occupied on the other side of the deck, either heaving on or sorting out his wires.

Eventually the net was over the side again, and as they lowered away the gear I scampered for'ard into the fo'c'sle to change into dry clothes as quickly as possible before I was missed and tormented again.

All too soon I was back on deck and climbing among the fish, my thin gutting gloves on and knife in my hand. I stood well for'ard in the fore-pound, out of the way of the other hands and the swinging fish. Only then did I take stock of the fish I was supposed to gut, and the size of them; some were four or five feet long and their heads were huge. Cod (for that's what they were) are a well-muscled fish and pretty powerful in the kicking stakes; with one hand in the gill and the other trying to slit the belly open with the knife, their jumping and wriggling soon had me spattered in blood. The orders were to head the first 500 kits (5,000 stone) but the heads on these were so big I did not have the strength to break them off. I had to drag them to the bollard and break them over the handrail, which made me very slow, much to the disgust of the skipper and the rest of the crew.

That's how I thought of my father now, just as the skipper, so indifferent had he been to my plight, usually referring to me as the kid or that snacker. The only time he had seemed concerned about me was when we were paying away the warp on the first shoot. I was standing unsteadily close to a warp in the pounds we were shipping up, and he shouted for me to move away from the whipping wire in case a splinter caught my frock and dragged me through the bollard.

That dark, miserable, strenuous day dragged on; with each haul we caught more fish and spent longer in the pounds as the skipper warmed (huh!) to his task. My wrists now were raw and nearly bleeding, chafed by the stiff, sharp stitching round the cuff of my oilskin when I reached for each struggling fish. After tea (half an hour), having been on deck for sixteen hours, the crew were split into four watches. Each watch was allowed six hours below, which meant the last watch wouldn't sleep for another eighteen hours. Fortunately, I was on the second watch below with the fourth hand; we were to go at half past midnight.

Those next six hours were the longest I had ever experienced, especially when we crossed the deck and had to wash the mountain of fish we had gutted through the earlier part of the day. Two hosepipes were thrust into the now-solid frozen fish and the water poured over them; we dug ourselves a hole to form a pool to wash the fish in by hand, rubbing the blood off each one before tossing them down the hatch, where four men below, including the mate, laboured to pack them in ice. The work was continuous and fast with constant back-bending for the next two hours till I thought mine would break. Then the telegraph rang to signal the next haul, with the previous haul untouched.

There was still some fish to wash, so it was decided that the two snackers, Charlie and I, would continue to wash, with Bill Steech remaining below to stow the fish, while the main crew were hauling the trawl. So while the rest went aft to change gloves for mitts, Charlie and I continued to bend and throw fish, which were swilling freely now in the man-made pool, down the hatch. We kept at it frenziedly: dip and throw, dip and throw. The ship lurched madly now that it was beam on to the weather again, and the knee-deep water rushed passed us as we grovelled for fish which were deeper now so that my arms were wet up to the elbows. With the increased roll of the ship, my dizzy, tired head and exhausted body could not cope, and I lost my balance and plunged forward into the water. The top of my head was protected with the sou'wester, but my face, neck and muffler were soaked, and the salt water stung my eyes, making me scramble to my feet amid a few cheers and jeers, which told me my clumsy dive had not gone unnoticed.

Bill Steech must have been working frantically down below. Although there were only two of us, the fish were really flowing down the hatch and for one man to crack his own ice, lay shelves and ice the fish, it must have been pretty hectic. But only once did he stop us, shouting 'Hold your hand', while he changed over from one side of the fishroom to the other, and we were able to stretch the kink out of our backs for two minutes and observe another three bags of fish pour onto the decks.

Soon the gear was over the side again and we were told blessedly to get for'ard out of the way of the warps for the seven or eight minutes it took to slack away. I staggered forward in drunken fashion through the hoodway door into the warm forecastle and sank down quietly onto a seat locker. I felt as if every joint in my body had come unhinged. I rummaged in my kitbag for a dry muffler to replace the salt soaked one that was chafing my neck, but my wrists and arms were so raw that I found a dirty shirt and singlet to wrap them in and ease the pain for a few minutes and my head fell forward and my eyelids closed ...

The fo'c'sle door swung open with a thump and I jerked upward as Bill Steech brushed in quickly to get another pack of cigarettes. He observed my drawn face and wrapped up arms.

'What the f-fuck are you doing with th-that lot wrapped round yer?' he muttered quietly, so as not to wake the watch below. 'Sore wrists, eh! Well, that won't do any good.'

'I've got some zinc ointment in my ditty bag,' I moaned. 'I'll put some on when I go below.'

'That won't do any good either,' he scoffed. 'It only makes the skin softer. Piss on 'em, kid. That's the only cure. Piss on 'em. Now play smart, we're blocking up.' And with that he swept out, allowing the noise of the deck and weather to flood in before he closed the door.

As always after a confrontation with Bill I was fired up; I quickly unwrapped my arms and stuffed the dirty gear back into the kitbag. Stretching the painful curve out of my back, I rose unsteadily to my feet and stepped out into the hoodway to retrieve my gutting gloves and take out my knife from my fearnought pocket. The wind was whistling a little and snow was driving across the outer doorway as another snow squall hit us. I stepped out on to the deck and the cold slapped my face.

The first of the men from aft were just digging their feet into this fresh mountain of fish, which were already stiff from the cold, and I climbed over the fore-warp and took up my position in the fore-pound ready for another two hours of frozen purgatory. Soon there were nine of us stooped over our task, with shoulders hunched. The snow stopped but the cold seemed to close in around us, subduing us all so there was none of the usual banter, and things were quiet except for the slap of fish and plop of livers into the basket.

After a while Grimmie stood up and, sticking his knife into a deck board, flapped his arms around him, trying to get some blood into his hands.

'Bloody hell! It's bastard cold,' he moaned, voicing the thoughts that were in all our minds.

'COLD?' echoed Jackie Brown, picking up the word. And then he slowly chanted a little ditty:

> 'COLD? YES, COLD!
> Cold as a fish in a frozen pool,
> Cold as the spunk on an Eskimo's tool,
> Cold as the fluff on a penguin's chuff,
> Cold as charity, and that's cold enough,
> COLD - DAMNED COLD!'

This brought a few chuckles from the rest.

'I can judge de cold by the size of dat icicle on your nose, Brownie,' chipped in Falk Amunsen. 'It grows longer by der minute. Ve must be mad cunts. I vish I vas at home in bed vid our lass now, under de lee of Bum Island.' And so the banter went on. It was vulgar but the more shocking the better; it took our minds off the pain in our hands.

Time stood still as I struggled on in these severe conditions, the occasional spray whipping over the rail to sting the face and eyes and snap me out of the dazed coma I think I was lapsing into, until the bosun shouted.

'Hey, Dasher! Go and call the watch below and do something useful, and don't forget to stoke the fire, and don't take too long about it.'

'Yes, and don't forget to turn the covers down on my bed,' giggled Grimmie. Keen as I was to get off the deck, it took two swings of my weary leg to get it over the pound boards before I could stagger forward to the fo'c'sle.

When you are next watch below, calling out the watch can cause mixed feelings, a combination of elation and dread. I stepped into the fo'c'sle, which was warm and beckoning, with a cheery note in my voice, careful not to be too enthusiastic when I called, 'Watch-oh, me hearties! It's twelve o'clock, the weather's fine, there's sixty baskets on the deck, and one hour before we haul, we think.'

I stoked the fire, cleared the ashes and stayed as long as I dare, just long enough to see one of the watch swing his legs out, and then I returned to the deck.

I had thawed out a bit and figured I could cope with another half hour easy enough, but I was wrong. It seemed ages before the watch appeared out of the fo'c'sle on their way aft, stumbling across the mound of fish we had piled on the port side, accompanied by some cheers and jeers from the lads gutting, as their white, drawn, dejected faces disappeared aft.

The next fifteen or twenty minutes were an eternity and my hands were dropping off before at last the first of them arrived in the pounds. Then, amidst more jeering and calls for us to give an extra half hour just for fun, our watch eventually moved off aft to hang our oilskins in the drying room around the funnel.

Once out of the cold and the stiff, wet, chafing oilskins, I didn't have to return to the deck for another six hours. I wanted to savour this time, so I decided to go aft to wash and get a drink of tea, as did the rest of the watch. While the others sat in the mess, smoking and yarning, I went into the galley and washed the caked blood off my raw wrists and face into the sink. I took my drink into the mess to listen to the chatter of my watchmates until I noticed by the messroom clock that twenty-five minutes of my precious watch below had already gone. With the half-hour call-out time, that left only five hours from now.

Jumping up, I made my excuses, hurried out as fast as my turned-down thigh boots would allow and stepped out onto the port side, striding quickly forward. This was now the weather side, the ship having come round; without my frock, sou'wester and gloves, the icy wind cut into my weary, defenceless body as I scrambled over the mound of gutted fish still waiting to be washed. My bare hands grabbed the slimy, frozen pound boards to steady myself as a chant came from some of the men still working on the other side of the deck.

'There he goes on his toes,
To the fo'c'sle I suppose,
Make it quick and hurry back,
Then it's my turn to hit the sack.
Wa-hey!'

I pressed on towards that rolling, dipping haven, which would take me away temporarily from this harrowing, freezing scene.

Inside the fo'c'sle, the warmth and comparative comfort made my desire for sleep increase, but I realised that I still had to clean my teeth. Taking my toothbrush and toothpaste from the locker, I hurried into the dirty, neglected bathroom. I turned on the cold tap but got only a slight dribble of water, then nothing else. Damn! The tank was empty. I would have to pump it up. I counted twenty pumps before I heard water pouring into the tank, but nothing was forthcoming from the tap. I knew a certain amount was needed before the syphoning effect would work, but time was precious. I put in twenty pumps more, and again, and again, before water gushed from the tap. But it was rusty. The bottom of the tank had been disturbed and it tasted foul. Blow it! Forget the teeth.

Hurrying back into the fo'c'sle, I tossed the toothbrush and paste into the locker and stripping quickly to my underwear scrambled into that beckoning cosy bunk. My wristwatch, which was hung there, showed that an hour of my watch below had already gone; the rest of my watchmates had already battened down while I was in the bathroom.

I pulled the blanket over me and coiled up in the foetus position. Ah, this was bliss!

Outside, I could hear the winch running; it was hauling time again. All the other sounds could be heard: the wind rushing and the water swishing, the clank and thump of the other operations as the men prepared to take the trawl on board again.

I was in another world. The warmth, the comfort, my head swam, this was great.... The sweet molasses of exhaustion slowly spread over me, my head sank into the pillow.... CRASH. 'Wakey, Wakey!' The door banged shut again as a wet, dripping frock swept past my bunk.

'Watch-o, me hearties!'

I was shocked. If this was a joke, it was disgusting when people were trying to sleep.

'What time is it?' a voice asked.

'Six o'clock in the morning, lads. The Old Man's found 'em this time. There's four bags on deck, the wind's freshening and we've been shot half an hour. But we've cleared all the fish on the port side, you lucky people.'

Perfect! This bastard is relishing telling us this, I thought. He must be next watch below. I can't believe it. I was just going to sleep. I started to move, but the stiffness in my limbs told me it was true. I had slept for over four hours, but I was still in the same position as when I climbed into bed. God! How was I going to climb out of this?

As I fell rather than climbed down from my bunk, every muscle and joint complained; my eyes were sore and my mind was foggy, and my wrists still raw and weeping, but the worst pain was in my fingers. They were so tender and dried out and cracked in the joints, they were curled up like claws. It hurt so much when I straightened them out, I could hardly put my boot socks on.

The rest of the watch had left before I was ready enough to step outside. The scene was still very similar, the men were working on the starboard side gutting. Fish slapped around me as I stumbled aft. The weather was fresher now, spray once again whipping over the rail, the wind whooshing faster overhead. The seagulls, wheeling and dipping, shrieked and cackled at my plight and the waves slapping the ship's side hissed at my heels as I passed.

Arriving aft under the shelter of the boat-deck, my hands struggled to undo the front flap of my fearnoughts. As I stood peeing into the scuppers, I tried to flex my stiff, tender fingers, but they were so painful I lowered them in front of me and allowed my urine to run over them. The relief was immediate as the warm liquid flowed over them in the frosty night air. Although I felt shame in what I was doing, my hands became flexible again. It was unhygienic, but it was the answer. I knew my shipmates were right and I realised I must pay more attention to their advice if I was to survive the next fortnight.

Chapter 3

THE HAZARDS INCREASE

Time was not measurable in the next few days, but they were a nightmare. My body was taken to its limit so many times, and I prayed more than I'd ever prayed before for the strength to carry on and not disgrace myself. The only memorable things were bad ones; when seas crashed on board during the worst of the weather, and men and gear sloshed around the deck. Often the men were cut, bruised and crushed, but usually a scream from the mate or a bellow from the skipper was enough to revive them. The most they might get was a bit of strapping or a dram of rum. But then there was an incident which broke the repetitive sequence

One morning, I think it was morning – the almost continuous dark made it difficult for me to judge – we were hauling and, as the warp was being hove through the fore-gallows, a splice picked up the derrick-hook tripping line, which had been blown over the fore-rail and was taking it through the block. The winchman stopped the winch while his watchmate ran forward to clear it. George Brunham climbed on the rail, put his arm through the rolling block and looked to have cleared the rope, so the mate, who was coming along the deck, instructed the winchman to heave away. But George was still struggling to pull the rope free; a splinter in the wire caught the sleeve of his oilskin and rove his arm through the rolling block, dragging it up to his shoulder.

The winchman stopped immediately, but not before George's feet had been lifted from the rail, leaving him hanging outboard, dangling from the gallows sheave. George let out only a strangled cry as the mate ran forward shouting to the winchman to screw down the spooling-drum brake and go and get help. Then, in an instant, he changed his mind. No, better stay where you are. He needed him at the winch in case there was a surge, putting an approximate ten-ton strain on the gear that could pull George's arm out.

The telegraph rang as the skipper automatically slowed the engines, but, once some of the weight came off the gear, the ship began to dip and lurch, swinging George around like a rag doll, while the relentless sea hissed and slobbered at him just fifteen feet below. The telegraph rang again in an effort to maintain the strain and reduce the amount of movement. A rapid popping on the whistle was the usual signal to bring the men on deck in an emergency, and they came tumbling forward, pulling on gloves and sou'westers. Men clambered on the rail and hung outboard from the bag ropes, risking their own lives in an effort to support George and take the weight of his body. Some climbed inside the gallows to disentangle his arm from the wire.

Suddenly the skipper was on deck and climbing up among them in his shirtsleeves, taking charge. He must have left the wireless operator on the wheel to follow his instructions from the deck. On orders from the master, the warp was allowed to run slowly back through the rolling block to extricate George's arm from the sheave, and sympathetic and willing arms gathered him inboard and carried him forward to the fo'c'sle.

As the immediate danger was past George's stoicism left him, and he moaned and yelped as the stricken arm flopped about on passage, when the group carrying him had to squeeze through the doorway into the accommodation. The arm was obviously broken and the hump on his back indicated a dislocated shoulder. George was laid on the fo'c'sle floor, while his frock was slit up the side and along the arm to remove it from his body. All the while, George moaned and rolled his head, muttering, 'Not my new frock, not my new frock', as it seemed to him his mates were adding to his misfortunes.

Since the arm was broken it was impossible to relocate the shoulder, and broad bandaging was used over the clothing to strap it up, with a table batten as a temporary splint to secure the arm. Almost everyone wanted to administer the usual medicine for pain, a dram of rum from their ration, but the skipper forbade it. Most thought he was being overbearing but he had other ideas. Nevertheless you could be sure someone would give George what he wanted when the skipper wasn't there. With difficulty, George was placed in the confines of a top bunk and laid on his good side. The watch below, who naturally were awake, were called on deck with all hands to retrieve the trawl before it fouled or caught the prop, and one man was left to watch over George and support and cushion him where necessary.

With the extra men on deck, the trawl was hauled quickly enough. Fortunately, there was no damage in spite of the delay, and three good bags were hove aboard.

Everyone, including the mate, expected we would get the rest of the gear inboard, and all looked towards the bridge, only to be surprised by the order to pay away, which we did in dazed disbelief. When the gear was down, the mate hurried towards the bridge.

'What's the score then, Skipper? Aren't we taking George in?' asked the mate, while the skipper was still lining the ship on course.

The skipper checked the depth on the sounder before replying. 'Yes, of course, Les, but the nearest port is Honningsvaag, at least ten hours away, and that means we will lose more than a full day's fishing before we can return. There are things to be done while the ship is comparatively steady. She'll be more stable towing than she would be laid or steaming. We're at the north end of the ground and we can tow back towards the land, shortening the distance, while the sparks contacts the shore, gets some medical advice and arranges for George's transport to some hospital. We don't know where that will be yet and anyway we have to move George aft somewhere more comfortable. We need a steady ship for that and if we pick up another haul while the fish is still here that will help our cause.'

'But what about the pain for poor old George,' insisted the mate, somewhat subdued.

'George won't be feeling too much pain right now, but when the initial shock dies down we'll have to counteract any excessive pain he will feel and that means morphine. I'll have to give him an injection. I hope he doesn't have any alcohol in him!'

This sort of callous logic is what makes a successful skipper, who is always under pressure to deliver, as Les was to find out himself in later years. There was a lot of sense in what the skipper said; carrying George aft across a deckload of fish would have caused some problems, whereas now all hands could clear it. And towing south at four knots for two hours with the tide behind us, instead of steaming all the way at twelve, would only cost an extra hour and a quarter, not crucial in a ten-hour plus journey.

Chapter 4

FROM MOUNTAINOUS SEAS TO MOUNTAINS OF SNOW

We were steaming now. George had been transported aft and put in the bosun's small berth in the after-cabin, where the engine room and galley staff could keep a more constant watch over him. He had received the necessary medication from the skipper and lay quietly now, with just the occasional moan between naps. The letter M was marked on his forehead as the *Captain's Medical Guide* dictated, morphine having been administered.

The gear on deck had been secured and the fish cleared. The skipper had decided to keep the four fishing watches while we steamed towards land. This meant I was allowed to take a watch on the bridge, mostly fetching tea and keeping a lookout, which I was enjoying because the sparks had tuned the bridge speaker to an overseas programme, and popular music was playing in the background, a real luxury on the fishing grounds.

I stood with my arms folded, resting on the bridge windowsill, my chin on my hands, staring with fascination at the mountains of Norway rising straight out of the sea as we approached Possanger Fjord, and listening dreamily to renderings of 'On Top of Old Smokey ' and 'Put Another Nickel In', which reminded me of home and my girlfriend, Pauline, who had been treating me well for the last couple of months; we had just got into petting.

The mood was a romantic one. The wind was on the port quarter and the ship was rolling to a following sea; a green phosphorous flashed and sparkled in the wash from the bow. The moon broke occasionally from scudding clouds and lit a shimmering path across the waves, picking out the snow-laden mountains, each with its pinpricks of light shining from the little doll's houses which were scattered in the sheltered nooks and crannies of the sheer shoreline.

This was my first visit to a foreign country and it was different to anything I had seen before. As we rounded each mountain, other channels or fjords ran off in different directions. In the flatter hollows, small clusters of houses formed little villages which appeared to have no connection with each other on the shore. No wonder that the main transport was by water, as the many small boats and snibbies chugging about proved. A snibbie was the fisherman's name for motorised small seine netters and line fishers, each with its own little wheelhouse, holding no more than one or two men and the controls, each with a stovepipe exhaust poking out the top and each making the same pop-pop-popping noise as they sped past. Small they may have been, carrying no more than three or four men, but beautifully seaworthy. It was clever to pass the exhaust through the wheelhouse and make use of the heat.

There was still some way to go when our watch was relieved, and I was able to get two to three hours sleep before all hands were called to tie up.

As we rounded the last mountain, we opened the entrance to a natural little harbour, which revealed a broad hollow in one mountainside where nestled the fairly large town of Honningsvaag. Every little rocky shelf near water level was used as a jetty for small boats, but we tied up at the mailboat quay, the one large, purpose-built wharf fronting the town.

Soon after we had moored alongside, the well-known, stocky figure of the agent Kora Hansen was clambering aboard, carrying a leather satchel packed with official papers and cigarette lighters, with an ambulance already in close attendance.

Kora acknowledged most of the crew standing around; they all knew him and greeted him on his way to the bridge. Many of the lads had written letters home which they passed to the linesmen to post with a fee of a few packets of cig papers – always in short supply in this region and always well received.

Pretty soon George was stretchered ashore and put in the ambulance, a doctor in attendance. But we were not ready to leave yet, it appeared, as the chief had revealed an engine job that needed attention.

'Just as usual,' the skipper remarked.

It required some work from the local fitting shop and would take two or three hours.

Kora had left the ship after doing what trade he could with the lighters, and most of the crew turned in to catch up with some sleep, as they were not allowed ashore. I couldn't sleep. I was too excited and interested in what was going on ashore; not that there was a great deal in the icy conditions that prevailed.

It was discovered that George Brunham had not taken all of his belongings with him; although he would not be returning to the ship, his wristwatch and some toilet gear still remained. As Jim Mullett, the third hand, was taking the deck watch at the time, and was considered pretty trustworthy, the skipper decided he could take these items to the agent's office. On hearing this, the few crew members who were still hanging around beseeched Jim to call at the local paper shop to buy some magazines for them, producing some English paper money and some Norwegian cash saved from previous trips for him to trade with. Norway's censorship laws were not as strict as our British laws and soft porn mags which were not available at home could easily be purchased here.

I had wandered into the wheelhouse, a better vantage point to view the shore, and in so doing I witnessed the skipper giving Jim his orders. My father glanced in my direction as he loaded up the third hand with George's belongings. He knew I had never seen a foreign country and guessed how much I longed to have a look around. In his first show of favouritism since I had been aboard, he instructed Jim to take me with him to help carry the things and act as a sort of chaperone – which Jim was happy to do, preferring some company to being on his own.

Pretty soon, I was striding down the quay alongside Jim in my turned down thigh boots and fearnoughts, with my blazer worn over an old guernsey for respectability. I was a little taken aback when the concrete quay gave way to the muddy tracks which served as roads in this built-up area. There was snow and slush everywhere and just about everybody was wearing waterproof boots, though more fashionable than ours, of course. The gaily painted wooden houses brightened up what might have been a pretty depressing scene, though some had fish hanging up outside to dry.

Some of the main buildings were of brick and stone. What we took to be the town hall and the post office or police station, for example, looked quite picturesque with a backdrop of huge, white mountains and fir trees almost overhanging.

We soon found our way to the Schipskandler which contained Kora Hansen's office, seeing as how he owned the business, and handed over George's belongings to one of his staff, who assured us they would be delivered to the hospital promptly. Now we were free to do our little bit of shopping before we returned to the ship. Jim appeared to know his way around a little and I guessed he must have been here before. He led me to a large single-storey shack with large windows on three sides which showed us a well-lit, roomy store inside, with three counters displaying the usual goodies one would find in a newsagents. One counter was completely covered in papers and magazines.

As Jim and I entered, our boots clumping on the wooden floor, the warmth was a welcome change to the biting cold outside. There was only one girl serving, a beautiful creature of about nineteen years old, wearing a well-filled Fair Isle-type sweater with Nordic design. She was attending to the only other customer as we entered. Jim moved over to the paper counter and started leafing embarrassingly through the sexy magazines which were stacked together; I moved down the counter and browsed among the more regular magazines.

I was turning the pages of a periodical when I suddenly came upon a full-page picture of a naked old man who was sat full frontal with his legs apart and sporting a huge set of genitals. His penis seemed extremely large, even in the flaccid state, and I was just reflecting how unfair it was for such an old man to be so well endowed, when I suddenly became aware that the young girl was directly in front of me behind the counter and paying me every attention. I looked up into those beautiful, twinkling almond eyes, which were obviously mocking me, and the knowing smile on that lovely fresh complexion sent an embarrassed shudder through me.

The fact that such an innocent-looking young lady should be standing her ground, glancing first at the open page and then into my shocked eyes, set my face burning. I quickly closed the mag and returned to the protective shield of Jim's presence, so she let out a little giggle and followed me along the display to stand in front of him. My shipmate was unaware of what had taken place and didn't seem to notice my embarrassed fidgeting. He just selected some of the raunchiest books and with a grin remarked, 'Some knockers there, eh?'(He pronounced knockers sounding the K.)

'Knockers?' repeated the girl. 'Oh! You mean kroners. No, not so many, these are 5 kroner each and these are only 3½ (pronouncing the half sounding the L). Only 59 kroner altogether.'

Jim glanced at me and with a knowing grin pulled out various denominations of Norwegian and English money. 'Will you accept pound notes?' he asked.

'I sink so,' said the girl. 'I'll just check.' And she moved into the back of the store for a few moments.

Jim turned and grinned at me. 'Jim!' I said. 'Did you have to be so vulgar with that young girl?'

'Oh, don't worry!' said Jim, with a brushing-away flap of the hand. 'These Noske girls take it all in their stride or should I say astride,' and he guffawed as the girl returned.

Her upper half bounced towards us as she said, 'Yes, I can take pounds but you will only get 19 kroner for them instead of the normal 20. Is that OK?'

'Yeah sure,' replied Jim. 'It's what I expected,' and he handed over three £1 notes and a 10-kroner note, ignoring the 1- and 5-ore coins in his hand.

Once again I was bewitched by the soft, feminine grace of her movements as she took the money and returned the change to my shipmate. I only realised I was staring when she glanced again in my direction over that half-hidden smile and I had to turn away and become interested in the planking of the cabin walls.

'Mange Tak,' said Jim, using probably the only Norwegian he knew, and then followed it with 'Auf Wiedersehen,' which even I knew was German, though it was probably well understood by someone who had been occupied by that nation less than half a dozen years before.

'Goodbye,' said the dream. 'Do come again,' and she gave me another knowing smile as we left. Gosh, I thought, *I'd* come again if only God and the skipper (probably one and the same) would allow it.

Back onboard ship, we found that repairs were almost complete, and Jim delivered the mags to the crew before reporting to God – er, the skipper! – which, as we had been quick, went down very well. Me, I decided I needed some sleep, but it was obvious I wasn't going to get it if we were about to leave, so I wandered into the mess, where Jim was recalling our jaunt ashore to some of the crew who were gathered there. As I entered, Jim was saying, 'and the boobs on this bint were terrific as she bounced around the store. Young Bob's eyes stood out like chapel 'atpegs,' and the group cheered and jeered as they looked towards me. (Chapel'atpegs, I later realised, meant chapel hat pegs. Only on a much later visit to the Fishermen's Bethel, when I observed the polished wooden coat pegs there, each with a bulb on the end, did I appreciate how graphic the description was.)

Steechy didn't miss the chance to embarrass me more.

'Did yer f-fancy giving her a length then, young 'un?' he leered.

'Well, I did think she was rather nice,' I replied.

'Ho! H-he did think she was rather nice,' mocked Bill, not for the first time. 'W-what he really means i-is he would have liked to give her a good shagging.'

This time, I didn't leave. I only turned away with a shy smile, the thought was rather warming.

Soon we were steaming back out again into those black seas and icy, whipping winds. To start fishing again, after that break, was even harder, but the skipper drove us on with a renewed frenzy to catch up on lost time. With great success too, as the day finally came when we were stamping fish down in the hatch coamings because we had actually filled the ship up, and we turned to head sou'-sou'-west towards home.

Clewing up the gear and clearing the decks took the last reserves of strength from the crew, but it was done with some elation as the worst part of this living nightmare was over. Eventually we all collapsed into those blessed bunks and finally passed out to the sound of the powerful, rhythmic heartbeat of the engines as they pushed us swiftly back towards civilisation.

An overnight sleep of some fourteen or fifteen hours had passed before I finally recovered consciousness, but I was so stiff in every limb that it took an extreme effort to move anything before I could force myself to even sit up. I was so filthy dirty that I desperately wanted to bathe. It was only then that I realised it was the banging of the bathroom pump that had finally roused me. Obviously everyone would be queuing up for the use of the one bath.

Once more I tumbled out of that top bunk, using mainly arms and elbows to grip. After such a long period of inactivity, my claw-like hands had dried out so much they were almost brittle, and urinating on them was not the answer this time. What they needed was a good soaking in nice, hot, soapy water. I discovered the only other moving occupant of the fo'c'sle was old Arthur Medlam, who was sitting on the seat locker next to the stove. He sat stooping forward with his elbows on his knees, staring blankly into the fire, half a rolled cig hanging loosely from his first two fingers. His wispy hair was fluffed up and snowy white, testifying that he had already had his bath. No doubt he had not slept as long, even after the gruelling finish to our eleven-day ordeal.

'Now then, Arthur!' I called, dragging him from his reverie. 'Reflecting on another job well done? By golly, she's got a bellyful this time, hasn't she? She feels pretty solid in the water now, not much bouncing about anyway.'

'I've seen it all before,' mumbled Arthur. 'Too many times in the forty-odd years I've spent at sea, twenty-six of them mostly with your father, too. I mind the time when he was pretty much like you.'

I doubt it, I thought, Father was a much stronger character than I, more aggressive and determined for sure. He liked the job, that he did, but I wouldn't be doing it again, I felt certain. Maybe the Merchant Navy, but not this filthy, dangerous grind.

'I was hoping to get a bath when whoever is in there has finished,' I said.

'You'll be lucky,' replied Arthur, quietly scratching his neck with a shaving motion of the back of his fingers. 'Sid Edwards is in there now but most of the others are aft playing dominoes and they are all waiting their turn. The watch on the bridge will take preference when they come off. None of 'em will be very happy if you nip in first.'

'But I'm filthy, Arthur, and my hands are so sore,' I moaned, examining the traces of fish blood still clotted in the creases of my wrists.

'Well, you'll have to get bathed in a bucket in the stokehold like we do in most other ships,' mumbled Arthur. I recoiled at the thought and decided to go aft and survey the situation. I looked around for my boots. It's a pity I had no clumpers (cut-down old boots) like the others; with the weather fine, no water on deck and a following wind, the lazy roll was a pleasant feeling as I trotted aft with the ship so deep in the water. The good old *St Apollo* had done us well, I guess, on this my first trip.

In the mess, most of the deck-hands were gathered around the far side of the huge table where the four domino players faced each other across the corner. Money was changing hands as the punters placed their bets on the down, or on the second, third or last larker. Gambling was still a large part of the precarious lives of these hard-bitten men. Having poured myself a mug of strong tea, milk already added, from the tin kettle stewing on the corner of the stove (tannic acid, the men called it), I sat alone on the opposite side of the table and observed, not the play but the number of clean hands and faces among the group, not many by the look of it. Falk Amunsen was telling the story of how he came to England and married 'Our Lass', while he continued to lay his dominoes in turn.

've had to get married between trips,' said Falk. 'I couldn't afford to have a trip off. She vent to get the licence from the registry office vile I was avay and took the necessary papers.'

'Ah! I see your fiancé was born in Sweden,' the registrar had said.

'Well, yes,' said Betty, 'but he has been circumcised!' She blurted it out.

Falk chuckled to himself. She meant to say 'naturalised', he explained.

'Oh!' says the registrar. 'Well, that's very interesting. I don't think it's a necessary requirement for marriage but I hope it helps.'

'By, she vas embarrassed ven she realised,' said Falk. He laughed out loud, his eyes sparkling in that merry, bewhiskered face, and everyone roared with him.

When there was a lull in the cheering and jeering, I asked about the bathroom.

'Who's next in the bath?'

'I am,' said Falk, 'I'm going in ven this hand's finished.'

'Well, I could nip in now, if you like,' I chipped in. 'While you're playing, I'd be very quick,' I added. This raised a jeer of protest from the majority.

'Not likely,' remarked Falk, with a cheeky grin. 'You can pump the tank up for me, if you like, but there's a few before you.'

'But you're wasting time. I'll not get bathed today at this rate,' I complained.

'Serves you right. You should have got up earlier,' snapped Bill Steech. 'Anyway you're last on the list. You'd come after the ship's cat, if we had one,' he sneered.

'Why don't you ask your old man if you can use his bath?' piped up Freddie Nott.

This remark angered me more than any other. Fred had no axe to grind with me and he had always been sympathetic in the past, not much older and in the same position only the trip before. Yet, even though I had swilled and spilled and worked alongside them, and was shown no favour, I still wasn't accepted as one of them. For a decky to ask such a thing of the captain was, of course, unthinkable, and he should know it.

'Well, you can all go and get fucked,' I screeched, in my falsetto voice, swearing for the first time. 'That's a ridiculous suggestion.'

For a moment there was silence and then a chorus of 'Ohhhh!' from everyone.

Then Steechy cut in first with, 'Now, then! Swearing, eh! Daddy won't like it if he knows Bobby is using f-f-f- bad langwidge in the mess-deck in front of his crew, will he? Especially when we tell him. Setting a bad example, that's what he'll say.'

This raised a laugh. Someone chipped in with, 'Don't start that, Bob. Remember who you are.' Once again I rose and left.

I decided to go forward and sweep out the fo'c'sle to make amends.

Charlie, my contemporary, remained in the mess, sitting unnoticed with his pack of cigs and his drink in front of him on the edge of the gathering, completely accepted and ignored by the rest. I had never used that language before that I could recall and I didn't know why I had used it now, except that I had constantly listened to this sort of talk and must have started to accept it as the norm. I would have to watch it. I was starting to fall into the same habits and didn't know if it was a good thing or bad.

After the day of rest which the skipper had allowed us to recover, the voyage home still kept us very busy. The trawl had to be dismantled, cleaned and repaired, and the whole ship had to be cleaned to rid it of the smell of fish (if that were possible). Even the decks were scrubbed with chloride of lime to remove the algae which had formed near the scuppers.

We daymen worked a full ten hours each day. After our breakfast of fried fish, we worked through, apart from a half-hour break for lunch, until tea was called at 1800 hrs. Fried fish again, and usually a second choice of maybe hotpot or stew, and baked doughboys; then we were able to relax and enjoy the evening entertainment of great stories told while cards or dominoes or both were played around the large mess table.

Jim Mullett told a lovely story of his days in an old ship called the *Cape Tariffa* at a time when navigation by some skippers was still a little primitive, discipline was sometimes lax and the booze still flowed.

They were steaming round the west coast of Iceland, running off to the fishing grounds, and there was still some drink to be had. The ship had been delayed by weather, and now that it was fining away they were driving on at full speed to catch up on time. The *Tariffa,* Jim informed us, was a coal-burner of very heavy consumption, and it was common for firemen (stokers) to do one trip and finish because it was so hard to maintain steam. Feeding the furnaces was a very demanding job.

One night, while skirting the coast, the ship grounded on a shoal, came to an abrupt stop and laid over a little. The skipper had been entertaining the sparks and the chief engineer in his berth when she hit and all rushed to the bridge. The skipper took charge immediately and after observing the situation, showed his experience by ordering the mate to go below and check the bilges and the hull for leaks. The bosun was instructed to sound around outside the ship to determine where the deepest water was; other members of the crew were directed to loosen the lashings on the lifeboats, just in case.

In the midst of all this activity, the skipper was in full flow directing operations from the bridge window, when much to his annoyance a dirty, bedraggled, exhausted, semi-naked fireman, with a sweat rag bound around his forehead to staunch the flow of perspiration, burst onto the bridge skipp. Apologetically, he stood wiping the sweat from his neck and asked in a faltering voice, 'I'm sorry, skipper. But do you think you could ease her in a bit while I catch up on the steam pressure?'

The skipper paused, then looked in horror towards the telegraph, which still showed FULL SPEED AHEAD. Quickly composing himself, he turned towards the stoker and said, 'OK, son. Just for you I'll stop her for a while but be sure to give me full steam when I start again - because I'll be going full astern!'

The stories went on into the night and they were amusing because they were true, though some seemed quite unbelievable.

Our days were full but they passed quickly. As the daylight increased on our southerly passage more cleaning was achieved on deck until Charlie and I found ourselves polishing the brasswork which we had plastered with grease – oh so long ago! There wasn't much grease on it now; the heavy water and ice had removed most of it, especially the deck-level portholes, now covered in green verdigris which had to be scoured clean with a mixture of colzer oil and bath brick powder. This job was left mainly to Charlie and I, while Steechy occupied himself with the more important job of chopping the worn wire grommets off the steel becket bobbins. All of us were working forr'ard when Bill decided to go aft, supposedly to get his chisel sharpened. As Bill was passing the bridge the skipper leaned out of the window and shouted to him, 'Bill! Just see what's on the log while you're aft, will you?'

'Aye, aye, Skipper,' responded Bill, and continued aft, with his legs-akimbo (lost me 'orse) rolling walk.

The log which the skipper referred to was the Walker's log, a geared, clock-faced mechanism that was fitted to the boat-deck rail, towing a revolving log-line with a propellor fan on the end, thus recording the nautical miles.

Shortly we witnessed Bill hurrying back along the starboard deck to stop by the winch barrel and shout up to the bridge. The skipper's head appeared again.

'Yes, Bill,' queried the master. 'What's the log say?'

Bill stood by the winch barrel pointing aft and, in his apparent excitement, started to stutter again.

'Ff-fuh-ff-ffuh,' offered Bill.

'Forty-four?' suggested the skipper.

Bill shook his head and still pointing aft, started again.

'Ff-fuh-ff-fuh.'

'Fifty-four?' offered the skipper.

Bill gulped and, still pointing aft, tried again. 'F-fer-fuh-f-fuh ff.'

'Fifty-five?' encouraged the skipper, louder this time, in an effort to extract an answer.

Once again Bill shook his head, gulped and, taking a deep breath, finally blurted out, 'F-fuh-fucking lóg's gone.'

The skipper raised his eyes to the skies, searching for the strength to control himself, and slammed the window closed. Both Charlie and I collapsed in silent mirth in a corner of the deck. When he was excited, Bill just had to start every sentence with his favourite f-word.

Two days later and at last the vessel was rounding Spurn lightship and entering the river Humber again. For the last few days I had been thinking constantly of the comforts and safety of home, and of my mother and sisters and my girlfriend, Pauline Mitch. I fantasised about how much prouder she would be now that I had started to go to sea, and I thought about her worried remarks before I left.

This time I should be able to take her out to the pictures and dancing or wherever she wanted to go. I relished the thoughts of what we might do in her front room when her parents were out. Coming home from the sea was going to be good.

Already the moon was up as the *St Apollo* glided through the calm, black and silver waters of the river, and I watched the lights of Grimsby slide silently by as I scurried back and forth across the deck, helping with last-minute chores, like coiling the lifelines away and knocking the clips off the hatches, or preparing the mooring ropes. In between times, I was finishing my packing, rolling up my bed and trying to make myself as smart as possible in my shore gear, while listening to the light-hearted banter from the rest of the crew, who were all doing the same.

'I know the first thing I'm going to do with our lass when I get home,' said big-nosed Brown, his thick lips slobbering a little.

'Oh! We all know the first thing you'll do,' chipped in Grimmie, 'but what's the second thing you'll do, Jack?'

'The second thing I'll do,' retorted Browny, a dreamy look in his eyes, 'the *second* thing I'll do is drop me kitbag off me shoulder.'

The usual raucous laughter followed.

Then the order came from the bridge to stand by for swinging. As we were approaching the fish dock area and the ship was being swept down on a full flood tide, we had to turn the vessel around to stem the current, prior to moving alongside. The same group that had been there when we left the dock over three weeks before accompanied the mate onto the fo'c'sle head and stood by while it was our turn to approach the quay.

Chapter 5

HOME THE BRAVE HERO – LET'S DO IT AGAIN

As we stood there high up on the whaleback, the evening breeze cut through us, and we stamped our feet and kicked our heels with our hands in our pockets in an attempt to keep warm.

'Bloody hell!' snorted Freddie Nott, who was sporting a new flat cap, one size too big for him.

'It's colder here than it was up north.'

It was strange but it seemed that way to most of us. No one considered that the reason might be that we were no longer dressed for the cold weather. Most were wearing lounge suits with open-necked shirts and skimpy underwear beneath, the latter for obvious reasons with loved ones waiting not far away.

Watery eyes stared constantly towards the shore trying to see who had braved the freezing night to meet us, no doubt concerned that all had returned safely. It was sad to think that one of our number had not made the journey back with us, though most likely George Brunham was in good hands now. He could possibly have been flown home before us, though that was unlikely; the gaffers wouldn't spend that kind of money repatriating a crew member. He was more likely to get a passage on some other returning trawler when he was fit to travel, but his money would have stopped as soon as he was put ashore.

As we glided silently towards the stone quay, snow began to fall. As usual it drifted almost horizontally across our faces so that all heads canted in the same direction and thus, as the heaving lines snaked ashore, my first trip as a fisherman was completed.

The next morning, although the weather was still very cold and plenty of snow covered the scene, my mood was buoyant. When I arose, I approached everything with confidence and a sense of achievement. The journey home the night before with my father in the taxi had been a repeat of the one I had made before the voyage out, even the taxi was the same, but we had arrived home to find my ailing mother confined to bed, with my sister in attendance.

My mother had a weak heart and a few weeks rest in bed was not uncommon. It was to her room that I now went to tell of my adventures and to reassure her how well I had coped. A bit of an exaggeration, I feared, but Mum listened intently, her serene, cherubic face smiling proudly at her youngest as she lay propped up with numerous pillows. Finally, as my exuberance waned, she stopped me by saying, 'Would you mind removing my breakfast tray, please, Robert? Then I think I'll take a little rest.'

'Of course, Mum' I said, and leaned over and kissed her.

Then, snatching up the tray, I turned to leave too quickly and upset the condiments so they spilled onto the floor. Immediately I cursed. 'Fucking hell,' I blurted out, and was shocked to hear the words come out myself. I bent down quickly to retrieve the pots and I knew my face was crimson. How could I say such a thing at a time like this, after avoiding the use of such language (with one exception) before. I hoped Mother hadn't heard properly, and tried to cover up by over-using the word flipping in the next couple of sentences. 'Flipping thing!' I muttered. 'I think the ship is still rolling.'

I grinned weakly as I turned back towards her. Mum was still smiling gently, her face unchanged so that I thought she may not have heard, but her eyes stared rather pointedly into mine. I made a hurried retreat.

Father had already left the house, taking the car, presumably to do some business or go to the bank. Neither he nor I had to go early to the fish market to collect the fry of fish which was allowed to every crew member of every trawler. The mate always organised it so that the skipper's fish was sent home to him, and my entitlement would have been included on this occasion, so my first job was to smarten myself up and go to the barber, before heading to the offices for the pay-out of the trip's settling, which was usually ready by about eleven o'clock.

I made my way to my usual barber on Hessle Road but it seemed strange to be going in the middle of the working day instead of after school as before. As I entered I wondered if the barber would realise I was now a fisherman because only fishermen and pensioners normally turned up at this time of day. But, as I was wearing a sports coat and flannels instead of the lounge suit and wide trousers that the seamen usually wore, he seemed undecided. He probably thought I was unemployed so I decided to give him a big tip of 2s. out of the £3 15s. my mother had returned to me as it was my first week's wages. (She had, of course, kept my other two weeks' wages for my board.) The barber was impressed with the tip, and the difference definitely showed as he did overtime with the clothes brush around my shoulders before I left the shop.

I strode on down Hessle Road, walking tall and confident, with a feeling of satisfaction and a sway of my body which had followed me ashore from the rolling deck. I passed people who were familiar; not that I actually knew them, but many were those I had often passed on my walks to school. Yet this was different; I felt sure they would pick out my fisherman's swagger, as I had easily picked out fishermen in the past. I felt comfortable now as I walked through this family of Hessle Roaders because I knew their main topic was fishermen and fishing. I passed the top end of the South Boulevard, where stood the proud statue of a fisherman, erected in memoriam to those who were lost in the Russian outrage of 1904. He stood there with arm raised and palm outward, wearing sou'wester, guernsey, fearnought trousers and boots. Was his arm raised imploring his mistaken aggressors to desist, or was his hand merely sheltering his eyes from the sun in order to see what the next ship was catching, as I had heard one cynical fisherman suggest?

I realised now that no fisherman would see the need for a sou'wester if he was only wearing a guernsey and trousers, but somehow it seemed right; the proud stance of an adventurer was there. For the rest of that walk down the dock I thought of the previous three weeks and remembered how hard they had been, but I realised also that every waking hour had been full of emotions. Not all had been fearful and painful, some had been amusing and satisfying, and I reckoned that as far as emotions go I'd been living life to the full and in the company of a fine set of hardy men.

But now I was on the dock again and approaching the company offices. Most of the crew were outside, shuffling about, hands in pockets and puffing on their shag tabs, laughing and jibing with each other, and with the usual sprinkling of hangers on, all waiting for settling time. Arthur Medlam, Dad's loyal deck-hand, was the first to approach me. 'Now then, young Dasher,' he started. 'How do you feel now? Ready to pack your hand in, eh! Like your old man?'

I was startled. 'What do you mean, Arthur?' I gasped.

'Well, the skipper's not going back this trip,' Arthur spoke a little quieter now. 'His legs are playing him up a bit, I think, and the gaffer's offered him a shore job, I understand. He's been after him as ship's manager for some time now. Anyway the mate's taking her this next trip.'

A familiar voice interrupted from the group. 'I don't think he'll be going back without Daddy to look after him,' chortled Bill Steech.

'Don't you be so sure, Steechy.' Big-nosed Brown was among those waiting. 'You're prepared to give it another bash, aren't you, Dash?' he said, turning to me with a grin and giggling at his own quip. Most heads turned towards me, waiting for my response.

'Yes! I'm going back,' I blurted quickly, not wanting to display any hesitation. 'One skipper's as good as another to me.'

There were grins all round and then Arthur said, 'Well, we hit a bad market and only made £5,000 with over 3,000 kits but if you're sure about going back you'd better get into the runner's office and tell Jack Gibson what you intend doing before you settle upstairs. If it's OK he'll tell you the sailing time.' He slapped me on the shoulder and turned away.

I was shocked and puzzled. Father had never given me any hint of his intentions and Arthur had told me things about my father that I should have known, proving that he knew him better. Still it was not surprising really; Arthur had spent more time with him in my lifetime than I had. Anyway it explained why Dad had been missing all the morning. I guess that's what he had been trying to sort out with the boss and he had finally been persuaded. It obviously didn't suit Arthur that he'd deserted us.

I moved on past the large, wooden double gates into the covered company yard and headed towards the small runner's office on the left. I wondered if I was doing the right thing when I thought about the sickness, freezing and exhaustion I had experienced. But, then again, maybe it wouldn't be so bad this time. Everyone said it had been a hard trip. Anyway, when I thought about facing Dad and my family and friends and Pauline, there was only one answer.

The only occupants of the little, windowless room were Jack Gibson and his assistant Benny Cargill, Jack was standing at his chest-high desk, marking off the ship's register, while Benny sat on the high chair that went with it, writing something in his notebook. I was thinking that the desk was a replica of the one that Bob Cratchit sat at when working for Scrooge.

Jack removed his glasses and turned to me when I entered.

'Now then, young Bob. How'd it go? Are you ready to pack it in?'

'No!' I said hastily. 'I want to go back again.'

Jack's eyebrows shot up. 'Going to give it another try, are yer? Your dad can't have pushed you hard enough then.'

'He did,' I insisted, 'but Les as skipper might make a difference.'

'Nothing will make a difference this trip,' said Benny. 'You're going to the Norwegian coast and that's always hard going.'

'Right oh then, Rob!' said Gibby, changing the subject quickly. 'If you're going back, there's nothing to sign as you remain on articles. But, as you're under normal age, there's a record of service sheet here which you have to take personally to the Mercantile Marine Office and get it stamped each trip until you're sixteen. You'll have plenty of time because the ship will have to blow down for a quick boiler survey, and that will mean two extra days for you before the ship sails. Now off you go upstairs and collect your cheque.'

Jack walked out of the office with me and was confronted by one of the many hopeful deckies looking for a job.

'Have you got a ship for us, Jack?' pleaded the out-of-work mariner. 'You promised.'

'Not today, Harry,' apologised Jack. Jerking his thumb at me, he continued, 'He's the last one on this ship and he's going back.'

'But Jack,' persisted Harry. 'You said if I came down this week you'd give me a ship.'

'Well, I can't give you one, if I haven't got one, can I?' snorted Gibby as he shuffled along. Digging in his waistcoat pocket with two fingers, he pulled out a small penknife and opening it up he quipped, 'Here go and fetch me a piece of wood and I'll carve you a bastard.' Jack cackled and Benny's giggle in the background had the distraught mariner turning away dejectedly.

'Never mind, me old china,' said Jack, sobering quickly. 'Come down again next week and I'll do me best for yer. Can't say more than that, can I?' And he slapped him on the back as he departed.

My visit to the cashier's office rewarded me with a cheque for £12, as much money as I had ever had at one time. I left the dock elated and made my way to the Yorkshire Penny Bank at the top of Eton Street, not far away, where I had a small account – something I felt sure most deckies didn't have. There I deposited half and took the rest in cash, starting a habit I maintained throughout most of my career. Then the world was at my feet.

As I walked down Hessle Road I wondered what I might do with my newly acquired wealth. I was looking forward to the evening, of course, when I would see Pauline, my girlfriend, after she had come home from school, where she had stayed on. I relished the thought of taking her out to the pictures or somewhere cosy. We had arrived home too late the night before for me to see her, but I felt sure she would know I was back from sea. But what to do until four o'clock? I had to go to the Mercantile Marine Office, of course, to get my service sheet stamped, whatever that meant. Jack had told me it was in Posterngate, in the old town centre, so I reckoned I'd better make my way there soon. As these thoughts were passing through my head I was suddenly aware that I was passing a greengrocer's shop and I spotted, up on top of one of the stalls, something I'd wanted ever since the war had finished. They had just started to appear in the shops again – a large juicy pineapple. Without hesitation, I advanced and claimed my prize, my hand diving in my pocket to pull out my little wad of notes.

With my reckless indulgence tucked under my arm, I decided to take it home to share with Mum and maybe get a bite of lunch before proceeding into town to do my business. I had been out a few hours by this time in nothing but my sports coat and flannels, the best I had to wear. With the previous night's snow still laid on the ground, I was starting to feel the sharp wind biting, so with hands stuck in my pockets and shoulders hunched I trudged towards home. On the way I passed a small group of schoolboys, also homeward bound for lunch, and was amazed and disgusted to see them frantically scooping up snow to make snowballs and pelting them at each other. How insane this seemed to me now, although a few weeks before I might have done exactly the same. But the frozen nightmare I had experienced recently had cured me of touching the stuff unnecessarily forever.

Pauline Mitchelling was a lovely girl with dark hair that curled under, just short of shoulder length. She had high cheek bones and lovely almond-shaped eyes with natural long eyelashes in a heart-shaped face. Women would describe her as having a full figure, with a large well-shaped bust above a nipped-in waist. The large bust was the feature that most interested us young men at that stage of our development. Pauline was probably well aware of this because she tended to wear cotton blouses with a pleated bodice which emphasised the curves of her ample breasts – thrusting the best of her features to the front of the stall, so to speak.

She tended to wear full-flowing skirts, probably to hide large hips, but they also served to emphasise her comparatively narrow waist. I suppose she wasn't a beauty in the classic sense, for her loveliness came from within, in her kind and loving nature and soft approach to people. Her lips were very sensuous, her top lip shaped in a lovely Cupid's bow and the bottom lip full and pouting. Pauline didn't wear lipstick, but the satin sheen on that beckoning mouth was always there and caused a tightening of desire around my heart. Her eyes were her greatest attraction because they were always directed at me.

The evening of that first day, I rushed through tea. Dad was still missing, which was not unusual on his first day home from sea. He was probably in some club renewing acquaintances and catching up on local news, but I wasn't worried. I had done my awkward business earlier that day when I reported to the Mercantile Marine Office, which was awesome, with its highly polished teak counters and austere personnel. I wasn't sure of the reason for my being there and when I was asked if there were any problems I thought they were questioning my behaviour. I didn't realise they were checking on my treatment and conditions, so I answered, 'No, sir' to everything and was relieved when they finally stamped my paper and returned it to me. My business was done and I could concentrate on enjoying my evening and the couple of days to come. Things may have been more complicated if they had known I was working eighteen hours a day and more, in dangerous conditions.

After tea, I quickly smartened myself up and greased my hair with Brylcreem, putting a quiff in my forelock, and went out into the back ten-foot, where I had spent most of my schoolday evenings kicking a ball about or playing cricket with my friends. I was hoping to see Pauline out there, standing as she usually did on her own back doorstep, with arms folded, thrusting out her bosom and watching the boys skylarking and showing off in front of her.

As I approached, with my new worldly-wise swagger, Pauline's face lit up. That beckoning, intriguing smile and those limpid eyes immediately consumed my rational side, and for a moment our eyes locked on to the same wavelength of mutual desire. Then quickly our gaze was broken before it could be observed and ridiculed by the friends around us.

I was to discover that two of my best friends, Terry and Charlie, were not among them. Both were a little older than I, but Charlie had left school two terms earlier and had started work on the fish dock as a barrow boy – a fate that was also planned for me. On hearing of my great adventure, he couldn't resist following, and had managed to sign on as a galley boy a couple of weeks after I had sailed. Terry, who was supposed to stay on at school, had also succumbed. He too had signed as a galley boy, the normal start for beginners, except myself, and by far the most sensible way to begin a life at sea, working in a warm galley until you get your sea legs. But my traumatic experience had faded temporarily in the presence of my first love, as I managed to get close enough during the general buffoonery to inhale her heady perfume.

Soon there was a call from Pauline's house, as her mother announced it was time to help get the younger children to bed before both parents went out and she, Pauline, was required to baby-sit. I was crestfallen. I had been hoping to find a moment when I could ask her to come out with me to the corner cafe or some place where we could be close. But I realised all was not lost when, after replying to her mum, Pauline quickly turned to me and whispered, 'Come to the back door about eight thirty after they've gone out. I'll leave the back gate unlocked.' Then she turned and scampered in.

For the next half hour or so things stagnated, with us lads not having someone to play up to. We shuffled around and chatted for a while; there was only one respite, when Pearl, a girl of similar age, small and neat but shapely, who lived next door to me, minced her way to the corner shop before it closed, flashing coy and embarrassed glances in our direction, in response to a few catcalls and wolf whistles from the boys. I was quite friendly with Pearl but I had never considered courting her; our families were too close.

Eventually it was decided through boredom to pool some money, go to the beer-off and buy some drink. Although we were under age, it had been done before and thanks to my extra contribution we agreed to get half a bottle of rum to share. That, we thought, would give us a kick. We all moved down to the other end of the street where the local off-licence was situated. At first I was elected to go in and purchase because I was the tallest, but then it was decided that I would be recognised and probably refused and the chance would be lost. So we picked Geoff, a pal who had joined us from a neighbouring district, who would not be known by the proprietor, and who was actually the oldest by a few months.

Poor Geoff was physically thrust towards the shop to make the purchase, the rest of us stood back at a safe distance to observe through the window Geoff's confident approach to the counter. We had been careful not to furnish him with small change that might cause suspicion, and to our delight the sale was quickly made and Geoff returned with a half-bottle of Lemon Hart rum. Everyone took it in turns to swig from the bottle. It seared our throats and set fire to our stomachs and had some of the boys coughing and spluttering. It was heady stuff and the fooling around began again, but I was conscious of time passing and kept checking with the nearby fish-shop clock. I was desperate now to make some excuse to leave and join Pauline at the agreed time without drawing attention to myself. I finally used father as my reason, as I always had in the past – everyone knew how strict he was – saying he wanted to speak to me before he went out for the evening. It's not surprising that I was allowed to leave without much fuss, as the gang realised there would be one less to share the rest of the rum with.

I tried to stroll nonchalantly away until out of sight. In the darkened ten-foot I scampered the length of the alley towards Pauline's back gate, thrusting a peppermint into my mouth to kill the smell of rum on my breath. When I reached the gate I looked around in the dim light before trying to ease the latch, but the resounding clack when it flung clear, I fancied, must have alerted the neighbourhood, especially Pauline's parents if they hadn't yet left. I quickly stepped inside, closed the gate behind me and slid the bolt home in case anyone should consider following me. I couldn't be sure the boys wouldn't put two and two together and I didn't want anything to spoil this evening.

I made my way down the unfamiliar path towards the well-lit scullery and on my uncertain approach the door was flung open. Pauline must have been impatiently awaiting my arrival, but she tried to display a nonchalant air as she lounged in the entrance. She had loosened the draw-string on the neck of her blouse and slipped it down over her shoulders, exposing a bare upper chest and a necklace with a pendant that nestled in the top of a very delightful cleavage. I noticed also that her lips were enhanced with a rich, ruby lipstick which no doubt had been quickly applied after her mother had left.

Pauline smiled but hardly spoke a word as she ushered me inside and led me to the sofa in the cosy lounge. I decided to start the conversation by speaking my mind and telling her how pretty she looked.

'That's a very nice blouse you're wearing,' I ventured. 'You look lovely with your shoulders all bare.' I sat upright in the middle of the couch, all correct and proper with my hands tucked between my knees.

'Thank you,' said Pauline. 'I got the idea from a bridesmaid's dress I wore at my cousin's wedding. Would you like to see some photographs?'

'Yes, sure!' I enthused. Sharing an album would give us a chance to sit close together right away.

Pauline quickly brought a large book and sitting alongside me opened it up across both our knees. With heads bowed close, she continued to explain the pictures while I inhaled her scent, until a scamper on the stairs and a stifled giggle told us the children had sneaked down to view the boyfriend. This caused Pauline to jump up straight away, leaving my arm, which I had just slid along the back of the sofa, suspended with nowhere to go. I decided to leave it there until she returned, which she quickly did. This time, more relaxed, she sat closer still, with our thighs touching.

Pretty soon came another disturbance from the kids for the inevitable glass of water.

My desire for Pauline was building up and as she plonked down beside me and bent forward once again I leant towards her, brushed her hair back with my hand and kissed her on the neck behind the ear. Pauline shrugged her shoulders with a little shudder and, as she turned her head towards me, I cushioned my lips on hers. My arms enveloped her as we fell back on the couch. I plied her with little, light kisses, little sips from those surrendering beckoning lips, drinking in the wine of love. We varied the kisses, pecking around the mouth and cheeks, nuzzling like horses and delighting at the sensitive response from each other. Another cry from above broke the spell and we separated reluctantly, Pauline sucking in a great juddering breath before rising reluctantly, face flushed but eyes sparkling, as she went off to tend to the children again.

For a few moments I sat·quietly, breathing deeply, my body was aroused and my stomach muscles were aching a little. I must have been holding them tense during our love play, partly to avoid putting too much weight on Pauline, I fancy, but that was not the only cause. Presently Pauline returned, tugging and smoothing down her skirt. 'I think those kids are going to be awake all night until Mum and Dad come home at this rate,' she said. 'The trouble is you never know if they might come downstairs again and I don't want them blabbing on what they've seen.' Moving across the room she turned the radiogram on low and taking my hand pulled me off the couch. 'Come on,' she whispered, and led me out of the lounge into a darkened front room.

I had to watch my step. What little light there was came from the street light shining over the lace half-curtain across the window and reflecting off the wallpaper. I could just make out an old fashioned chaise-longue facing the fireplace, with the toe towards the window. Pauline guided me towards this and we sat down, with her lying back on the arm. Then she pulled me down on top of her and we started a serious wet smooching session. As I closed with her, my chest pressing against hers squeezed out the warm air in her blouse, and the mixture of her perfume and body scent was intoxicating. This time the kisses were long and lingering and the tongues came into play. Our bodies undulated as we each concentrated on arousing the other, but as our feet remained on the floor this was confined to the upper body only. Had the contact been further down Pauline would have realised how successful were her efforts.

It is difficult to say what excited me most at this stage. The softness of her body was so enthralling. I had wrestled with girls before and although there was never much muscle to contend with they had always been pretty strong, resilient and resisting, but this was different, I was finding out just how soft a female body could be, so responsive and surrendering. Pauline's flesh seemed to melt into every contour of my own body. My right arm was across her shoulders with my wrist supporting her neck and head while I gently tweaked her earlobe, fingering a diamante stud.

'You're not trying to steal my jewellery, are you?' she murmured, with a throaty chuckle.

'No,' I croaked. 'I'm after taking more than that tonight.'

'Hummm! I think you'll be lucky,' she moaned, not too convincingly.

My left hand was massaging the line of her right shoulder blade, sweeping down occasionally to her waist and easing her blouse gently out of her waistband.

'As a matter of fact,' I half whispered, 'I was thinking of buying you another piece of jewellery after my next trip, a bracelet or ring maybe.'

'Oh, I would love a ring!' enthused Pauline.

Was this bribery? No, I was just speaking words really, trying to preoccupy her, hoping she wouldn't realise my fingers were now massaging the lovely, smooth flesh of her tummy. I murmured on with other possibilities, punctuated with sloppy kisses, but my mind was concentrating on the hand which was now massaging that beautifully shaped breast through her silky bra, the nipple so hard that it almost scoured my palm.

After a few moments more of gasps, moans and simmering, I sensed that Pauline's legs were squirming as she rubbed her knees together. I chose this moment to slip my fingers under her brassière and push it up to expose this wonderful, smooth, delicate, spongy orb to my exploring fingers... A clatter against the window and an exchange of words outside made us both stiffen immediately. I turned my head, glanced over my shoulder towards the cause of the disturbance and saw a small figure jump up again and try to balance on the narrow window ledge, I recognised the voices of Terry's younger brothers, who had followed our group around earlier in the evening. They must have sussed out what my early departure meant. Maybe someone had called for me and found I hadn't been home. Anyway they had worked out where I was likely to be. With his next jump, the younger one managed to balance on the ledge, supported by his brother, and as he peeped over the lace curtain I could hear him say, 'I can see them. They're laid on the couch.'

I was sprawled across Pauline almost completely, shielding her and hiding the position of my hand. We froze. 'Stay completely still,' I whispered. 'They'll soon lose interest if there's no action.' The would-be voyeurs changed places a couple of times, trying to report on the scene, but as there was no movement it was obviously difficult for them to make out any detail. I wished them in hell!

We lay quiet for a while. The radio in the next room sounded clearly; Teresa Brewer was singing 'Put Another Nickel In.' Pauline stealthily extricated herself from her compromising position, removing my hand and restoring her clothes. We both cooled rapidly and became aware of the passing time; it may not be too long before her parents returned. We waited a while longer and, as soon as there was a lull in the activity outside, we quickly rose and scurried back into the lounge. We didn't settle again, choosing instead to take our time on a long, lingering, smoochy goodbye, during which we agreed I would take her to the pictures the following evening.

Pauline followed me down the darkened garden path to bolt the gate – a final kiss and I quickly slid off into the night.

The next day, though pleasant and relaxing, was a long one. None of my friends were available, being either at school, working or away. I mooched about the house a while, helped with a few chores and played some records on our radiogram, something that every fisherman's house had at that time. But I didn't have any records of my own.

The house was full of drying sea gear. Mine had pride of place on the ceiling pulley as I was sailing next day, but other clothes were draped over everything else. The clothes horse and fireguard were covered. It made me restless and I decided to go into town and buy myself a record. I was keen on boogie, and 'Hamp's Boogie-Woogie', played by Lionel Hampton on piano, was a popular record I was keen to buy. I still had most of my £6 left and could easily afford it. Sydney Scarborough's was the place to go; you could listen to your selection of records played in a booth before purchasing. After that, I thought I might look round some of the big stores and price some cheap jewellery.

Quickly, I dressed in my best clothes, caught a trolleybus into town and spent the best part of an hour in Sydney Scarborough's. I purchased a record and then made my way into Whitefriargate, the main shopping centre, to look around. Halfway down was the Monument pub, a dingy place nestling among the tightly crammed shops, and as I approached a small group of drunken deckies tumbled out of the doorway, accompanied by two or three freeloading women. As they stumbled and staggered about in front of me, laughing and joking, I was suddenly confronted by Freddie Nott. His grinning, beer-sodden face lit up as he recognised me, and he lurched towards me, arm outstretched to rest on my shoulder.

'Well, if it isn't young Dass-sher,' he slurred, still grinning. 'Hey! We're gonna be mates next trip, yuh know. Charlie's signed off and I'm back decky learner. So doan worry, I'll show yuh the ropesh.'

I was surprised. I didn't know Charlie had finished. In fact I'd never thought about any crew changes.

'Lishen,' continued Freddie. 'These are some of my mates off the *Cape Tariffa* and we're all going to a dommie at Mart's house. Why doan' you come along?'

I didn't know what a dommy was, but one look at the two younger women, with short skirts – in this cold weather – and diamond-etched stockings, teetering on perilously high heels, gave me a good idea what a dommy was liable to be, and I wanted no part in it. It appeared at this stage that another member of the party was also reluctant to proceed. He kept arguing with a little fellow named Frank that he wanted to get a new suit and that was what he had really come out to do.

'You can get a new suit anytime,' argued the little chap. 'Don't spoil this chance to have some fun.'

'No! I've got to get one now,' insisted the first decky, swaying precariously.

'OK! OK!' conceded the ebullient little Frankie. Steadying his friend, he glared at him for a moment with bloodshot eyes. 'Wait here a second and I'll get you one,' he assured him, and turning away he dashed across the road.

Directly opposite the Monument was Jackson's, a well-known, high-class tailor's shop, frequented by fishermen. Into this ran the intrepid little Frankie to appear immediately in the shop window display. He then grabbed a dummy sporting a nice grey suit, which he dragged out of sight only to reappear a second later coming out of the door, carrying the mannequin and slamming it down on the far side of the road, where it took a list to starboard similar to the character for whom it was intended. A rush of outraged shop assistants exiting from the door behind Frank had the whole riotous little group precariously scampering down the street, while I retreated self-consciously in the opposite direction, trying to display no connection with the unruly mob of revellers.

That night I sat in the back row of the Langham Cinema with my arm around Pauline's shoulders, watching 'For Whom the Bell Tolls', starring Gregory Peck and Ingrid Bergman. Pauline fitted snugly under my arm, with her head resting against my jaw, and once again the smell of her hair and other cosmetics enhanced her femininity and softness and made me feel so protective. The film was a good one, but at times I lost concentration in it as I savoured the closeness of our bodies. Ingrid Bergman was beautiful and the love scenes had us both squeezing closer in sympathetic union with the characters on screen. Pauline occasionally placing little kisses on my cheek and chin. Both of us were sorry when the film finished and we had to leave the warmth of the cinema for the cold outside, but we walked home hand-in-hand, our arms around each other, until we reached the back streets of our neighbourhood and I guided Pauline into the familiar darkened ten-foot alley dividing the back of our homes.

I chose a sheltered spot in the garage compound behind Pauline's house. I was already aroused and bent on a conquest on my last night at home. Pauline was also aware that this was our last chance to love each other before I left again the next day, but her natural modesty constantly fought a battle with her obvious desire for me, so that when I tried to hold our bodies close she always thrust her hip bone into my groin rather than let our pelvic areas merge.

My left hand was inside Pauline's coat, massaging her waist and back. When I sensed that the hypnotic atmosphere had her weakening and the undulations of our bodies were in unison, I slid my hand down over her buttock to the bottom edge of her skirt, searching for the forbidden area of her thigh above her stocking top, so firm and smooth and warm. The explorations became more exciting for us both as a gasping moan from my willing partner confirmed. Frustration with a suspender was hampering things when a loud enquiring call of, 'PAULINE?' from Pauline's back garden sounded surprisingly close. And then, 'Pauline, are you there?'

It had the intended result. Pauline thrust me from her and then, with her hands still on my upper arms, she whispered, 'It's my mum. She knows we're here.'

'No, she doesn't,' I whispered in reply. 'She's only guessing.'

'I'd better get back,' she murmured again.

'OK,' I agreed. 'But not too soon or she'll twig. Better go round the front way.'

Pauline composed herself. We moved down to the end of the alley and paused in the light from the street lamps where we could have a last look at each other. As we pressed close, murmuring our goodbyes, I looked into her adoring eyes and felt ten-feet tall.

'Be careful,' she said, 'be sure to come back to me. You're so close to the water out there in those small ships and so many have been lost before.'

I was surprised at her perception and my memories of the last trip made me realise for the first time how right she was.

Chapter 6

DESPAIR AND TRIUMPH

Packing my bag was something I had to do myself; I could not bear the thought of not knowing exactly what was in there when I came to use it at sea. It was one thing I continued to do throughout my sea career. Mum would have all my gear laid out, neatly ironed and stacked in little piles, but I would select from these piles and pack each item in the order I would require it, and that is what I was doing on this, the last morning before we sailed.

I think all the family were surprised that I was going back for another dose of purgatory. I was surprised myself, but these last few days had been great, being more or less my own boss with time and money to spend as I wished. There was also a certain esteem attached to being a sailor who risked the perils of the deep. I was part of a revered band of men with an exceptional sense of comradeship which was well known and accepted.

My sisters, in particular, bemoaned the fact that I had succumbed to the call of the sea, saying they thought I would have been a doctor or lawyer, though how this was to be without an education, I do not know. The die was cast when I failed to progress to college, I think. Anyway, here I was again preparing to prove a point.

This time I left in a taxi, on my own and in daylight, and this time the streets were busy. I don't remember exactly what thoughts crossed my mind on this occasion, except a little sadness at leaving behind this close-knit community of Hessle Roaders going about their business, as once again we thundered through the cobbled tunnel leading to that other world

As we drove across the swing bridge over the lock I looked around again in amazed excitement at the vast scene of frantic activity. So many trades were involved – planning, preparing, repairing and discharging the many proud ships that littered the dock. Many were on the move, some under their own steam, some being towed across the dock by the little dock tugs, and some being pulled along the quay physically by the men working in the shore gangs. I couldn't help feeling proud to be at the heart of this great industry.

It was the coast season and this trip we were heading for the Norwegian coast. These grounds were nearer than the previous trip and in normal conditions should have taken only three and a half days to reach, but not this time. Although the cold was ever present the major problem was the raging gales and snowstorms. The winds struck us from the north and made every yard of progress a battle over mountainous seas. I was sick again.

I learned from my previous voyage and had managed to acquire two important things. On my way to the ship I had stopped the taxi at the fishermen's stores again and, apart from replenishing my supply of cotton gutting gloves and other necessities, I had bought myself another thirty-bob flock mattress. What was even more important, I was on board early before the newcomers arrived and was able to select a fore and aft line bunk that had been vacated. It's true that the bunk was right at the fore-end of the fo'c'sle, in the eyes of the ship, but I thought at least I wouldn't be sliding up and down when the ship rolled.

But rolling on this occasion was not the problem. We were heading directly into the weather, and the pitching of the ship was horrendous. As the powerful engine tried to force us over every pinnacle that rushed towards us, the ship would balance for a moment on each peak before plunging down twenty or thirty feet into the trough, and the aquatic avalanche which followed, with an almighty crump that tested every plate and rivet in that noble British vessel. The bunk I had chosen was one that headed this dedicated charge into the earth's natural, aggressive elements.

For two days of this maelstrom, no work was possible either on deck or below. I was not able or allowed to go aft to eat or drink and, as there was no drinking water forward, I sustained myself between bouts of sea-sickness from a bottle of lemonade which I had brought with me from home – not the ideal refreshment if one was trying to calm an upset stomach in such circumstances.

The pounding we took in those bunks throughout this intense struggle was horrific; my body was slowly being pulverised. The *St Apollo* threw her head up so quickly when each wall of water rushed towards her that my body just about left the mattress. When she then headed down before I did, I met her coming up again on the next sea with such an almighty slam and always that bounce and shudder as the impact traversed the ship from stem to stern. Time after time this violent motion dragged me from unconsciousness and the oblivion that I sought, all the time accompanied by the sound of that powerful wind, which had gained such velocity, as wind does over such a wide unrestricted expanse like the ocean. How does one describe such a sound? It rushed, it screamed, it howled, it sighed, and it whistled through the cracks around the fo'c'sle door, constantly reminding you of its power when you are unprotected against its ferocity.

Eventually every nightmare comes to an end, and you can be sure that the people responsible for the success of any venture will be observing and monitoring the situation and looking for a chance to progress. The skipper and his officers on the bridge were looking for just such a chance.

The weather on that trip never did fine away, but as soon as conditions were workable the skipper had us on deck coping with the elements to prepare the ship and the gear for our next attempt at wresting our living from the seabed.

As consciousness once more came back to me in the confines of my bunk, I was aware immediately that the scream had gone out of the wind. There was still plenty of motion in the ship but not so violent, and no crashing as it rose and fell. Laying there now was more like laying in the bottom of a swingboat rather than enduring the violent battering of an armoured tank, but still the movement was sufficient to keep my weakened stomach churning. The fo'c'sle door was hooked back, probably to clear the air from the smoke billowing from the coal stove, and the stale smell of a dozen sweaty bodies. It appeared to be mid morning as we were still far enough south to have the sky brightening at a fairly early hour.

A large, bewhiskered face suddenly rose over the bunk side close to mine. I had a top bunk. The stubbly lantern jaw was instantly recognisable as Bill Steech and he leered at me.

'Hayeee! It lives,' he cried, to no one in particular. 'I was beginning to wonder, after two and a half days without a movement and never been out even for a piss.' This was not true, especially the latter, and I had staggered out a few times to be sick as well.

'Well, that's your lot,' continued Bill. 'The captain requires our bodies on deck and that includes you! You've missed your breakfast, but I'll make sure you don't miss the work, so get your body out of that shit pit and let's have you on deck in fifteen minutes.' As Bill turned away he called back after him, 'There's tea aft but if you want a drink you'd better look lively because I'm not waiting for you.'

At this point, a voice from behind a curtained bunk said, 'Do you mind doing your bullying on deck, Steechy? Some of us are trying to sleep.' But Bill just grunted and clumped out into the bleak daylight.

I tumbled, aching, from my bunk and wondered how many months had passed since I spent those two evenings with Pauline. It appeared as long ago as that now.

Fishing the west coast of Norway is different from fishing anywhere else. Most of the trawling is done at great depths, 200 fathoms (1,200 ft) or more, and there is a constant current flowing from the south. It is not practical to tow at these depths against such a strong flow and so to repeat a tow you have to steam back after every haul. One would think that this was easier for the men on deck, giving the crew time to clear some fish, but this was seldom the case, as the net had to be overhauled and repaired first, and the constant lifting of the trawl doors and gear inboard and out again was very wearing. Working on the net, which had to be stretched along the bulwarks while steaming at full speed in bad weather, presented greater risks, especially to the men aft side. Lifting the gear and steaming back every haul or two hauls also cost valuable time, so the skipper had to make every haul pay extra, and hauling and shooting had to be done at near record speed every time, especially this trip with so much time lost running off.

Normally the first contact with Norway was the light on Stadtland corner, known to fishermen as Svino, usually reached in forty-eight hours. This trip it was over two and a half days before we even sighted it. The next landmark was Skomvaer light in the Lofoten Islands, normally after three days. The skipper chose to shoot at Andaness about seventy nautical miles beyond this. It turned out to be a good choice. There was plenty of fish and the ships were massed there. A large bight in the sheer edge of the bank caused the fish to gather in a small area, and the Anda light close by was in sectors – some white, some red or green – making it easier to pinpoint the bad ground and rocks.

But the greatest problem was the number of ships, all trying to put their gear through such a small area, and in weather that made it difficult for intricate manoeuvres. With everyone towing only one way, dozens of ships were queuing up, one after another, to put their gear down in the correct place, some nipping in ahead of you if they could. And with the tide carrying you away when the ship was stopped it meant that speed was of the essence. I was bemused to see such a confusion of lights surrounding us in the almost constant dark.

Shooting, hauling and lifting the gear rapidly meant that we used every wire we possessed, so I was dispensed on the port side to clear the wires for the fishroom man. Bill Steech welcomed me with almost open arms and had me running the length of the port side constantly stretching out wires. I have to confess, although necessary, it was an easy job compared with the frantic and dangerous activity on the other side of the vessel, and I wondered if Les, the skipper, my father's mate of many years, wasn't trying to protect me a little.

Well, you could be sure that Bill would turn this to maximum advantage. During the occasional lull in the proceedings, Bill would call me to him and tell me to fetch him a cig from for'ard. For me, it meant a few brief moments in the warmth of the fo'c'sle while I rummaged through my locker, opened the packet of Woodbines I had bought from the bond issue for my mother, and lit one to return it to him and place it in his bewhiskered mouth. He received it ungraciously and, closely watching events on the other side of the deck, waved me back to my duties clearing the confusion of wires that had piled up there.

This became a regular issue and was costing me my present to my mother. I resolved to put a stop to it somehow. But how was I to refuse Bill, now that this was started? On the next pause in the crashing and banging of the gear while we were hauling, Bill called me to him, dispensing me once more to get him a cigarette. I started forward, then returned to him and asked, 'Where do you keep your cigs, Bill?'

He gave me a startled, exasperated snort and snarled, 'Never mind, just get on with your job.' It did the trick; he never asked me again. Bill only had baccy in his locker.

The fishing was hectic – no, desperate – that trip, and when gutting the fish, which were large, there was an extra consideration. As this was a breeding ground, all the fish carried inside them either roes or chitterling (fish eggs) which had to be saved and bagged apart from the livers. So exhausting was the work that I don't think my eyes ever had a chance to focus for the last couple of days, and some others may have been in the same state because Freddy Nott had a little accident towards the end of fishing. While taking the gear in after hauling, with the usual mad rush, Fred let his hand linger on the bulwark rail when the bobbins were brought inboard. As the bobbins struck the rail on their way in, none of the twenty-inch balls actually caught Fred's hand (they would have crushed it completely if they had), but one of the smaller iron beckets which spaced the bobbins did tap on Fred's mitt, causing it immediately to swell up like a balloon. Even though it was strapped up, it was obvious that Fred couldn't grip anything properly, so he changed places with me and I worked the starboard side aft for the last thirty-six hours of fishing.

The weather was still foul and we all constantly watched those unpredictable, prancing waves. On one of the last hauls, I was working with Jim Mullett, the third hand; we were lifting the after wing inboard on the Gilson wire. The skipper rang the ship full speed to hasten back to the starting position, but before the exercise was complete, and as the ship gathered speed, Jim was just releasing a lashing on the rail to allow the gear to come in when the familiar shout of 'WATER' was hailed.

I instantly sprang for the comparative safety of the engine-room casing above, as I had been taught, when she shot a dollop of water over the bulwarks, smacking Jim front on and knocking him back on the seat of his pants. And, as the water rushed up the deck, I watched helplessly as it carried Jim with it, still sitting upright, arms and legs spread wide like some child going up a slide in reverse. Jim's face bore a look of horror until he came to an abrupt stop when the onrushing water slammed his back up against the edge of the steel-clad spare trawl door, which is strapped to the casing side. Then his face changed to show excruciating pain as he slumped over in the receding slop.

I jumped down, splashed towards him and grabbed his arm, trying to lift him to his feet, but he waved me away with a groan and gasped, 'Free that lashing, Bob, and lift the gear inboard, clear of the water, or she'll scoop another dollop at us.' I turned away and dashed back to the rail where the gear was still suspended on the Gilson swaying above my head. I saw the lashing had jammed, and now *I* was in the vulnerable position as the ship raced on, dancing over the seas. I lost no time trying to clear the rope, instead I flung my mitten off and scooped my oilskin above my waist. I dragged my knife out of my pocket – it was open in a flash – and I slashed through the lashing, indicating to the winch man to heave away until the gear was inboard. The others rushed from for'ard to secure it and help Jim from the deck.

There was a few minutes' respite while we caught our breath before returning to the deck, and I pushed into the mess-deck to see if Jim was alright. He had always been kind to me and I was concerned that he might be badly injured. They had propped him up in a corner of the mess. Although he was holding himself rigid, he was breathing easily and smiled when I approached. 'I'll be alright eventually,' he assured me. 'But you did well, Rob. You acted quickly and fearlessly when danger threatened, and I think you'll go right to the top.' These were the kindest words spoken to me since I had launched myself into this doubtful profession and it gave me great heart.

Jim did return to light duties for the rest of that trip but I was never to sail with him again.

On the journey home, the weather was still bad but this time, with a following wind, the passage was much quicker. When we landed the fish, it sold for £7,500, nearly £2,000 more than the previous trip, but on this occasion my store bill and other expenses had to be deducted so I finished up with the same amount of money to draw, about £12. Still, I was rich once more.

Although my father had agreed to take the shore job offered to him, he was to return for one more trip. He asked me if I intended to pursue a sea career. Having survived two trips, I seemed to be hooked. The money had a lot to do with it, but what I saw as the swashbuckling aura of the job was the decisive factor. Anyway, the alternative, as a barrow boy on the fish market, was unthinkable, so my answer was yes.

'Well, in that case, as you're so green about the job, you'd better stop ashore and get your decky learner's ticket before you do another trip,' he insisted. So it was decided that I would sign up at the Nautical School for the next course, which would last three weeks. Two days later, the *St Apollo* sailed without me and I signed up at school to learn my trade.

I took to my schooling very well. I was lucky enough to be taught by a fine old ex-skipper called Jack Glanville, with whom I had a great affinity. I learned very quickly about net-mending, the construction of a Granton trawl and the way it towed on the sea bed, and many other things, including most knots and splices and how to read the compass – skills I had already learned in the boy scouts. Meanwhile my relationship with Pauline, which I had been looking forward to so much, unfortunately foundered.

While I was away I had conjured up a picture of my girl, true to me and impatient for my return. I think she was. But maybe Pauline's generous nature got the better of her because, according to some of my friends, she had been a bit free with her kisses, and some claimed to have had the occasional hand up her jumper. I guess there were some exaggerations, but a number of the stories jelled. Maybe I had aroused something in Pauline which she couldn't completely control. Anyway, I was devastated and I told her we were finished.

Now it was Pauline's turn to be devastated and she beseeched me to forgive her and make it up, contriving every possible way to bump into me. She hung around the outside the house on an evening, hoping I would come out to walk the dog. She even let it be known that she would let me do anything to her if only we could be as we were before. Very tempting, but that was the trouble. She let it be known and anyway my mind was made up. Fortunately, I had plenty to occupy my mind with my studies and another young lady called Audrey Hepwood who had come to live nearby.

My schooling had gone well. I was so far ahead of the others in the class that Jack had to give me first-class net-mending work, which was really intended for bosuns' study. I enjoyed my time at school. It made sense of most of what I had seen at sea, and I passed my ticket with flying colours. Now I was impatient to put it into practice.

I had completed my exams just in time for the return of the *St Apollo*, and Jack Gibby was kind enough to sign me back on that ship, but this time with an entirely different skipper. This was one Thomas Nightingale, or Tommy Nighty, 'the bastard with an angel's face,' as he was known throughout the company. Every skipper had some crew members who followed them around, and Tommy Nighty was no exception, so there were quite a few new faces when I joined. Freddy Nott had signed off with the promise of another start as deck-hand in one of the smaller, older ships. Thankfully, Bill Steech was no longer with us. He declined to sail with Nighty, whom he did not regard as a good enough fisherman. Bill's place as fishroom man was taken by a mouthy character called Bunker Carmichael, who had a hump on his nose caused (so I was informed) by poking his nose into other people's business.

Our new bosun was not a Nightingale regular, as I understood it, although he had sailed with him many times. Jack Gordon was a tallish, gaunt, square-shouldered man, whose mouth took a slant to starboard, the side he spoke out of, so that I never really trusted him. His nephew, Alan Gordon, out of a similar mould, at twenty-one years old was my fellow decky learner, much favoured by his uncle. The real character amongst the new crew members, as far as I was concerned, was the mate. Arthur Munzer had stuck with Tommy Nighty like glue through thick and thin over the years; he was a workaholic – probably not surprising with a German-sounding name like Munzer – and perhaps one of the main reasons behind any success Nighty had achieved. He was to have a great influence on my attitude towards the job or any job that I undertook.

Early in the first trip with Tom Nightingale, a couple of incidents occurred which were to speed my progress in my drive to get to the top.

We were into April now and, though there were plenty of grey days with occasional sleet showers, there were also some fine days when a watery sun shone through and the sea was not so choppy. Our destination was the Barents Sea, or the White Sea as it was more commonly known to Hull fishermen. It would take us five or six days to reach, depending on where the skipper chose to shoot the gear, and with this extra time in hand Nighty wanted his bridge kept clean on the run-off.

Alan and I took it in turn from day to day to take up the bridge mat, scrub the deck gratings and polish the brass for an hour or two each morning.

I was scrubbing the bridge on the first fine morning when the skipper turned out. It was easy to see how he got his nickname. An average-size man, a bit on the chubby side, and close to fifty years of age, he had what one would describe as a boyish face, with a charming smile, but also a livid scar that slashed across the right temple. The story goes that this was caused when he was blown up during the war while skipper of a minesweeper, a splinter entering that part of his skull which had to be repaired by a metal plate. It was generally believed by most deckies that this plate attracted the compass, which in nearly all trawlers was situated in the deck head in front of the wheel. Many a wheelman who had just been bollocked for not keeping her straight could just be heard muttering under his breath for the little, fat bastard to stop pacing the bridge under the damn compass.

It was also suggested that it was this injury to Nightingale's head that caused his rapid change in personality. One moment he was all smiles and apparently concerned for his crew; then without warning he would change. His face would turn bright red and he would be shouting and screaming and frothing at the mouth as he demanded more effort, more work from every man Jack. Often when I was alone with Tommy I witnessed this rapid change take place. It was as if some violent pain in his head started up, causing him to thrash about on the bridge. He would actually bang his forehead violently against the bridge windowframe to try and shake off his torment; then woe betide all hands. Fortunately, this did not happen too frequently.

On the morning in question, I was cleaning the bridge and the skipper was in a good mood, having slept well and risen to a fine day, but he was concerned with the distance run overnight, according to the figures in the officers-deck logbook, and he ordered the mate to take the group working on deck and pull in the log-line to see if it was foul or faulty. It takes a lot of men to pull in a log-line when the ship is steaming full, so Tommy sent the wheelman aft to help and took the wheel himself. Still the men aft were struggling – the line is thin, wet and slippery – so, as I was scrubbing near the telegraph, he suddenly ordered 'half speed'.

I was startled. 'Pardon, Skipper?' I enquired.

'Half speed, half speed,' roared Nighty. 'Didn't your old man show you how to work the telegraph?'

'Oh yes, Skipper!' I spluttered, and jumped up to ring the ship expertly on half speed.

'Can you steer? Do you know the compass?' he demanded.

'Yes, Skipper,' I replied quickly.

'Then take the wheel while I look aft, and steer north by east three-quarters east.' He gave the course in points.

I complied hurriedly.

Nighty watched the proceedings aft, regularly checking the compass. He seemed impressed. 'Good,' he muttered on a couple of occasions, as I happened to be spot on and passing each time he looked. The log-line was eventually hauled and a small piece of rope yarn cleared from the fan before it was streamed again. The skipper appeared pleased with my performance until the wheelman returned and I handed over the wheel and the course. My effort was to stand me in good stead later.

The long run-off should have given the crew plenty of time to prepare the gear, but the skipper decided we should prepare two gears, one on each side of the ship.

With the abundance of fish generally available during the prolific years after the war, most skippers had given up using a port gear as it was difficult to shoot, or so they said, needing to swing constantly to port against the turn of the screw. But Nighty wasn't going to miss the chance of working two gears, changing over as soon as one was damaged, and thus keeping a trawl on the bottom at all times, even if it meant twice the work for the crew. It was confusing too as everything has to work the opposite way on the port side.

The five and a half days' steaming off were full days, with the extra gear to prepare and set up. Working two gears was always demoralising for a crew. They knew what it meant when fishing began. For us daymen, the two decky learners and the fishroom man, they were tiring days, working from seven in the morning till six at night, with just the half-hour break for dinner.

When we did shoot, it came after another full day's work. We had just staggered forward to the fo'c'sle after tea to lie down in our blessed, comfy bunks, now that everything was ready, including the fishroom. Then the order came to down trawl, and all hands had to turn out to shoot for the first tow on Skolpen Bank.

We were into the fish straight away, hauling three good bags of haddock, and the skipper decided, as apparently he often did, to work all hands for the first twenty-four hours' fishing before starting the watches. At the end of that period it meant that, with the twelve hours I had done as a dayman, I had been up thirty-six hours, working practically non-stop, before the watches were started.

Then came the next shock. Nighty wasn't going to work the normal eighteen plus six, that was eighteen hours on deck and six below. He elected to work twenty plus four, which meant that he had all hands on deck for four hours every day but everyone else lost out. Then came the last straw, when Munzer finally sorted out the watches. He wanted me on watch with him and he was to take the last watch below. After thirty-six hours I still had another twenty hours to do and already I was shattered. Once more, I was asking the Good Lord for help to stay the distance. At fifteen years of age I wasn't built for this level of work.

To say the least, it was dangerous working in that environment in such an exhausted state. A number of times I fell asleep on my feet, often to collapse into the fish, but only to be dragged to my feet by the scruff of the neck and reminded that only a couple of years before there had been no watches below while fishing. The deck-hands were expected to work almost non-stop till the ship was full.

For two or three days we fished well and during this time Arthur Munzer kept me working close to him. Seeing that I was easily manipulated and quick on my feet, he insisted I live up to my nickname of Dasher and had me dashing around the deck faster than anyone else. He taught me how to prepare the cod ends for paying away after each bag while he tied up the cod-line. He advised me how to look good in the eyes of a skipper by keeping myself busy during small stoppages while a shackle was being tightened or a small hole mended in the net. Most men would take the chance to stretch their backs and stand with mittened hands hanging down by their sides, motionless in yellow oilskins or black rubber frocks. They looked like penguins, or so Arthur said. 'But you want to keep moving. Throw out the small fish or pick up a piece of twine and bend it on the hand rail. It doesn't do any good but it looks good,' he explained.

If he wanted a spanner or bar from for'ard or aft he would tell someone nearer and then send me in the opposite direction to see if I could beat them, and more often than not I did. It all required more effort and more work on my part but I followed his advice. It became a habit that did impress most observers and in time it made me more alert.

After a few days, the fish began to disperse and the hauls diminished. Then one afternoon we hauled with a cable stranded and Nighty decided to steam for a few hours while the fish were cleared off the deck and repairs effected. Surprisingly, the skipper called me to the bridge to steer.

No one heard his high-pitched voice at first with the winch running. Eventually Bunker Carmichael on the wires shouted, 'Hark a nightingale sings,' and the word was passed down for young Dasher to go to the bridge. With wet gear off and boots turned down, I clumped on to the bridge and Nighty greeted me with a benign smile.

'Come on, young' un! Now's your chance to do your stuff. Grab the wheel and steer ESE,' and he walked to the window and left me to it while he watched the proceedings on deck.

The weather was fine and clear and the *St Apollo* steered easily. Tommy Nighty watched the fish cleared, and checked the sounder and our position on the chart a couple of times, while the men on deck changed their gutting gloves for mittens and proceeded to change some of the wires on the gear. Tommy, having found my steering satisfactory, checked our position once more and looked around the horizon. There was no one else in sight. 'Keep your eyes open, Bob,' he said, 'while I slip down below, and give me a shout if you see any ships.' Then he scampered down the companionway to his berth.

After he had gone, I slouched easily on the wheel, watching the compass closely and glancing occasionally around the horizon. In this relaxed state, the muscles in my body tweaked and ached a little, reminding me of the intense activity they had maintained in the last few days. The skipper was gone longer than I expected, and I guess I was starting to feel dippy, when the telegraph suddenly rang to the stop position and I heard the engine cease. I answered the telegraph immediately and instinctively moved to the front of the bridge to see what was happening on deck. The engine-room voice pipe whistled alongside of me and, removing the whistle, I answered. I heard Tim Hartley, the chief engineer, telling me that he had observed the dormant messenger wire on the port side running out over the port quarter. He had run down below to stop the ship before it could foul the propellor, and advised that someone should check it immediately. I thanked him and replaced the whistle.

As I stuck my head out of the window with the engines stopped, I saw everyone looking quizzically towards the bridge and informed them of the problem. Some of them reacted right away, running down the port side as the skipper reached the bridge.

I explained to the skipper that the ship was stopped because the messenger wire was running out over the port rail and that I had despatched some of the hands to retrieve it. Nighty moved to the port bridge wing and looked out of the window in time to see the wire being hauled back safely on board.

Tom was so relieved to see no harm had been done and turned away pleased and delighted with me.

'Excellent. You did well there, young Bob,' he enthused. 'That was quick thinking on your part.'

'Well-er, it was the chief that spotted it,' I tried to explain, as the skipper rang the ship on.

'Nevertheless,' he interrupted, 'you reacted quickly and saved the day. I've been watching you on deck lately and you're getting pretty sharp. Keep it up.'

After that I could do no wrong in Nighty's eyes, and he called me regularly to the bridge whenever there was a short steam to be done. Munzer too seemed delighted that his protégé was being recognised, but the rest of the crew were not so pleased that a decky learner was given such responsibility instead of a more experienced deck-hand.

Alan Garton, my contemporary, would have given me a hard time as well if it hadn't been discovered that he was the cause of the near-disaster. It was he who had tied his blood-stained gloves to a length of twine and thrown them overboard to tow them clean, tying the other end to a bight of the messenger wire laid on the deck. This still might not have caused a problem if he hadn't weighed the gloves down with a shackle. This was a pretty stupid thing to do, it was agreed generally, but it made Alan resentful and he constantly looked for a way to discredit me.

We continued to fish well that trip, but Nighty kept us hard at it regularly changing gears whenever they were even slightly damaged. Eventually we settled at a place called the North Deeps, some distance off the Russian coast, catching six bags of jumbo haddocks. Fortunately, the weather remained pretty fine and warm for the time of year, but the big wooden-headed haddocks were hard on our hands. They also contained a sandy type of sludge in their stomachs, which spewed out when we were gutting, causing haddock rash between our fingers and on our wrists, forming little scabs which dried up and broke off leaving raw flesh. There was no treatment for this in the medicine chest. Some, who had their own bandages, strapped up their wrists to stop chafing; others cut the sleeves of their oilskins short, thus ruining expensive gear which would then be useless when the cold weather returned. But still the work had to continue, clearing the constantly loaded decks regardless of pain.

The crew remained cheerful because the weather was so fine and we were earning a living. When the decks were laden and we were waist deep in fish, we took to a favoured pastime of sailors over the centuries, chanting ditties and singing popular songs old and new, including 'Barefoot Days' and a top-of-the-chart song by Joseph Locke called 'Goodbye'.

Everyone joined in the chorus and went on forever to drown out the screeching of the giant Russian seagulls which dived and swooped around us. These massive birds would often sit on the ship's rail, not more than a yard from you. With their beaks wide open, they would defiantly scream and screech directly at you, demanding some fish liver – which they loved – until someone threw some guts or offal at them. Then they would simply drop off the rail into the prevailing air stream and swoop up and around to return to the same position and continue their torment.

We clewed up with 20,000 stone of mostly prime haddock that trip and set off for home.

Nighty, with his vast experience and expertise, judged that we had just six days' passage to catch the end of Wednesday's market. Having a cargo of haddock, he assured everyone that the end of the market was the position to be.

'You see,' he explained, 'on the Hull market they start at the first ship and move down the line of ships selling the cod first, and when they reach the last ship they work their way back up the market selling the haddock. Therefore the last ship on the market has the first sale for haddock and gets the best price!'

Unfortunately, the weather chose not to fit in with the plan. Almost from the second day steaming the weather turned foul and persisted for the two or three days we traversed the Norwegian coast, until it became obvious that we could not catch the tide for the Wednesday market at all. Even though the weather fined away nicely crossing the North Sea, it seemed likely that we would arrive at the Humber in time for a middle of the market position on the Thursday. Still, Nighty was not to be dissuaded from his plan. He eased the ship down in order to catch the last of the tide.

Well, it was another day on the trip which was a pity, adding to expenses, but things were going fine when we met up with the *Yorkshire Belle* while crossing Bridlington Bay. The *Yorkshire Belle* was a pleasure steamer which took holidaymakers across the bay and around Flamborough Head. The captain of this fine little cruiser, spotting us idling by, took advantage of this extra attraction for his passengers and dodged up alongside us for a natter.

Tommy Nighty, flattered by this attention to his comparatively new, streamlined vessel, stopped the ship to allow the crowded holidaymaker to close with us. We, in turn, the scruffy, grimy, tired crew welcomed the chance to shout and wave to the gaily dressed young ladies crowding the *Yorkshire Belle's* rail.

Nighty enthusiastically reiterated our experiences in the Arctic Circle until he suddenly realised that too much time had passed. We said our hasty goodbyes and he rang the engines on again. But the tide had already turned against us in this position and progress was not so good. By the time the skipper realised that full speed was essential, it was too late, and we entered the river Humber with the ebb against us. We missed that tide also and were first for the Friday market. Tommy was right; apart from another extra day on expenses, we also took the last sale for haddocks – another poor return for an excellent, hard-fought voyage. When was I going to make the big money that was promised when I took up this profession?

I spent over a year with Nighty and Munzer and although we never made the big time, moneywise, my standing with them grew. Nighty constantly promised that I would be promoted to deck-hand. However, I was still only sixteen years old and unbeknown to me such a promotion at that age was impossible. Still, the skipper and mate continued to make their promises while I and the rest of the regular crew members continued to suffer various deprivations in search of the big settlings. The trouble was that the vast shoals of fish were now being hounded by an increasing number of sophisticated fishing vessels and were abandoning the traditional tows for different and deeper waters.

In the summer months, when they left their breeding grounds, the large schools of fish became more difficult to find, and the trawler skippers had to use their experience and expertise to greater effect. As we struggled to find fish through that slack summer some of the trips became longer and longer, in some cases considerably so. After two or three mediocre voyages, Nighty became more frantic to chase after good fishing reports, wasting more and more time steaming.

On one occasion we steamed all the way from Bear Island to the White Sea and back again with very little fish on board. After eighteen days at sea, we finally found some heavy fishing at Bear Island. Our time was up and we should have been steaming for home, but Nighty wasn't going to leave fish now that he had found it, even if it meant writing off what little we had caught in the first week. This was tough because the crew were already tired and weary, having spent so long on the fishing grounds, and the food was almost finished.

We had a well-known little cook called Tommy Kenyon. He was a gaunt, slim-built workaholic, but also quite eccentric. Tom was known for his tasty meals and excellent baking, but he had a wild look in his eyes all the time and would listen to no one. With Tom you were liable to get steak and onions for breakfast if he felt like it, and any complaint would see him chasing you with a meat cleaver, so you accepted gratefully what he prepared for you.

It was good, but the trouble was Tom would provide for three weeks only. At the end of that time there was nothing left, not a slice of bread or a spread of butter. He would simply sweep out the pantry and prepare himself for going ashore, regardless of what anyone else was doing. Such was the case on this occasion when after three weeks we were still fishing, heavy fishing. The only thing left to eat was the fish we caught but with no fat to fry it in, all we could do was boil it – we didn't even have an onion to put in with it.

Boiled fish was not enough to sustain a body for the long hours and heavy labour we were now having to endure, and the attitude of the crew was starting to turn ugly and resentful, myself included. I had never been without food before and trying to force down boiled fish three times a day, when you were working with it all the time, was more than I could manage. I felt myself getting weaker by the hour and still the fish poured aboard. We all wished it would take off so that we could go home, but it didn't.

I think it was Munzer who finally approached Nighty and told him enough was enough; that if he didn't pack it in and set off for home, he would have a mutiny on his hands. This, coming from Munzer, whose greed for fish was well-known, must have shaken the half-crazed skipper, and we at last took the gear inboard. But we still had five days' passage back to Hull.

With most deep-sea fishermen the main topic on the homeward journey was sex. But this time it took second place to food; until, of course, on arriving ashore we were able to stuff ourselves with the first big meal of our choice, and then things reverted to normal.

Chapter 7

MORAL RISKS AND PHYSICAL DANGERS

I was pleased to discover on this homecoming that my two schoolboy chums, Terry and Charlie, whom you remember had also chosen the sea for a career, were both home at the same time. It was the first occasion we had all been home together since we left school. In those days we had always competed for the same girls and it didn't look as if things had changed.

According to Terry and Charlie, the current object of their desire was to be found at a local roller-skating rink that had been set up in the Empress Dance Room in Gypsyville, a west Hull suburb. I didn't even know it existed; the only recent roller-skating available in the city prior to this was a travelling rink that set up periodically in a large marquee on the Walton Street fairground. Both Terry and Charlie were keen that I should accompany them to the roller rink in order to ogle this little cutie with whom they had struck up a relationship, or so they claimed.

'Well, it's OK by me, if we can get a drink there,' I agreed.

Oh! There's no booze there,' chipped in Terry, 'only a soft drinks bar. But we can get a bottle of beer to share before we go, and maybe smuggle in a half-bottle of spirits to spike the drinks and liven up the proceedings.'

That night, after a visit to the beer-off – where we purchased a bottle of Moor and Robson's mild and a half-bottle of Gordon's gin, which we figured would stand less chance of detection than our usual rum – we caught a bus to Gypsyville, disposing of the large bottle of beer on the way.

Gaining entry was no problem. We were all smartly, though casually, dressed with open-necked shirts and flannels. We climbed the stairs to the first floor and entered a large room with a parquet floor covering the large circular centre. A flimsy wooden handrail surrounded most of the perimeter; outside the handrail were a couple of rows of tip-up seats; and on the right of the room was a small area with tables and chairs surrounding a semi-circular bar. Behind this I clocked a tall, glamourous blonde, with a rather large nose. But the main attraction was a young sixteen- or seventeen-year-old dolly bird doing pirouettes and figures of eight in the centre of the floor, showing off her expertise on skates, with a couple of semi-accomplished males circling in close attendance.

This girl was also blonde, with short, bobbed hair and an elfin face. She wore a red leotard, which restrained pert breasts above a very slim waist, and a short, pleated white skirt enhanced tight, rounded buttocks, below which full thighs and shapely legs terminated in white lace-up skating boots.

The three of us remained rooted to the spot for a while watching the sensuous undulations of this pretty girl whose name I was told was Audrey Stamford, and then a smile or two in our direction had us scurrying to the skate-hire counter.

At our age none of us had forgotten how to skate, but not one of us was proficient. A couple of swigs of gin in the gents might have steadied our nerves but it did nothing to steady our legs. For a while we circled the outskirts of the rink, crashing regularly into the handrail when we got over-ambitious with our speed, and all the time striving to get nearer to the centre of the rink, in order to get closer to Audrey. But each time any of us nearly made it we were frustrated either by some whiz-kid flashing close by us and sending us into a death spin or by one of we three deliberately tripping the other. The best we could ever achieve was to fall splat at her feet, causing her to burst into fits of laughter.

Eventually someone started a chain which gathered speed and gathered people until we, again struggling around the outer edge, were caught up by it too. Taken by the hand, we found ourselves being whipped around at an ever-increasing speed at the end of this line. It was Terry who had grabbed my hand in passing and I who brought Charlie along outside me. As I was being dragged along I had to keep crossing my legs one in front of the other to stop myself falling, which inadvertently increased our speed still more. Charlie, meanwhile, just sped along wide-eyed in crouched position with knees bent and bottom stuck out; his free hand extended searching for some salvation, he appeared a most unwilling partner.

After two more circumnavigations of the floor, the inertia became too great for me to hang onto Terry's sweaty palm, and Charlie and I departed the throng, heading straight for a gap in the rail. Charlie tried to arrest our flight by grabbing the end of the handrail but it just tore away, uprooting the endpost as we ploughed through a plywood screen that hid the entrance to the ladies' toilet. We crash-landed in this female domain amid screams from the occupants. There must have been some wet panties as the users tried hurriedly to retrieve a compromising position from our shocking intrusion.

Two or three stewards immediately descended on us and dragged us to our feet, remonstrating and threatening. I think we would have been ejected from the premises there and then, if we had not clearly been in a state of shock ourselves.

I appeared to have come off worst in the pile-up, being the one who finished up underneath and mostly breaking Charlie's fall. Apart from a bump on the head, I had a badly twisted knee and a few other cuts and scrapes. When we had recovered, and the giggling onlookers had moved away, Charlie gave me a knowing wink and a grin and then moved off gingerly to exploit the attention we had attracted with Audrey.

It was typical of Charles to take advantage of the debacle but I was too embarrassed. Not wanting to appear a buffoon or a lout in Audrey's eyes, I moved off stiffly in the opposite direction towards the little bar for a soft drink, my enthusiasm for skating somewhat dampened. The area was quiet when I arrived – just the tall blonde behind the bar, looking bored as she wiped down the top for the umpteenth time – but she gave me a lovely smile as I approached.

'Hi!' she said. 'Had enough for the time being?'

'Yeh! It's getting a bit hectic for me,' I answered ruefully.

'I should think so! I've heard of gatecrashing but it's the first time I've seen skate-crashing,' she giggled. 'What can I get you to drink?'

I decided on sarsaparilla; it was the nearest they had to beer, in appearance anyway.

She served me, then rested her elbows on the counter. Her face cupped in her hands, she stared into my eyes. I admired her make-up as I sipped my drink – the glossy lips, the pencil-line eyebrows, the platinum-blonde hair.

'My, *you're* big!' she finally spoke. 'How tall are you?'

'Six feet two and a half and still growing, I think,' I grinned.

'Mmm! I like tall men,' she enthused.

She was easy to talk to and showed a certain elegance. Her name was Elaine and she was twenty years old. My age increased by three years to nineteen. I would have preferred to be older than her but didn't want to push it too much.

We talked on with few interruptions. Elaine seemed very keen to know me better, and when she came out from behind the bar sporting a waitress' costume with short, flared skirt, my enthusiasm increased even more. And even more when she bent over to wipe down a couple of tables, showing long, shapely, black-nylon-clad legs, in stiletto-heeled shoes.

The tables didn't really need wiping and I wondered if she had done it just for my benefit.

Elaine was surprised to discover that I was a fisherman and said I didn't look the type. I wasn't sure whether this was good or bad, but I decided it was good and asked her if she wanted me to take her home. She said she would like that but that she didn't finish until ten thirty. I said I didn't mind and I would wait.

As the night's skating was drawing to a close Terry and Charlie came to the bar for a drink, all hot and sweaty, with red faces. Both appeared a little frustrated. Audrey, it turned out, was being escorted by her skating partner but didn't mind if they tagged along. It was decided that we should retire to the gents to finish off the gin, and that's when I told them I was taking Elaine home – alone I emphasised.

'You sly dog!' snorted Terry. 'While we've been flogging it around that floor on rollers, you've been smoothing it with that sex-bomb behind the bar.' 'Yeh, well! You'd better hope she's not too nice or you could be wasting your time. Anyway, she's too tall for me. I'd rather have Audrey, and I bet I'll finish up taking her home before the night's out.'

'Well, we'll have to see about that,' butted in Charlie.

I was pleased I wasn't involved in this dogfight and I was delighted with my prize. In fact, that last gin seemed to have heightened my perceptions and I realised Elaine was very pretty. Actually, when I studied her again she was beautiful. In fact, thanks to the gin, everything was beautiful.

When the night was finished and the room cleared by the bouncers, I waited outside for only ten minutes, before Elaine came hurrying out. We caught the same trolleybus as everyone else and climbed onto the top deck so that Elaine could smoke. We chose to sit near the front, but I was conscious that Terry and Charlie were sitting at the back with a little gang, giggling and cheering and making ribald remarks.

When the conductor arrived, I fished out the handful of change I had left and paid for our two tickets for the town centre. I was relieved, some stops later, when the gang got off, with Terry and Charlie pointedly shouting goodnight to me. After that I moved closer to Elaine and put my arm around her. It wasn't until we got off at the bus station and got on another bus that I thought to ask Elaine where she lived. I was shocked to find out she lived in the village of Cottingham, some distance from the city, and when the price of two more tickets took most of my remaining change I was a little concerned about getting back. But Elaine snuggled closer and gave me a kiss on the cheek, dissipating any doubts I may have had.

We disembarked on the outskirts of Cottingham and walked down a well-lit, open road of urban terraced houses with well-tended, small front gardens. Elaine told me her mother, who was a widow, would be waiting for her, but not to worry. 'You'll like her,' she said, as she led me down the short path and opened the front door with her own key.

We stepped up into an unlit hallway. I made the mistake of closing the front door behind me before she could switch on any lights, which left us in total darkness. As I edged my way forward with the back of my knuckles on Elaine's rump, someone rushed past her and thumped me hard in the chest with such violence it threw me flat on my back. I banged my head on the floor; my shoulders were pinned to the ground with a great weight and I was aware of foul, heavy breath in my face. I sensed Elaine trying to restrain my assailant, as she screamed, 'Larry, you fool, get off.'

Who was this? I thought. Some jealous boyfriend? An over-protective brother? Elaine stepped back and threw open the door to the living room, casting a shaft of light and revealing a Great Dane slobbering over me. Its front paws were planted on my shoulders, as it tried to get a firm footing for its back legs in my groin, leaving me squirming until a squeaky, aged female voice in the room called him to heel and he obeyed immediately.

I scrambled shakily to my feet with Elaine's assistance and through the open door observed her mother, who had risen from her armchair at the side of the fireplace and was anxiously peering in my direction as she gathered her cardigan about her and smoothed her skirt. The only other occupant of the room was an elderly gent, who had also risen from the other armchair.

'This is Rob,' said Elaine, introducing me. 'He kindly escorted me home and he's come in for a coffee.'

'Oh, do come in!' said Mother. 'I hope Larry hasn't hurt you. He's harmless really, just playful mostly. Only I shut him in the hallway because he was such a nuisance snuffling around George all the time.'

George, meantime, was already gathering up his scarf and overcoat off the sofa. 'Well, I'll be going now, Margaret, now that you're not on your own. All being well I'll see you tomorrow. Nice to have met you.' He beamed at me as he passed. Margaret followed him out to the front door.

Elaine beckoned me to sit in the chair that George had vacated. 'Just relax there for a couple of minutes, Rob. I'll make us a couple of coffees. DO YOU WANT COCOA, MOTHER?' she called, as she moved out to the small kitchenette at the back.

I studied Larry, who was stretched out in front of the fire in typical lion pose, his eyes fixed unerringly on me. I considered joining Elaine in the kitchen, but then decided that Larry would not appreciate any sudden moves and it would be better if I remained where I was until the women returned.

After a few minutes, I heard the front door close and Mother passed through the living room with a benign smile at me. Out in the kitchen I could hear some muttering and whispering, interspersed with the tinkle of spoon in mug; then they both returned with three drinks, Mum leading the way with her mug of cocoa.

'Well, I'll be going to bed now, if you don't mind?' she said to both of us. 'If you'll excuse me, Robert, I'll just get my medicine,' she added, as she pushed past me to the tall built-in cupboard (situated above three drawers) in the recess alongside the fire breast. She reached up and opened it – revealing four widely spaced shelves, the upper ones holding a near-full Victorian dinner service, with tureens and a large meat platter, barely used but waiting for that great day when they would come into service again to celebrate a wedding or a birth.

Mum took a small bottle from the bottom shelf, crammed with oddments which were obviously used on a much more regular basis, and as she turned away she paused to look straight at me and emphasise, 'It's alright, I've got everything now. I won't be coming down again. Goodnight!'

I was a little taken back by this pointed remark and as she left the room Elaine advanced with my coffee extended and a knowing, sexy smirk on her face.

As the sound of her mother's footsteps receded up the creaky stairs, Elaine kicked off her shoes and draped herself over one end of the couch. One leg was tucked under her, the other shapely limb stretched out along the seat, so that her short skirt rode up enough to reveal her stocking top with suspenders and an inch or so of white, silky thigh.

Nothing is more arousing to a man than the sight of suspenders stretched across a soft, fleshy upper thigh, and I was no exception to the rule. But as I rose from my chair to join her on the sofa and take advantage of this obvious invitation, Larry beat me to it. Suddenly jumping up, he leapt on to the sofa, occupying the remaining space alongside Elaine. This seemed to amuse my date for the evening no end and she made no effort to remove him, enjoying instead my impotent attempts at coaxing, cajoling or dragging him from my chosen berth. Valuable time was lost as I became more frantic in trying to pull this giant from the couch by his collar, only to be discouraged by a low, throaty growl. Despairingly, I appealed to Elaine to remove him as I retired to my armchair. Otherwise we'll get nowhere, I pointed out.

A snap of the fingers and a sharp command from Elaine was all it took to dispatch Larry reluctantly back to the hearth, as I quickly took his place and pulled Elaine's outstretched leg across my thighs. I wasted no time. Hitching myself as close as I could and putting my right arm around her shoulders, I placed a gentle kiss on those glossy lips while my left hand massaged everything, starting with her cheek and throat and ending up on her satin thigh.

Elaine responded enthusiastically, thrusting her body to every touch until we were so entwined with each other and exchanging such juicy, passionate, tongue-searching kisses that it was almost difficult to breathe. Meanwhile, our hands probed and explored the intimate, secret parts of each other's bodies. As I rolled over on top of her, my free hand starting to unbutton and remove part of the clothing that covered this sexy, seductive siren, the clock on the mantlepiece struck twelve. My feverish mind was planning my next move, as my hand slid around her naked waist, my body fully aroused and TWELVE!

The clock had struck twelve! I froze and glanced up at the timepiece. It was true. It was midnight and I was sailing early that morning. I had to be on board by 1.30 and I had to collect my kitbag from home first, not to mention gear from the fishermen's stores.

I thought of the few pence in my pocket, barely enough for the bus fare back to town.

Elaine, suddenly aware that the action had stopped, opened her eyes and stared up with consternation into my worried face. 'What's wrong, Rob?' she gasped. 'What's the matter?'

'Is that clock right?' I faltered. She looked across at it, her arm still hanging around my neck.

'More or less,' she answered suspiciously. 'Maybe two or three minutes fast, that's all. Why?'

My mind was racing, my thoughts were in turmoil. Here was the best opportunity I'd ever had for a sex session, all laid on with an attractive and willing partner, but no time to take advantage. I didn't have enough money for a taxi and I couldn't walk back to the city in time. My only option was the bus, unless I missed my ship! That didn't bear contemplation, when I thought of my father's reaction. He and the company would disown me.

'What time does the last bus leave?' I asked tremulously. My heart was pounding, stirred up by my racing thoughts and mixed emotions.

'Why? You're not thinking of leaving now?' asked Elaine incredulously.

'I'm sorry, Elaine,' I apologised. 'I should have mentioned it before but I was so full of desire for you I even forgot myself' – I was trying to repair the damage – 'but we're sailing at 1.30 this morning. I have to catch the last bus. When does it leave?'

'It passes the end of the street about ten past,' she replied in a low monotone, head down, concentrating on fastening her buttons.

I glanced once again at the clock. 'I'm sorry, I've got to go now,' I stressed. Thrusting her legs from me, I rose and, barely pausing to adjust my own dress, set off down the hallway, closely followed by Elaine. As I opened the front door and paused on the doorstep to say goodbye, she made one last-ditch effort to change my mind. Closing with me, she put both her arms around my neck. She thrust her body close to mine, rubbing herself up against me and planting kisses on my mouth and neck.

'Are you sure you have to go?' she moaned. 'I want you so much!'

God ! This nearly broke me. My knees were trembling. Should I go back and see what happened? I was conscious that precious minutes were ticking away. I thrust her away.

'I'm sorry, darling, but I must go,' I nearly sobbed. 'But I'll come to you next trip as soon as I get home, I promise. Goodbye, love.' And I scampered down the short path and out into the street back the way we had come.

As I set off, almost trotting, down this open road, which seemed so much longer now, I heard the door slam behind me. But my eyes were fixed on the end of the street. I was praying I would be in time, but three-quarters of the way down I saw the lights of the empty bus go flashing by. I slowed to a steady walk as I realised that plan number one had failed, and turned round deciding to retrace my steps.

What now? If I hurried maybe I could catch Elaine before she retired, while she was still hot. Perhaps she would ring a taxi for me in an hour's time after we had made love and maybe lend me the money. Or I could get the cash from my mum when I picked up my bag, though that wasn't so desirable. Either way the next hour could be very satisfying. Now that I was approaching the approximate area, I concentrated on the houses, which were all very similar, and I suddenly realised that I didn't know the number of Elaine's house. In fact, I didn't even know her second name!! How could I contact her next trip if I couldn't look her up in the phone book? In dismay, I ran my eyes up and down the row of silent houses, looking for something I might recognise or a dull glow of light through the curtains that may indicate the house I had left only a few moments ago. Come on, Larry, why don't you bark? I thought. Hummph! No good expecting you to help, I guess.

Suddenly the night was cold and damp and silent. I was stranded in a wilderness and further from home than ever, and time was even more limited.

Once again I retraced my steps towards the main road, and then turned towards Hull at a brisk pace, though I knew I'd never make it walking. Then, in the distance, I saw a phone box on the other side of the road. I headed for it. When I was fifty yards away a taxi cruised past me and stopped next to it. The driver entered and made a call – back to base, I guessed. As I approached, he left the box and made to get into the car. I called him.

'Excuse me,' I shouted, 'are you going back to town?'

'Yeh, sure!' he answered, his hand resting on the open door.

'How much is it from here?' I asked.

He paused for a moment. 'Well, it'll cost you four shillings.'

'Look!' I stammered. 'I'm a fisherman and I'm stranded. I have to join my ship in less than an hour and I've only got 1s. 10d in my pocket. We're both going the same way. If you'll give me a lift and drop me anywhere you like in the town, I'll give you what I've got.'

He paused again; then recognising fresh-faced innocence, he gave a sympathetic nod. 'OK, get in,' he condescended. I scrambled into the front seat alongside him. During the remarkably quick trip into town, I explained my dilemma.

I was fortunate that Cream Cabs were in the centre of the city and my cabby dropped me on Ferensway. I was so grateful to him as I dug my hand into my pocket, scooped out the last of my change and thrust it into his hand.

'Thanks a lot, pal,' I enthused. 'You've saved my life. I'm sorry I've had to short change you. If we meet again, I'll make it up to you another trip. All the best and thanks.' With that I leapt out of the car and set off on another walk home against the clock.

As I stretched my long legs towards home, confident now that I was going to make it, I had time to reflect. I was mortified at the thought of the golden opportunity I had rejected, which left me still a virgin. I knew if any of my mates or shipmates had been given such a chance they would have succeeded, risking any possible stigma or embarrassment that may have followed.

Filled with chagrin, I thrust my hands deep into my pockets, my shoulders hunched as I strode home. It was then I discovered a coin in my right-hand pocket and retrieving it I saw it was a sixpenny piece, which had been amongst the change I'd intended to hand over to my cabby friend. I realised, with yet more embarrassment, that I'd only given him 1s. 4d. for his kindness. If he counted it he would think that I had deliberately deceived him – not a good image for a fisherman. This left me even more morose as I approached home and let myself quietly into the house. I tiptoed upstairs into my back bedroom and undressed just in time for my alarm to go off. I started to dress immediately in my seagoing clothes as Mother's footsteps could be heard tripping towards me down the landing. I knew she would turn out to see me off – better ruffle up the bedclothes.

The next few trips were very eventful and instrumental in furthering my education in the unconsidered dangers of my chosen profession.

It was late in September. I had now spent nine months constantly sailing in the same ship, apart from the one trip when I stopped for my decky learner's ticket, and I felt like a seasoned fisherman. I was certainly making a full contribution on deck and during this time I had been to most of the fishing grounds, including Iceland, Bear Island, the White Sea, the Norwegian coast, and even the Faeroe Islands. On this morning, after another trip to the Barents Sea, I was walking down the dock for another settling at the company offices.

I crossed the swing bridge that spanned the entrance to the dock and traversed the familiar cobblestones which paved the south side of St Andrews Dock. I acknowledged the occasional wave from some of the shore workers, who now knew me by sight.

A small cluster of the ship's crew and out-of-work hopefuls were gathered at the end of the company yard. One of the first of the shipmates I approached was old Arthur Medlam. Standing with his head down and hands thrust deep in his pockets, he was saying to another of the lads, 'Well, I won't be going back this trip. I'm too old for Greenland and, anyway, I wouldn't pass the medical, I shouldn't think!'

'What do you mean, you're not going back, Arthur?' I interrupted. 'We couldn't do without you. What's the problem?'

'You'll find out, kid,' said Arthur, raising his droopy eyelids towards me.' Get into the runner's office and see Gibby. He'll tell you she's going to Greenland and Nighty's dipped out too. Munzer's taking her.'

Greenland! Here was a cause for some extra excitement and not a little trepidation, I thought, as I moved off further down the yard to the runner's office. Not every fisherman out of Hull had been to the west coast of

Greenland, on the other side of the North Atlantic. It was regarded as an extra hazard, not only because of the distance (5,000 miles round trip to the northern banks), but also because it was inaccessible for a large part of the year with icebergs, heavy pack ice and growlers surrounding the whole of the coast.

Even in the late summer season when this ice broke up, there was always the chance that the entrance to the few Eskimo havens would be blocked. They therefore could not be relied upon for support in the event of accident or illness. In any case, this small nation was virtually disease free at this time, so landings ashore were strongly discouraged. This also meant that every man had to pass a fitness check before every trip.

Jack Gibby didn't take a gamble by offering me a choice when I entered his office. He just informed me that she was going to Greenland and I would need to pass the doctor. He gave me a chit to hand to Ginger, the doctor's assistant, and told me it would give me priority in the waiting room.

Doc Burns, the Trawler Owners' Mutual Insurance Company doctor, had his surgery situated in the Insurance Building on the riverside quay, just outside the dock entrance. Well-known and mostly well-liked by all the dockworkers, he knew how to handle the rough docker or fisherman by not standing on ceremony and knowing when to bend the rules. His chief assistant, Ginger, who had been in the services with him, was no less popular because he too would call a spade a spade or a case of VD a dose of clap, if appropriate.

It was Ginger who took the chit off me with a grin and pointed me towards the waiting room saying, 'There's some of your lot in there. Just follow on and providing you haven't got crabs or a hernia, you won't be long.'

Some of the lads informed me that we would be carrying four days' extra food this voyage and that we would also need a navigator to take us across the wide expanse of the North Atlantic. They also volunteered the information that the previous year one ship got caught in a following westerly gale on the return trip across. The seas were so huge that she had taken a sea down the funnel, which put the boiler fires out and caused them some serious distress until they could be lighted again. But that ship had been a coal-burner; the *St Apollo* was an oil-burner and more modern, so I hoped that would make a difference.

The trip out was pretty normal. The weather at this time of year was usually fine and sunny, which allowed us to carry on with our regular duties, preparing the gear and fixing spare trawls. I was assured these would be needed at this 'dump,' as the experienced members of the crew referred to our destination. It was a bit strange seeing Munzer constantly on the bridge as the skipper. He didn't look too happy to be there either; there was always a distant, worried look on his face whenever he was at the bridge window. I was used to working alongside him all the time, with him cajoling and driving me on. He was happy enough forcing the pace to get the fish on board, but now he had to find it and keep in mind the safety of the ship and crew.

We had a new mate, of course, an experienced chap called Biff Smith, well-known by the rest of the crew. He was in his forties, tall and heavily built, with a bald head and a happy disposition. He paid no attention to me even though he knew my father, who had now taken up the position of outside manager for the company.

It was after we had passed through the Pentland Firth, and left Cape Wrath and the Butt of Lewis on our port quarter, heading due west, that I noticed a difference from other trips. Even though the weather was still fine, the lazy swell that met us was huge. It seemed to take a minute and a half to steam over each long, surging wave as they rolled incessantly towards us. Although the motion was not violent, it tended to make the ship roll heavily and wallow as she dropped down into the huge troughs, making work down the fishroom more dangerous than usual. When we were balancing on the three-inch wide battens while stowing boards on the shelves, the ship was nearly on her beam ends with each roll.

However, regardless of the large swell, it was a fine passage with clear visibility and, after about six days or so, we finally saw the mountains of Greenland on the horizon, way in the distance. They looked at first like a ridge of clouds peeping up out of a grey, distant sea, until you studied them for a while and realised that the edges were too firm. Then it became obvious that they were ice-clad mountains, so large they were still sixty or eighty miles away.

We eventually closed with Cape Farewell on the southern tip before the light of the day had gone and could see there was still plenty of field ice flowing along the coastline, stretching ten to fifteen miles out, with clear water inside. But, as darkness closed down, we skirted around the edge, picking our way amongst the loose, bergy bits and growlers. Bergy bits, as they were commonly known, were large chunks which had broken off larger icebergs, forming little mini-bergs which had a fair amount showing above the surface of the sea, easily spotted and picked up on radar if the weather wasn't too bad. Though picturesque, where water and weather had carved some wonderful shapes and designs, some of the field ice, which had ridged and pushed up on top of itself, posed a formidable threat.

But the worst threat came from the growlers. These lumps of ice were really solid, containing little air and little buoyancy. They floated just below the surface, with just a little patch visible when the weather was fine. But when there was any swell they bounced up and down in the water, a movement which usually made them global in shape, like giant mines. Often their colour was a light bottle green, indicating compressed solid ice, and the swell would thrust these growlers several feet down. Then they would come rushing up to the surface with a wooossh! Often close to the ship as well, if you were not very careful and vigilant. You only wanted one of these to clip you under the bow and it would punch a hole in you without any bother.

That is why we kept well outside the icefields, or tried to during darkness. The only trouble was that the current on the west side of Greenland had pushed the ice out to forty miles or more from the land and from the fishing banks, so we had to force our way through to the clear water inside at some time. When we did the poor old *St Apollo* really struggled, and the sound and feel of the ice grinding and crunching against the plates, and the ship lurching and bouncing, made sleeping in the fo'c'sle near impossible.

We were very lucky with the weather. Usually the icefields in these latitudes encouraged dense fog banks; we had some murky days and plenty of pitch-dark nights but generally speaking conditions were good, and most days we could see the mountains clearly as we made our way northward along the west coast in search of cod, for there were no haddock here. I often gazed at the mountains. There was no flat ground, and they appeared more sombre and forbidding than any I had seen in Norway or Iceland. In those countries there was at least some sign of vegetation when the snow or ice broke away; with these titans, only grey slate or black rock frowned down on you, along the coastline anyway.

There was more open water as we moved up on to the main banks, with less field ice but more bergs. Some of them were very large and would run aground in waters up to 70 fathoms (420ft). One we measured on the radar was over a quarter of a mile long.

Munzer still followed Nighty's way of calling me to the wheel when we were steaming between grounds, if there were repairs to the trawl and he was remaining on the bridge. At such times, I was able to observe the nervous strain he was under. The bridge floor was always covered in the little pieces of depth-recorder paper he habitually tore up while pacing up and down when deep in thought. He had to find a good return of fish each haul because fishing time was more limited when the extra steaming time to and from these distant grounds was deducted. He had also to find this fish clear of ice and if possible clear of foul ground. This was not easy as the Greenland grounds were comparatively new and there was not a lot of knowledge of the sea bed in these areas.

And so we worked further north, picking our way through the ice, past the aptly named Cape Desolation and No Name Bank, up to Frederikisharb, where a massive ice glacier could be seen on the shoreline. This was one of the places where the great bergs were formed as they broke away from this gigantic ice shelf. We caught fish at most of these places, but we did a lot of damage to the gear too, often coming fast on the bottom. This is expensive and time-consuming, apart from being very dangerous. Some of the strong currents that flowed would often cause a cable or warp to part, sometimes making it fly or whiplash across the deck. Then the resultant one-ended job would cause more danger, necessitating heaving all the mouth of the trawl and tons of ironware to the mast or derrick head, while the crew worked beneath it all on a rolling deck, trying to connect a new wire to the broken wing of the gear.

It was small wonder that our temporary skipper was worried when we steamed further north each time while the gear was being repaired. It meant more distance from home and more time needed to return; but still he had to find a more consistent reward for our labours.

With Munzer promoted to skipper, I was not selected for the mate's watch on this trip, and found myself on watch with the bosun, little George Lomas. He was Nighty's regular bosun and had replaced Jack Garton some trips past. George was a lively, stocky little fellow with a ready grin which lost its sparkle during fishing when he always removed his false teeth to avoid spitting them over the side while screaming at the men. But like all good bosuns he was a taskmaster, who would drive you hard, with a rapier tongue and a ready wit.

George's main failing was getting out of his bunk at watch time, a problem he shared with our other watchmate, big Harry Troon. Harry was a big, hefty, barrel-chested young man with a happy disposition, a booming voice and a laugh that would start an avalanche. Harry was powerful and relied on brawn rather than brain to promote his standing in the ratings. That Harry was a good worker was never in dispute; he would pull and lift and drive himself to exhaustion. So when he slept, he slept solidly. It usually took considerable physical effort to rouse him once he was away with it. In fact, there was a favourite story that deckies used to tell about Harry when he was a decky learner.

They were heavy fishing in one of the old ships – probably before there were any watches below – and had been working non-stop with deckloads of fish for a couple of days when, during one long session in the fish, Harry announced he needed to go to the toilet properly. Clambering out of the fish, he dragged himself for'ard to the toilet, which opened on to the fore-deck, and climbing inside closed the metal door behind him. After some time, the boys in the pounds suddenly realised that Harry had been in the toilet longer than even someone with difficulty should take. A volunteer went forward and opened the door and found Harry fast asleep on the toilet, with his trousers round his ankles. Even the giggles didn't wake him.

Quickly a couple of the lads took some livers from one of the liver baskets and tiptoeing for'ard dropped them in Harry's trousers. Then gently closing the door, they waited a second or two before banging on the door and demanding to know what Harry was doing. Of course, Harry, ashamed, quickly whipped up his trousers and scrambled out to don his frock and return to the pounds. Everyone watched the look on his face. His discomfort was obvious, as he wondered if he had maybe had an accident he was not aware of. When they could contain their mirth no longer, they revealed the truth and Harry was allowed to go forward and clean himself up. In spite of his good humour it would be a brave man who would try something similar today.

Being on watch with these two cheerful stalwarts suited me fine except at watch times, when I was expected to make sure that they didn't miss the boat after we had been called to turn to. Munzer had set watches of sixteen hours on and four off because this rotated the watches and, with the best fishing usually in the daylight at Greenland, evened out the workload. The trouble was that you often missed a meal. Also, with only four hours below, there was only a fifteen-minute call-out, during which time I was expected to get myself out and dressed and give Harry, who slept in a top bunk, an extra call.

That was a job in itself. Shouting at Harry would provoke no response, even if you were close to his ear. You had to grab him by the far shoulder or arm, and shake or rock him violently. This would cause him to grunt or maybe even give a muffled OK or alright, but his eyelids wouldn't even flutter. You didn't have time to spend more than a few seconds at this, so I used to rock his huge frame, gathering momentum until I could roll him on to the edge of the bunk board. Only when he was in danger of falling would he wake up enough to grab hold of something to preserve himself and then his eyes would open.

'Are you finally awake, Harry?' I would say.

'Yes,' he would bark, before his eyes began to droop again and I had to dash out, leaving him teetering on the edge of the board, hoping that if he did fall off it was outside rather than inside his bunk. Running across a littered deck, watched suspiciously by a watch going below with only ten minutes to go, I then had to rush aft to the bosun's berth to revive him, and that was a different kettle of fish. Although George slept just as solidly as Harry, and shouting brought about as much response, touching him physically was a dangerous practice.

George had experienced a couple of nerve-shattering moments during the war when two of the minesweepers he was sailing in were blown up and sunk, practically beneath his feet, the last while he was watch below. So to shake George while he was deep in sleep would have him leaping instantly from a prone position right out of his bunk and on to his feet. The first time I tried this, he leapt right out on top of me and had us both rolling around on the berth floor, which didn't do my nerves any good either. Nevertheless I didn't have time to spend shouting myself hoarse, so I just used to give George a shake and then run. Invariably he was on his feet before I reached the door. Then, for me, it was straight into the galley to pour three pots of tea and hope my mates would arrive in time to drink some of it. It was a period that certainly taught me how to turn out quickly.

We continued to move north between speculative attempts until we finally moved clear of the field ice and finished up on Great Hellifiske Bank, where the fishing was good. It was here I first caught sight of some fishermen whose job was even more onerous than ours.

The weather was still quite fine, though overcast and grey, and when the light breeze swung round to the north it was very cold. It was while we were towing along with 150 to 200 baskets on deck. I was gutting in the fore-pound, when I glanced over the rail and saw in the distance what looked like a plank of wood bobbing up and down in the slight swell. Even with only two- to three-foot waves, I often lost sight of it. I thought little more about it until we towed along further and I spotted another, and shortly after another. But this one was much closer and I was shocked to discover it was a narrow little open skiff with a man in it, although we were some thirty miles from shore.

This little boat was crammed full of cod, nearly to its gunnels, and the fellow was standing up in it, maintaining good balance while his little craft rocked and bobbed in the light swell. He didn't appear to have any particular protection against the elements, apart from wearing thigh boots which were made from I know not what – not rubber like ours, probably leather. He wore doeskin-like trousers and a pea jacket, with nothing on his head or hands. He was obviously long lining, as he was in the process of paying out a thin, strong line which was interspersed with dangling hooks, and one of considerable length judging by the substantial coil still at his feet.

The other lads in the pounds had seen him, of course, but as most had witnessed this kind of thing before they were not as amazed as I. I looked on in baffled admiration.

'So that's what a man in a boat looks like!' chirped Bunker Carmichael, and there were a few chuckles that I didn't understand. A couple of the older hands ignored the wisecrack but explained he was a dory man – one of a few dozen put out by a parent ship at the crack of dawn to return at nightfall, unless he filled up and had to return during the day to unload and start again. Sure enough, as the explanation was forthcoming, a three-masted sailing vessel came into view, and majestic she looked as she lay among the mini-bergs making herself available for her offspring to return.

'A sailing vessel? Where did she come from?' asked one of the younger ones.

'Portugal, most likely,' was the reply. 'They're the only ones who still use sailing vessels for deep-sea fishing'.

'Crikey! It must have taken some time to get down here!'

'It doesn't matter. They spend most of the summer down here anyway. They're salting.'

'God! Fancy spending every day for three or four months in a little boat like that. Do they do it in all weathers?'

'Well, they wouldn't put out in a gale, I suppose, but I bet they often have to try and get back in one. You know how quickly the weather can change at sea. Funny enough, I think it's fog they fear most. They're expected to fish in that and it must be terrifying not knowing what's coming at you because big ships can't pick you up on radar and it's so frightening to lose your bearings. I think that's how a lot of them are lost.'

Fog! Perhaps we shouldn't have mentioned it because, now we had, it came down like a blanket as we towed into a fog bank. It was easy to see why dory men hated it.

There is nothing more depressing than dense fog. It's not the wetness of it as it drips off everything, or the chill that seems to eat into your bones. It was the loss of vision, not being able to see anything; that in itself was the reason for the increased activity on the bridge, as windows were banging open and closed all over the place.

We had been lucky to avoid fog for so long in these regions, but once with us it was reluctant to leave, and visibility was poor for the rest of fishing. It did lift at times, enough to see half a mile, but for the most part you were lucky if you could see a hundred yards.

Poor old Munzer! He had just got rid of one worry – finding fish – when this lot came down to cause him another. It was much more difficult to haul and shoot, manoeuvre among ships and bergs and put her in position without visibility, even with radar to help. And then came an additional problem to cause us all stress; the radar packed up. Sparks said it was the magnetron

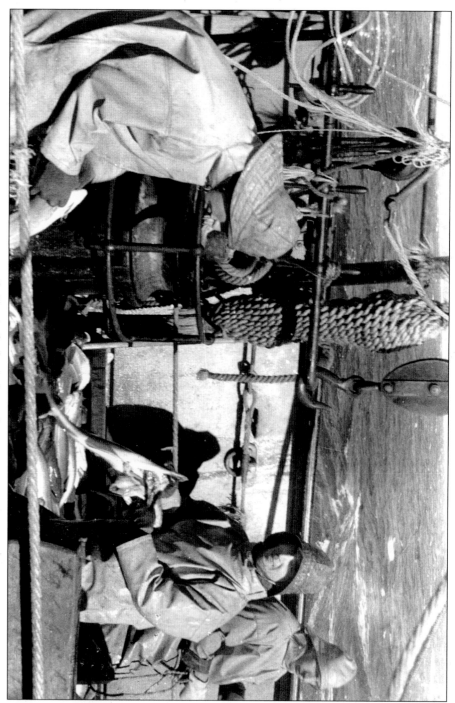

Gutting in the forward pounds.

that had burnt out, probably with the extra range changing. Anyway, we didn't have another so it meant contacting the office by radio and reporting our plight. After checking, they informed us that there was another company vessel on its way out that carried a spare. We were to carry on fishing until it reached us, which would be two or three days at least. It was up to Munzer to keep on the fish so the other vessel wanted to join us; otherwise we would have to chase him.

Munzer was already exhausted. He had felt it necessary to remain on the bridge almost constantly since we arrived in Greenland waters. Now, with the extra strain, it was dragging him down. You could really see his face shrinking into a little walnut, and his eyes getting very red around the rims.

As fishing slacked off during the night, when there were only thirty or forty baskets to be caught at most, the skipper decided that he would have to take at least one tow below in his bunk. So, after midnight, when we had hauled and shot the gear, he called the mate to the bridge and explained the depth of water he wanted him to follow along the edge of the bank. Although we had no visual aids to detect things above sea level, at least our sounders enabled us to keep position by following the seabed.

Arthur didn't waste too much time talking, but explained to the mate that there was another Hull trawler fishing close by who was keeping an eye on us by radar. If he saw us getting close to any bergs, he would warn us by popping rapidly on his whistle, and then he would inform us by radio. The fish from the previous haul was soon cleared and, as there was no work to do on the spare nets, the lads were keen to take advantage of an extra hour in their bunks and all dashed for'ard. All except our watch, the bosun's; we were on deck watch and had to keep an eye on the warps and the winch. The bosun went to the bridge to support the mate in his unenviable task.

'Make some tea and bring a couple to the bridge, Bob,' he called, as he climbed the casing ladder. 'There's some swag in my locker, if you need some extra.'

Half of Harry's face was hiding behind a cold fish 'banjo', when I passed the mess-deck. He was content to sit by the door and listen for any surge of the warps while he mopped up what was left of supper, so I decided to take *three* pots of tea on the bridge and maybe spend half an hour up there keeping a lookout.

Both senior deck officers were grateful for the hot liquid to warm their bodies through, as each had a window open and kept thrusting their heads out alternately to take full advantage of all their senses when sampling the murky night. Each in turn listened intently for any sound audible above the steady pulse of the engines or the slight swish of wavelets on the bow. The mate kept half his attention on the depth sounder and gave the wheel half a turn one way or the other as he strove to maintain the depth marking on the paper. Only the light from the screen of the depth recorder and a little from the rudder indicator illuminated the bewhiskered faces of the two men, as they quietly discussed the prospects for the trip and the hostile area we were operating in.

We knew there were icebergs scattered around us; they had been mostly in the distance when our radar packed up, but the constant west side current was always carrying fresh ones up to the banks from Frederikisharb, as the mate explained. He also told us of the arrangement with the *Swanella*, the other Hull ship who was watching for us on his radar when he wasn't too preoccupied with his own problems, and explained the whistle signal if we were standing in to danger.

The deck lights had been turned off to eliminate the glare reflecting off the fog. There was a moon shining occasionally somewhere up above; you couldn't see it but you could sense a glow from time to time, which suggested the fog was mainly at sea level. My two superiors were quite happy for me to stand on the port side of the bridge and keep a lookout while I listened to their chat, grateful for a younger pair of eyes, no doubt. I, for my part, was intrigued at the thought of bergs or ships passing close to us, unseen and undetected, and I stared intently into the murky dark looking to left and right, expecting to see the glow of a light or a dark shape lunging past us.

I hated passing close to icebergs; they gave me the creeps. They were so large, most towering above you in ominous fashion, and all so silent, rising sheer, straight out of the water, with their strange, craggy shapes. In failing light, they looked just like ghosts creeping up on you. My mind continued to wander when suddenly I heard a sound in the distance, way in the distance, a ship's whistle; *whoo-op, whoo-op, whoo-op* – rapid blasts but only faint. I pulled my head inside the bridge.

'Did you hear that, George?' I asked the bosun. Both men immediately broke off their conversation, thrust their heads out into the dank night and waited silently.

'It was a ship's whistle!' I puffed it out into the cold night air.

'Sssh,' was the only response.

Then it came again – *whoo-op, whoo-op, whoo-op, whoo-op* – faint but clear.

'It's someone popping, alright,' snapped Biff, as he hurried towards the wireless room. 'Watch her for a minute, George. If it's the *Swan* I've got to contact him.' He disappeared off the bridge.

Traditionally, the wireless operator always went below between midnight and breakfast, so Biff would have to work the radio himself.

'Do you think that signal was meant for us, George?' I queried. 'It seemed a long way off.'

'Must be. Too much of a coincidence not to be. Keep your eyes peeled, Bob. You should see better than me, if you concentrate.'

Next minute we heard the mate's voice calling on the bridge speaker – a pause but no response. Even when he repeated the call, there was no answer. The ship throbbed on.

After another couple of attempts, the mate hurried back. 'He's not answering for some reason. I can't afford to mess about just now. Just keep your eyes open, lads. We need to be vigilant now.'

I stared out over the bow; we all stared out over the bow ahead. My concentration was total as I blinked away the tears from my watering eyes. The dark fog swirled beyond the hiss of the bow waves.

'We must have passed it now,' muttered George, almost to himself.

As I looked on, I fancied the sky ahead was lightening a little. Yes, I think it is. The tension in my body was easing a fraction. Maybe the moon was coming out again. I looked up to confirm it. Oo-er! Something stung the sphincter muscle in my bottom. The sky above was as black as ever beyond the masthead, but it had a pale, jagged edge to it! 'Look up there,' I shrieked. The realisation came to us all. 'The bastard's on us – hard a-starboard.'

The mate rove the wheel over, hand over hand until it hit the stop point. Starboard was the obvious way to turn – with the weight of the gear pulling on that quarter, she turned quicker that way. Sure enough the *St Apollo* seemed to sit back on her arse and her proud, high bow swung rapidly to the right. When the mast and rigging swung out of the way, and my brain could assemble all that my senses were telling it, I could see the monster quite clearly alongside us through the haze, its sharp edges and the dark hollows of the caves at the water's edge. But as we swung broadside on to it, it appeared to go on forever. It enveloped us. It was like we were in a bay and this white Ku Klux Klan-like horror was reaching out to us. My tormented imagination was running riot; we still had to clear the outer ridges.

The mate's left hand was still tugging at the inert wheel, his right hand hovering over the telegraph, as he stared fixedly ahead. With the warps now pulling nearly at right angles, the ship was hardly turning any more to starboard, and she was crabbing towards this spur of ice protruding off the port bow. It looked as though we *might* just clear it, but how much did it extend under water?

We passed very close to this saw-toothed ridge, almost scraping it. If it did extend underwater, we hoped it was deep enough for us to pass over; silently we watched it slide aft and fade into the murk astern.

'That was too fucking close,' gasped the bosun.

The three of us were breathing deeper when the mate turned back to the

Irregular berg.

depth sounder and let out a yelp, 'Shit! the water. We're dropping off the edge of the bank.' He spun the wheel back to port to regain ground before our gear came off the bottom.

A sudden squawk from the bridge speaker and our name was being called; it was the *Swanella*. Once again the mate handed over to the bosun as he dashed into the radio room. This time contact was made on the correct frequency, and George and I could hear what was being said by the *Swanella's* skipper.

'Are you alright, Biff? We've knocked out halfway through the tow to come to you. We thought you'd had it. We watched you on the radar and both targets merged into one. I tried to warn you. Did you hear me popping?'

Biff assured him that we were alright and had cleared the danger without mishap, although he knew not how, and said he would be calling the skipper in ten minutes. He thanked him for his assistance and support and said we would probably report back to him when we had hauled. Then he shut down and came back on to the bridge. 'Right, lads, I'm calling the Old Man in a few minutes and we'll be hauling shortly. So, if you want to get your gear on, we'll hope the trawl's OK when we get it up. I'll break things gently to him when he's fully awake.'

'Aye, OK, Biff,' said the bosun. 'We'll leave you to it,' and he and I trooped off the bridge, calling in the drying-room on our way aft, saying nothing to each other, as our minds juggled with the past events.

As we entered the alleyway aft, Harry came tumbling from the galley where he had been clearing away.

'I've got some bad news, George,' he solemnly addressed the bosun.

'Oh, fuck! What now?' George spat out wearily.

'There's no milk left for the next brew. It's not my fault. The last watch used it all but the watch turning out are gonna kick up a stink!' He waited for a reaction.

The bosun looked at Harry for five long seconds. Then turning to me with a twinkle in his eye he said, 'I dunno, Bob. It's just one crisis after another. I don't know how we're gonna survive the night,' and with a shake of his head he donned his frock.

It was alright George making a joke of it, but I thought Harry was right. It was a problem.

It remained foggy for the rest of our fishing time, which caused a few tricky moments, but we eventually got the spare part for our radar in time for the return journey home and the steam round the icefields. We had managed to catch a bare 2,000 kits, which was a fair trip; we were glad to round Cape Farewell again, and set off back across the North Atlantic with a feeling of relief. But the pressures were not finished yet. As we suspected after a long, fine period, the wind built up behind us from the west and before long we had a full screaming gale raging up our stern.

It continued for two or three days until a swell built up of gigantic proportions. As we were running away from them the seas didn't batter us to a standstill as usual, but built up high above our boat-deck and then charged down on us at twice the speed we could muster, threatening to swamp us. But the neat, watertight cruiser stern of the *St Apollo* would just rise up and allow each massive sea to zip the ship forward like a big surfboard, until we crested the wave with engines racing and slipped down the other side into the trough, and the next sea picked us up for a repeat performance.

With one foam-flecked ski-slope after another building up astern, the daymen were restricted to working forward because the ship's rail kept dipping and scooping up great slices of green, solid water, which rushed along the after-deck and crashed against the bulkheads of the casing and the liver house, testing the watertight door leading to the after accommodation. From the fo'c'sle door you could look aft across this corrugated ocean and watch the spume fly from the crest of each wave, before dropping down in front of the next row of white horses, leaping the hedge above us. In my mind's eye, I could see a pack of white hounds among them chasing down after us, the bob-tailed rabbit, scurrying petrified across the watery plain.

The danger was in one of these curlers pushing the stern round to one side, allowing the ship to broach beam on down the side of a high wave to be rolled over and swamped. It took considerable skill from the wheelman and constant attention from the officer of the watch to prevent this. Aft-side in the mess-deck or cabin, where the beat of the engines dominated the sounds, you could feel the surge and the tilt of the ship as each sea caught up with us; and when the peak swept under us, leaving the propellor nearly exposed, the engine would race like the ship's heart was pounding with apprehension, until the roller had passed and the beat slowed down.

It was easy to see why other ships had been damaged when returning across this great ocean, as we had heard in the doctor's waiting room before the voyage. It would be a wonder if we were to escape on this occasion. In fact we didn't as the last night of the crossing was to prove.

During the early hours of the morning, while I was enjoying a sleep that only the weary young can muster, there was a *crunch* on deck that woke all hands. This was followed by a shuddering throughout and an unnatural slow tilt of the fo'c'sle that told us our gallant little vessel had taken some serious water and was struggling to resurface again. Behind each bunk curtain, men were poised in the dark, reading the sounds and signs, ready to leap out if there were further indications that the situation was deteriorating. Most did not wish to show alarm, but a couple did draw back their curtains and put their bunk lights on, and one of the hands, Jocky Roberts, who had probably had more narrow escapes than most, climbed out and went to the fo'c'sle door. When he opened it to the early light what he described didn't reassure anyone.

Only the bridge and the forward part of the port rail were visible above the water, sticking out of the slop at an angle. The rest – winch, starboard rail, and foredeck and hatches as far as the mast – were beneath the swirling sea.

But already you could feel the life returning to the intrepid little lass as the buoyancy was restored beneath us. The ship was swinging, with a struggle, back on to her course, the skipper having elected to try and press on rather than head back into it.

'Who's on watch?' chafed Jocky, as he swayed his way back to his bunk in his grubby John Ls. 'That'll keep their arses bubbling till breakfast, anyway. Maybe they'll watch the job better.' He rolled into his bunk and the ship continued its precarious surf-riding.

At breakfast, with the swell still running, full daylight revealed that the port lifeboat had been stove in. Strangely enough, on the opposite side, the pipes to the liver blower on the starboard fore-deck were also twisted grotesquely out of shape. We had got away quite lightly really. The journey across the pond was nearly over now, but we still had to navigate the Pentland Firth with its narrow passage, strong currents and boiling reefs.

With the wind easing and the sweeping tide with us, the passage through the narrows past the Stromness lighthouse was uneventful, although it was a bit like whitewater rafting. Another twenty-four hours down the east coast of Britain and we were rounding the Spurn light vessel into the supposedly calm and safe waters of the river Humber. But even that was a fallacy, as I was later to find out.

Chapter 8

NEVER MIND THE ELEMENTS, WATCH THE ELEMENTARY

This particular spell at home between trips was uneventful except that I no longer had to go to the Mercantile Marine Office to get my paper stamped, as I was now over sixteen, and I also got measured for my first suit. The suit was being made by a little Jewish tailor friend of my mother from some material bought from another Jewish contact. I had to go to his home to be measured up, which I was not too keen on; that was until this gorgeous, sylph-like nymph, with black hair that shone like my grandmother's grate, wandered through the room apologetically and flashed a coquettish little glance, with a flutter of the eyelids in my direction. 'My daughter,' muttered the little tailor, as he looked meaningfully into my wandering eyes. No chance there, then; still, it would make subsequent visits more interesting, I thought.

We did get an extra day at home on this occasion. Possible damage by ice meant the ship's annual dry docking was brought forward, but the only dry dock available was in Grimsby. Come sailing time, all the crew had to catch the ferry across the Humber and then the train to Grimsby docks. Crossing on the ferry at 7.30 in the morning, the crew became very suspicious when they spotted the company steam-raiser on the boat with us, particularly as the skipper (Nightingale, again) was not.

Disgruntled questioning of the poor ex-engineer confirmed that he was going to the ship to flash up the boiler, which angered the crew. Everyone knew it would take at least twelve hours to get up enough steam to sail, meaning the ship could not sail until the evening tide at 22.30.

Why were we ordered so early, when we could have had another twelve hours at home?

As the ferry was deemed to be at sea, although in fact she was crossing the Humber, more than twenty miles from the North Sea, the licensing laws did not apply once we had left the pier. So some of the crew, or rather most of the crew, decided to have a dram of rum with their coffee while they discussed whether to return to Hull on the same ferry until later in the day, or press on to Grimsby and find out exactly what was happening with the ship. Inspired by two or three more drams, the majority decided that there must be some reason for us being ordered so early. Maybe we were required to help bring the ship out of dry dock; so all agreed to continue.

The train journey along the south bank became much more jovial as more booze was produced from various kitbags, so the boys were much more relaxed by the time we arrived at Alexandra Dock and found the ship tied up alongside – with no steam, no heating, and not even a galley fire for cooking. Not much point in returning home now. The lads' craving for solace became unquenchable. Once kitbags were dumped aboard, everyone reasoned they had better find somewhere that was warmer, and return for tea when the cook had been given a chance to produce something.

There were numerous places suggested where it was warmer – all frequented by ladies of the town and so not considered suitable by myself, the other snacker or the galley boy. We decided to have a day at Cleethorpes.

Whereas a day at home flies by before you know it, a day at Cleethorpes, seaside or not, is inclined to drag, particularly if you're not geared for it cash-wise or dress-wise. After a mooch around the amusements, beach and gardens – and nearly all our money going on snacks – we didn't even have enough to take us to the pictures for the afternoon. In fact, we'd only just enough for the train journey back to the docks; which was just as well, as the galley boy had orders from the cook to be back for four o'clock anyway.

Once back on board, we two snackers decided to light the fire in the fo'c'sle and make a start of our brasswork-greasing job. We were so much nearer to the river entrance here at Grimsby and would be at sea in no time once we let go. There were no other deckies aboard at that time, but the skipper, mate, and fourth hand (who was the skipper's brother-in-law and already the worse for drink) turned up. They were surprised, and a little perplexed, to find hardly anyone on board and immediately resolved to go and tour the pubs and clubs and round up the crew.

There were only a handful for tea, including a fireman, the chief and the sparks. After eating, my mate and I decided to turn in, now that the fo'c'sle was warm, and catch up on some snooze until we were due to sail, some time after nine o'clock.

I slept heavily for the time of day, partially disturbed on a couple of occasions by someone staggering in and collapsing into the handiest bunk, but I was finally aroused later by a number of thumps and bangs on deck, accompanied by lots of revelry and drunken singing and shouting. I looked at my watch; it was 10.45, much later than I expected. We should have been away over an hour ago. I jumped out of my bunk and went to the fo'c'sle door in my stockinged feet. Looking out on to the floodlit deck and dockside I could see that the majority of the crew had returned together – most of them the worse for half a day's drinking with their Grimmy chinas.

Two deckies were rolling around the deck on their backs near the rail, with their hands and feet kicking the air. They looked like two beetles that had been turned over and can't get back as they struggled to get a purchase, burbling incoherently. On the dockside was the skipper, surrounded by a little entourage, red-faced and swaying. Oblivious to the two men on the deck in front of him, he was complaining at full volume, with hands waving, about the ship being moored facing the wrong way – heading up the dock instead of towards the lock entrance. Unusual, it's true, but maybe someone was hoping to make a few extra pounds when the skipper called for a dock tug to help to turn him round. If so, they were due for a disappointment.

Either side of this group, deckies were teeming like lemmings from the dock wall as they tried to negotiate the three- to four-foot drop to the ship's rail. An assistant ship's runner was in attendance, sent through from Hull to make sure the crew were on board and the ship got away. He was very agitated at the late hour and was trying to encourage everyone, especially the skipper, to get on board as quickly as possible. 'Come on, Tom,' he chided. 'If you're not away in twenty minutes, the dock master says he'll close the gates on you to allow the ships in the outer basin a free passage.'

'Doan you worry about that,' slurred Nighty, with a dismissive flap of the hand. 'If the chief's aboard with steam up, we'll soon have the bugger away.' And with assistance from Munzer, the mate, who was one of the few who still had control of all his faculties, he stumbled aboard and immediately ordered stand by.

Having donned my clumpers, I met this group on the fore-deck. Munzer turned to me and, grabbing my arm, he said, 'Listen, I don't want you for'ard with me this time, Bob. With most of the crew drunk and the bosun the worst for wear, I need you to work aft and listen out for me and repeat any orders I might issue from the fo'c'sle head and make sure they understand 'em.'

'OK, Arthur,' I murmured. 'I'll stay next to the bosun and watch out.' I hurried aft to repeat the skipper's order to stand by.

Soon, with a good-natured, if disorganised, little rabble gathered on the after-deck, the order came from the bridge to, 'LET GO FORE AND AFT AND HOLD ON THE AFTER SPRING.' A clang from the telegraph and the water swished and swirled beneath our feet as the propellor took a few turns astern and the bow of the ship could be seen swinging steadily from the quay. Another two clangs from the engine-room telegraph inside the casing behind us and the propellor stopped, and then began its thrust ahead as the final order from the bridge came to let go the spring.

Immediately, another clang from the telegraph and you could hear the thump of the engines as they picked up to full speed, and startled faces looked up towards the bridge in surprise as, with the wheel hard a-starboard, the ship rapidly arced out towards the centre of the black dock. I was no less alarmed. I had never experienced a ship proceeding at full speed within the confines of a town dock and ran to the starboard side to observe this dramatic manoeuvre. Suddenly the mate turned from his position right for'ard on the stem and, waving his arms up and down in a slowing-down motion, bellowed for the skipper to go astern.

'Go astern, skipper. There's a pontoon in the middle of the dock and you're not going to clear it. GO ASTERN NOW!'

Again the telegraph clanged; the engine went from full ahead straight to full astern, as only steam-trawler engines can, and the whole ship shook, shuddered and bounced on the turbulent water beneath. The reverse action of the screw caused the ship's head to swing quicker; pretty soon, the mate reported that we were clear and we proceeded ahead again at full speed. Not another thing was moving as we gathered momentum down the length of the dock towards the lock gates. A cluster of figures at the end of the dock seemed to be getting agitated and began shouting and gesticulating to the mate on the fo'c'sle head. From the bridge, I could hear raised voices as the skipper and his brother-in-law appeared to be having a heated discussion. The mate leaned out over the bow rail, his hand cupping his right ear in an effort to cut out the noise from the bridge and enhance the voices from the dockside. Suddenly he turned from the rail and ran halfway back across the whaleback, hands held up in front of him.

'GO ASTERN, SKIPPER. YOU'RE HEADING FOR THE WRONG LOCK GATES. THAT'S THE DRY DOCK.'

From the bridge – 'WHAT?'

By this time the distance had been halved and you could clearly see the closed gates rapidly approaching. The mate continued screaming, 'YOU'RE GOING BACK INTO DRY DOCK. ONLY IT'S DRY. YOU WANT TO BE TO PORT!'

I could hear the order repeated, just before the telegraph rang again. Surely, it was too late. We only had a ship's length left to stop.

The ship's head started to swing to port before the screw began its reverse thrust, but the second action counteracted the first and the ship swung back again towards the bullnose on the right of the entrance. I just had a glimpse of the little group scattering before the quay disappeared from sight beneath the bow and we struck! C!!R*U!*N*CH! The newly painted bow rode up with the impact, lifting a large capping-stone with it. Then, with engines still churning astern, the lovely *St Apollo* slid down again and backed away, allowing the capping-stone – the size of two tea chests – to drop into the dock.

The engines stopped.

'IS THERE ANY DAMAGE?' enquired the skipper. 'Well, we won't be sailing this tide,' I thought. The mate was laid on his stomach beneath the handrail, looking over the bow.

'NOT MUCH TO THE SHIP, BY THE LOOK OF IT,' shouted back the mate. 'A BIG DENT, THERE'S MORE DAMAGE TO THE DOCK SIDE.'

'OK! CHECK THE INSIDE WHEN WE GET INTO THE LOCK,' replied the now-sober voice of the skipper, as he rang the ship on at a more sedate pace.

I was amazed. Surely the soft-nosed bow of the ship must have been torn after such a collision. But, apparently not, for although there was a large dent in the stem and the dock master told the skipper there would be a case to answer on his return, we were allowed to proceed out into the river and down to the oft-threatening sea.

The trip to Bear Island was more or less without incident, except for some exceptionally bad weather which washed us about the deck in atrocious fashion, forcing the skipper at times to abandon fishing, pull the gear aboard and dodge the ship into the wild and racing seas. This was a situation that I would normally welcome, for fishing was heavy and I relished the time off deck, but on this occasion I was very conscious of the ferocity with which the ship slammed into the oncoming rollers. I feared that the bow might be weakened and would give way to the pounding, but my fears were proved groundless and eventually we were on our way back with an excellent trip of cod and some haddock. The ship was nearly full. Surely, this time, we would make the big trip we had been hoping for all year. With Christmas approaching, a big payday would be most welcome by the married men. But would it be good enough to get Nighty off the hook after the damage he had done in Grimsby? Time would tell.

The run home was good, with following winds from the north. The ship ran well – she was so deep and solid in the water – and five days later we entered the Humber, with bare chance for the evening tide. The night was clear but pitch black under an overcast sky; the ship was racing flat out through the calm, glassy waters of the river, the occasional shore light twinkling on either side.

Everything was ready on deck and the lads were jubilant, with a fine trip on board and the market reports good. Some of the crew were catching up on some sleep for the last couple of hours, expecting little later on, if we docked tonight. I had finished packing my kitbag and had only to get a strip wash before changing. I made my way to the bathroom next to the fo'c'sle, the throb of the engines beneath my feet as the engineers drove her home. I opened the door with my right hand and was just stepping over the lip when – WHAM!!!, C*R+U*N+C*H!! – over 800 tons of steel and stores came to an abrupt STOP!

Everything loose in the ship was shunted forward. I was catapulted off one foot straight down the dolly hatch of the fore-hold. I thank the Lord that I landed on a bundle of net at the foot of the ladder although I was on my head. Half-dazed and aching from the fall, I was up in an instant and scrambling up the ladder and was one of the first out on deck. It was so dark, with only the fo'c'sle light through the door behind us throwing a beam. The skipper was shouting from the bridge window, 'NO LIGHTS! NO LIGHTS!' Everyone thought he wanted all the lights out so he could see over the bow, so the fo'c'sle lights were turned off, leaving those inside and out stumbling about all over.

After a minute or two, a flashlight made its way forward along the deck – behind it, the bosun. I joined on behind him up the ladder onto the fo'c'sle head. Our engines had now been stopped and all that could be heard was the swish of water, which always sounded ominous at such times. The narrow arc of light picked out, way above us, what *I* thought was a large, white building; it had square windows and a veranda. I thought we had hit a quay or something ashore, but as the torch searched its way downwards it revealed the large, black, bulging stern of a ship, overhanging what was left of our stem, and written across it in large white letters, BRITISH CONFIDENCE, LIVERPOOL.

Lifting the torch beam up to the rail of the tanker (for that is what it was), we observed a black man in officer's uniform come strolling casually along the deck, his hands tucked in his waistband. Reaching the rail *he looked down on us*. The skipper's voice could be heard again from the bridge. 'NO LIGHTS! NO LIGHTS! She's got no lights.'

Responding to this, the officer drawled, 'Yes, sorry about that. Our generator has failed. We're just trying to rig up some emergency lights.' For the next ten seconds both George and I just stood looking up at him, open-mouthed, still suffering a little from shock.

Then came the skipper's voice again, 'How serious is it, George? Are we taking water? Is it safe to come astern?'

With the lights back on again for'ard it was quickly established that although the fore-peak had gone and there was a gaping hole into the fo'c'sle, it was well above the waterline and we could proceed. Nighty needed no more info. We were not far from the dock now and with the tide just turning he pushed her on full speed again. With the troubles stacking up against him, he could not afford to miss this tide and this market.

Further checks among the crew revealed that nobody forward had suffered any serious injury, even though the fore-end of the fo'c'sle had been smashed in and the top for'ard bunk head had been cracked. Harry, who slept there, still had to be shaken awake and told what had happened. When he looked over his shoulder at the state of his locker, he shot out of his bunk. His only concern was for the half-bottle of rum he had been saving, under great duress, for a drink going alongside. But so cold was the gale now whistling through the fo'c'sle that we deemed it necessary to issue it to us all to stave off frostbite and shock, and it was promptly dispensed.

On reflection it was considered miraculous that I had been thrown down the dolly hatch, which was only big enough for a big man to squeeze through, without hitting the sides, and landing on the net at the bottom was more than fortunate. In fact, the only serious injury aboard the ship was aft, to the unfortunate fireman on watch, who was at the top of the engine-room ladder, with two mugs in his hand, at the moment of impact, and was thrown down its full length on to the engine-room footplates. He sustained some nasty injuries to his ribs and back.

There was a shout to stand by. With all the discussion, I still had not changed. The strip wash was abandoned and I settled for a quick wipe round the face, while the rest of the lads dashed out on deck. As I came out of the bathroom, I felt a nudge as the ship made first contact with the quay. It set me rushing around quicker still, conscious of the fact that I was not at my station. Quickly removing my working trousers, I was hopping around on one foot in my little briefs, trying to get my leg into my shore trousers, when I was suddenly aware of some female giggling emanating from the fore-end of the fo'c'sle. Only then was I reminded that there was a gaping hole, framing a cluster of young girls who had gathered on the quay to observe the damage and found the extra attraction of a jumping jack tar in a box.

We did make a very good trip for money next day, but it was going to have to last longer than usual because the damage to the ship was going to take some weeks to repair. The amount of damage was staggering when observed in full daylight; the whole of the fore-end had been pushed back almost to the anchor windlass. This would have to be rebuilt and so it looked as if we would be home for Christmas. This sounded good to me, if the money lasted out, and my colleagues advised me to get myself to the Labour Exchange in town and sign on the dole. It was to be my first experience of the Labour Exchange and I didn't like it at all; there always appeared to be at least three queues you had to stand in to complete any business. I completed my application and attended three times a week, as instructed, but there was such an air of despair and despondency about the place that I vowed not to return again, unless I was desperate.

However, money was no problem for the first week or two and I indulged in a few purchases for myself. I splashed out on a portable electric record player, which I set up in my room, and of course I included some of my favourite boogie records – among them, Tennessee Ernie Ford singing 'Shot Gun Boogie'. His voice appealed to me and it wasn't long before I'd also added 'Mule Train' to my collection. Since I'd passed my sixteenth birthday I'd started smoking, unbeknown to Mum and Dad, not because I'd come of age but because it gave such satisfaction when there was a short pause in the long hours' working on an open deck. Anyway, I also thought it looked sophisticated, so I bought myself a nice, tortoiseshell Ronson Variflame lighter, which I flashed on all suitable occasions. My friends and I hadn't the courage to go into pubs as yet, but we still managed to acquire beer and spirits when we wanted it. Milk bars and cafes were the main venues on an evening. But, if we wanted to meet girls, the Newington Dance Club was the place to go, we were told. So after a little Dutch courage we made our way there one evening.

There was no alcohol on sale in the club, which was situated down Albert Avenue, but we were as usual relying on a half-bottle of gin, which was virtually undetectable, though one of the lads had a half-bottle of rum, which was much preferred for putting fire in the belly.

There were many pretty girls in the dance room, and a distinct shortage of young men, but the few who were available and could dance were kept very busy. None of *us* could dance, of course. We just stood there and ogled, and occasionally disappeared into the tearoom or the toilet for a quick swig at a bottle. Eventually, we got chatting to some girls who were more forward than any others. One of them, a redhead, with a nice, rounded figure and lovely white skin with a few scattered freckles, had caught my eye because she was so lively and bubbly. She had a coquettish way of standing close to you, almost chest-to-chest and looking up into your eyes, which was very arousing, particularly as she was wearing a dress with a square-cut neckline, which just exposed the beginning of her valley of desire. Rebecca's other friends were not so attractive, but just as forward. One of them, Irene, with hair that curled on to her shoulders, was particularly suggestive with her remarks and appeared to take a fancy to me, but I only had eyes for Rebecca.

Encouraged by the girls, we managed to get up and dance to 'Balling the Jack' and the 'Polly Glide', which allowed us to link up with arms round each other's waist and led on to more fooling around. I even managed to get Becky across my lap with the pretence of spanking her for her cheeky remarks, which both she and I enjoyed immensely as I became aware of the thinness of her dress and the softness of the curves between my hand and thigh.

After this exercise, Irene took every opportunity to plonk herself onto my knees whenever I sat down, drape her arms round my neck and look into my eyes with a smirk, while she wriggled around purposefully on my crotch. She was not unattractive; she had a good complexion with high cheekbones and bright eyes, but her nose was a bit hooky and her lips were thin. Still her figure was good, though not as full as Becky's.

When the dancing was finished, the girls were still keen to remain in our company and suggested we all went to a terraced house nearby, where one of the girls lived with her grandma, who was expected to be in bed at this time. This was enthusiastically agreed to, but Rebecca was unable to go. She said her father was a taxi driver and would be picking her up as soon as he was free, and she had to remain in the hall until he came. I was very disappointed and wanted to wait with her, but she declined and the rest of the gang wouldn't hear of it. And, as she pointed out, we could meet again here, as she used the place regularly. So, reluctantly, I left with the rest.

There was plenty of horseplay on the short walk to the little two-up and two-down that we all crammed into. There were four of us boys and three girls. Now that the competition was gone, Irene was playing the field a bit more, skylarking with all the boys in order to bring me on a bit, and then returning to me and messing about, tickling and such, to try to arouse me. One of the lads was also a decky learner and had a flat box of fifty Woodbines which he handed around from time to time. It gave me a chance to flash my new tortoiseshell lighter, which Irene took a fancy to, snatching it from my hand and teasing me with it.

Two of the guys had settled on either side of the couch, each with a girl on his lap, smooching; and the few drams we'd supped earlier must have relaxed some inhibitions because their hands were massaging the girls' thighs well up under their dresses, exposing plenty of stocking tops, white skin and suspenders. This was something I hadn't missed and neither had Irene, who was looking frustrated and deprived as she sat in the remaining easy chair, looking up at me from under her eyelashes. She continued to tease me with my lighter, offering it and then snatching it away when I tried to get it, passing it behind her back and under her legs so that I had to put my arms around her in pursuit, and bringing forth plenty of shrieks and giggles and some pretty heady perfume.

Eventually, I stood back grinning down at her and holding my hand out for it to be returned. Irene just held it up between index finger and thumb and then deliberately pushed it down between her thighs, close to her crotch, taking her dress with it, and dared me to try to get it before she did. After a slight pause, I made a dive for it with outstretched hand. Even though she whipped it away, I deliberately followed through and made a grab for whatever remained, which brought the biggest shriek of the night. But this only distracted the others momentarily.

A small radio was tuned to Radio Luxembourg, which was churning out 'Wheel of Fortune', by Kay Starr. Irene was still giggling as I grabbed her arm but she quickly dropped the lighter down the front of her dress. 'That won't stop me,' I warned, thrusting my hand down after it. With the feel of her pert breasts, I seemed to lose my concentration temporarily, which didn't upset my antagonist at all. Things were going just the way she wanted. She quickly clutched the bodice of her dress, pulled the chest band of her bra out and allowed the lighter to slip through down the front of her dress. After an extra rummage inside her bra, I withdrew my hand.

'Where is it now?' I asked.

Irene giggled again. 'It's here,' she indicated, holding her stomach, 'and it's going further down.' She pulled out the slack of her dress and chased it down towards her groin. I sat back on the arm of the chair, my arm across the back of it.

'You won't get it, where it is now,' she snickered, and lifting the hem of her dress she exposed her thin, white cotton panties where I could see the shape of the lighter nestled among the shadows. The excited challenge in her eyes launched me immediately into my next move, as I shot my hand down and slipped my fingers inside the waistband of her panties. After an initial recoil Irene pushed her hips forward with a little moan. Thrusting the lighter to one side, I cupped her vulva in my palm.

My mouth closed with hers. She wrapped her arms around my neck, pulled me to her and thrust her tongue searchingly into my mouth and down my throat, taking me by surprise and shaking me a little; no one had done that before. Suddenly I was startled by a Yankee-style hooting and hollering from the rest of the gang, and I realised we had taken centre stage. This was followed by a frail voice calling down the narrow stairs for one of the girls on the couch. My ardour cooled instantly; withdrawing my hand I gave Irene an extra little kiss of gratitude and rose to my feet. With Grandma's intervention, the others were also beginning to stir. Looking down at Irene, I said, 'I'd still like to have my lighter more than ever now. That lighter has been places that most lighters would never get. It'll be special.'

I had an ache in my lower abdomen I knew would not go away in a hurry. Having adjusted herself, Irene rose and dropped the lighter in my hand. With a little smirk on her face, she replied, 'Keep it close to you. It's still warm. Maybe it will lead you back for better things.'

It was now barely three weeks to Christmas. If I was intending to buy presents, then I was going to have to watch the spending money; a large withdrawal from the bank account seemed inevitable. I decided to go down dock to find out the latest on the ship and see how long I had to last before she was ready. I was also hoping to meet up with some old mates while I was down there. I went down in the morning, about ten o'clock, just before the usual settling and signing-on time, but the dock appeared almost empty of fishermen. There were plenty of shoremen and ancillary workers going about their business. But, at the entrance to each trawler-owning company, where you would usually see a cluster of out-of-work mariners standing about, there were none, except for the occasional down-and-out.

When I entered our equally desolate company yard and approached the runner's office, Jack Gibby greeted me very enthusiastically, with a beaming face – like a long-lost son, in fact.

'Now then, young Bob. Have yer spent up already, eh? Looking for a ship, are yer?'

'Not exactly,' I responded. 'I was wondering how long before the *St Apollo* was ready. How much longer I've got at home.'

'Ohhh! Don't you worry about the *St Apollo*,' bellowed Jack. 'She'll be ages before she's ready, way after Christmas. You'd have time to do a trip in another ship before she's ready, and earn yourself some good money too. This time o'year, you bet. In't that right, Benny?'

Benny was standing at Jack's shoulder, hands in pockets, beer-belly thrust forward. He nodded emphatically.

'Now, if you want a quick trip,' continued Gibby, 'we've got the *St Elstan* just landed this morning. There's a few changes there, if you want to go.' (There were in fact a lot of changes.)

'The *Elstan!*' I frowned. 'One of the old 'uns.'

'Not that old, and she's been converted to oil,' enthused Jack.

An oil-burning ship was a big advantage compared to others of her class still burning coal, the cause of a lot of dirt, discomfort and other restrictions. An oil-burner was what I was used to in the *St Apollo*, but this ship was much older, being built before the war. Still, she was regarded as a very fine ship until the *Apollo* and *Leander* Class came along. The company had already launched two bigger ships still this year; they always seemed to launch them in pairs.

I thought about the fact that I would be away for Christmas and the opportunities I would miss now that things were looking up on the girly front. Still that would take money, too.

'Well thanks, Jack, I know the *Elstan* is a good, sturdy ship and has a reputation for being a good sea ship as well, but I don't really want to miss Christmas.'

'Well! You might not, if she did a quick trip, and anyway you'd be back for New Year. I mean – *we are* talking about a deck-hand start here!'

I looked up at him quickly and stared into his face; Jack was such a joker. But, although the eyes twinkled with amusement, his gaze was steady. He meant it.

'You mean, you're prepared to sign me on as spare hand?' My mouth gaped.

'Better than that, I'll sign you on as deck-hand. You'll get a shilling a week more then.'

'But I thought I wasn't old enough. How can you do that?'

Jack looked down at his feet, 'Aye, well! There are ways and means. We'll have to pull a few strings, but you can do that at Christmastime. It'll be alright for this one.'

'Hell, Jack! I had plans but it's a big temptation.' I hesitated.

'Well, she doesn't sail until the day after tomorrow. So, if it's a girl on your mind, you've time to sort her out,' Jack cackled to himself, then thrust a pen towards me. 'Now then, are yer gunna sign today or let somebody else snatch the job afore yer.'

I took the pen and moved towards the logbook, 'OK, I'll sign. But who's the skipper?' I asked, pausing.

'Bernard Goodman,' said Jack, smoothing down the page.

'Never heard of him. Where's he from?' I frowned at the runner.

'Oh! He's sailed for this company for quite a long time, but he's semi-retired now. Only does a trip once in a while for a bit o' pocket money, but he'll look after yer.'

'Aye, like the rest of 'em do, I reckon.' I smiled grimly and turned away. 'OK, then. See ya.'

'Right-o, Bob! Five o'clock Friday morning, then. Don't be late.'

Chapter 9

ANOTHER STEP UP – OR IS IT DOWN?

When I swaggered back home and told my mum about my signing on and the promotion she was more worried than ever and seemed to think I would be at even greater risk, not to mention her disappointment that I was going to miss Christmas.

'Well, you never know, I might still be home in time,' I tried to reassure her. But she appeared to dismiss that out of hand; she had heard it all before with my father.

Over the next couple of days, I had mixed feelings about what I had done. I was still pleased at the early chance of promotion, but my friends thought I would be sailing with a load of 'Christmas Crackers' as shipmates, and in an old ship. Still they would think that wouldn't they, if they were jealous of my quick promotion.

On the day after I had signed on, it was lunch time and I was returning back home after signing off the unemployment and having my stamp card franked. I had just jumped off the trolleybus at the top of Walcott Street, and was crossing Hessle Road, when I spotted a group of young fishermen heading towards the Criterion pub, among them the easily recognisable young face of Freddy Nott smiling at me.

'Now then, young Dash. Where are you heading?' he called.

'Hiya, Fred! Long time, no see.' I grinned back. 'I'm just going home to pack a bag. I'm sailing tomorrer as deck-hand.'

'You're what? You'd better come and have a drink and tell us all about it. Come on.'

'You know I can't, Fred. I'm still underage,' I reflected.

'Underage be buggered,' retorted Fred. 'You're big enough, and you're spare hand now, ain't yer. If you're old enough to be spare hand, you're old enough to drink.'

'I'm deck-hand actually,' I smirked. 'Well, if I stay in the middle of you lot, maybe I won't be noticed – I hope.'

'Are you kidding? With you towering above us,' snickered Fred. 'Never mind. Don't worry, follow me.'

As we entered the pub by the side door, I tried to steer Fred into a small room at the back, away from the gaze of the landlord in the bar, but Fred stopped me. 'You can't go in there,' he said, grinning, 'that's the skippers' room. I don't think you've been promoted that much, have yer?' He and his friends cackled their way into the busy, smoke-filled bar. Fortunately, the bald-headed proprietor had his head turned away as he canted his ear across the bar to take an order from a bleary-eyed punter above the general din of banter and the rattle of dominoes.

Fred led the way to one of the few remaining empty little circular tables with wrought-iron legs and, as we settled ourselves on stools around it, a pretty young girl sporting a blue linen pocket apron approached us. Fred ordered for us all. 'Hiya, Stella! Pints o' mild all round, please.'

'Anything else,' asked Stella, expecting the usual additional order of rum chasers.

'Well, you can give us a pound out the till, if you like,' retorted Fred. There were guffaws from all as Stella turned away with a bored smile.

'Now then, Bob. What's this about you signing on for Christmas?' started Fred. 'What ship is it?'

'*St Elstan*,' I smirked, trying to appear casual as I handed around a pack of cigarettes, 'and Gibby's given me a start as deck-hand.'

'Well, sooner you than me,' said Freddy's mate, sitting opposite me. His young face looked hard, and I noticed his tattooed hand already had a finger missing, no doubt the result of an accident at sea. 'In a ship like that you're going to get a right bunch of down-and-outs.'

'You ain't sailed in her though, have yer Stiggy?' chipped in Fred. 'They're good sea ships that class you know.'

'That only means the skipper can fish in even worse weather,' snorted Stiggy.

'Who is the skipper anyway?' asked Fred.

'Somebody called Goodman,' I muttered through the froth on the pint of mild Stella had just served. 'Bernard Goodman, not heard of him myself.'

'What, old Better Days Bernard!' chortled Fred. 'He's alright, but he *has* seen better days as he'll tell you himself. You're OK. He won't wash you about unless he gets pushed. He's more or less finished in the rat race, only does the odd trip now. I doubt he'll be driving the job like the others do.'

'That's no good. I want him to drive the job if we're going to get back for Christmas. Gibby said there was a chance.'

Stiggy was quick to butt in. 'Don't fall for that one, Dash, or Bash, or whatever. You won't be back before, no matter how well you fish. The gaffers don't *want* you back before Chrissy because the markets 'll be rock bottom. Everyone's buying Christmas fayre, ain't they? Now get Chrissy well clear, when they're all sick of eating cold turkey, and they'll be crying out for a bit o' fish. You'll make a packet then.'

'Ruddy hell! That'll make it a long one, won't it? Especially if we go to Iceland!'

'Aw! Forget it, Bob. Do your celebrating now,' said Fred. 'Come with us. Stiggy's organised a dommy for this afternoon with Big Nell. 'Shave off. It'll be some dommy if she's involved.'

'You might have to shave off, if her mate Crabby Carole wraps herself around yer.' The third member of the trio spoke for the first time. He had a pale, flabby face with watery eyes and his name was Barry. 'I got a dose of crabs the last time I went with her, so watch it. She's hot stuff though and has a great body. She'll probably be OK now if she's been to Mill Street.'

Any ideas I may have had of going along out of curiosity were quickly squashed after this last remark, and I decided it was time I left. I called Stella over and ordered and paid for three more pints for the lads; then I rose and made my excuses. 'I'll see you around then, Fred. Have a good time, but I've got to go. There's things I must do. All the best.'

As I turned to go Barry spoke once more. 'I hope you have a good trip then, mate. But don't count on it. They still haven't got a cook for your ship yet, so you better take sandwiches,' and he cackled along with Stiggy.

'Thanks a lot,' I sneered, as I left. That greasy bastard had only spoken twice and he'd upset me on both occasions.

Barry was probably right. When I got home at teatime that evening there had been a phone call from Gibby to say they were still some crewmen short and the ship wouldn't be sailing till the following tide. At the time I was sorry, and yet relieved that I wouldn't have to get up so early in the morning. And now here I was, tumbling out of a taxi on the quayside at teatime the following day. As the taxi driver helped me pull my kitbag and mattress and huge oilskin, packed with my waterproofs and other heavy deck gear, out of the cab, I ran my eye over my new home for the next three weeks or so.

The *St Elstan*, and others of her class, I had, of course, seen many times before in my travels, both in the dock and at sea, but this was the first time I had surveyed her from a surviving or working point of view. The first thing that differed from the soft lines of the *St Apollo* was her square bridge, still painted up with mock wood graining, but a little grubbier and scruffier. She had a squat, hard-nosed stem with the keel bar continuing up from the fore-foot to the fo'c'sle head. Her fore-deck seemed wider, but once I'd boarded her I realised it was an illusion caused by the fact that her rails were much lower than those of the newer ships. In fact, later on when we had got away and were working amidships, I was a little alarmed to find the rail there only came halfway up my thigh.

The wing bollard for the after warp was amidships, opposite the winch, instead of in the shoulder of the deck under the rigging. This meant that the warp would cut across the fish-pounds when we were gutting. I wasn't sure what problems that may cause. I noticed also that the hatches were secured with tarpaulins and wedges, not the steel hatch-covers that I had been used to, and the coamings were not as high, creating a greater risk of shipping water when the decks were awash.

I dragged my gear towards the open, walk-under whaleback and round the centre cenotaph companionway which led down below, passing the open door to a double toilet on the starboard side which I didn't like the look of at all. Humping my gear over the weather step, I let it all drop down the ladder, with a shout of 'STAND CLEAR BELOW,' and then I followed it.

At the bottom of the longish ladder, I looked round in the dim light at a square box of a room. It was just like a big tank, with bunks three high surrounding three of its sides. The usual single plank seats were connected to the lower bunks, and the coal-fired stove, with its deep ash pit, stood next to the ladder in the centre. The only other occupant was stooped over the bottom bunk, directly in front of the stove, spreading a grubby-looking eiderdown over a distorted, lumpy flock mattress. He was wearing a shapeless, stained suit, with the double-breasted jacket hanging open and the pockets weighed down, bulging with odds and ends. As I descended to the coconut matting on the fo'c'sle floor, he turned and stared blankly at me. With red, watery eyes peering through steel-rimmed glasses, he looked a bit vacant. I guessed he was about thirty. I was a bit taken aback as I had never seen anyone in a deck crew wearing glasses before and I wondered how much he would see after the first salt spray had hit them.

'Hi!' I said, breaking the silence. 'What's your name?'

'Roland,' he replied defensively, with a sniff. 'I'm a decky learner.'

'OK, Roland. I'm Bob. You seem to be one of the first to sort a bunk out,' I added, as I surveyed the mostly empty bunks and the heaped-up bags of gear at the foot of the ladder, where other deck-hands had thrown their kit down and trooped aft in search of booze. I decided to select a bunk before going aft myself, although there was no shortage. At three bunks high the fo'c'sle had been designed with eighteen bunks for the big crews before the war. Now there were only ten men sleeping for'ard, the top bunks were unlikely to be used – except for gear.

I selected a bunk on the starboard side away from the stove. I knew how these fires could belch out smoke when the ship was pitching and I selected one on the second tier. I didn't like fellas above me planting their sweaty feet on my bunk side when they were clambering down. Although there was no sprung frame on the bottom of the bunk, just bare boards, I was pleased to see there was at least a little bunk-light, obviously fitted in recent years. These ships wouldn't have been built with them, but they were an important factor in a seaman's off hours, when reading was a major leisure pastime. After laying out my mattress and bedding, I threw my kitbag on top for safekeeping and, leaving the sniffing Roland fussing round his little domain, I made my way aft.

As I swaggered along the deck I noticed other differences between this older ship and the one I'd just left. The engine-room casing top was lower – much more accessible when escaping from heavy seas; the wheel race that ran along it a foot above the main deck was for real, and the open channel contained a steering chain that came down from the bridge and ran aft to a massive tiller arm. This was under the boat-deck, covered only with a large wooden grating which prevented anyone from stacking things alongside it and obstructing its movements.

Behind this, on the very arse end of the ship, was a deckhouse which contained, for the most part, the liver boilerhouse, except for a door in its port end which led to the toilet for the after accommodation. All of this was open to the elements, as the main housing finished five yards away, although the boat-deck was suspended above it. I would hate to think of having to use the toilet with a strong breeze on the port bow. Every time the ship dipped her rail, several tons of water would be blasted aft to hit its ill-fitting steel door. There would be no need to flush it after that.

All of this and more I took in as I moved towards the galley, but my general impression was of a well-worn, homely and mature ship that had probably seen every watery terror and survived them all.

The noise and chatter that echoed down the alleyway as I approached the mess-deck suggested that the tide at this time of day was good for getting the crew aboard early, but what I saw when I looked into the mess was not your usual crew. They were a real mixture. Gnarled hands and tattooed arms indicated a few seasoned salts who were probably past retirement age, but the majority were younger and had the sparkle of adventure in their eyes. If there were to be recriminations in the future at their incompetence or ignorance of the job, it did not show now while they had booze to share. And they had, as the large table proved, with its litter of half-consumed and empty bottles.

There were no faces I knew but that didn't matter. When the heavy work started it threw men together as if they were lifelong chums. I joined the happy throng to find out who was who and was immediately plied with a tot glass full of whiskey and a bottle of Moor and Robson's mild ale. Such generosity at these times was common and I thought nought of it as I joined in the merriment, caused mostly by the greenhorns' accounts of why they had signed on, or how the clever Gibby had shanghaied them.

As I weighed up my new shipmates there was one lad who impressed me. No more than two or three years older than I, he was obviously very street-wise or should I say deck-wise. He was heavy of shoulder; they heaved when he chuckled, which he did often, with a kind of yuk-yuk like a yokel. He had short-cropped, dark curly hair and a constant twinkle in his eyes. I watched him when he screwed up his face in mock pain as he gave me a knowing glance and cocked his head towards the maker of some naive remark. Later, when I had chance to talk to Nick, I asked him what he was doing aboard a ship like this, sailing at this particular time, when he could probably do much better.

'Well, I can't afford to stay at home,' said Nick. 'I've got our lass in the pudding club and we're gonna have to get married, and I'm trying to get myself established in the company again. I've been a naughty boy and missed a couple of ships in the past when I was too far gone enjoying misself. I did a few trips for one of the smaller companies, and now I'm having to do a favour for Gibby to get back in. And by the look of this lot, it's a mighty big favour. You know who's skipper and mate, don't yer?'

'Well, I know the skipper's name is Bernard Goodman, but I don't actually know him. I understand he's pretty laid-back.'

'LAID-BACK!' yukked Nick. 'He's practically horizontal. I thought he was more or less retired. Still he should catch a trip. He knows his way round Iceland and that's where we're going, and what *he* lacks in drive is made up for by the mate, Jumping Jeremy, the mad bugger. Jeremy Bywater, not exactly a Yorky name, is it? Actually, I think his family is pretty wealthy. His grandfather made a lot of money from fishing in the Brixham area, I think, before they moved up here. Anyway, don't worry too much about Chicken Head. He's pretty excitable but there's no harm in'im.'

I was to get to know Nick pretty well on that trip; we sort of chummed up. We had a similar sense of humour, but to Nick everything was a joke and he craved excitement. He'd pull any stunt for a laugh – a bit of a rogue, really. I think if Nick had been born 200 years earlier he'd have been a highwayman.

One other shipmate that caught the eye was the worried-looking young man who was mooching around the galley, picking up the various grimy, battered pots, pans and large tin trays, and shaking his head with each examination.

'Our cook doesn't look as if he has an excess of confidence or experience,' confided Nick, as he handed me another tot of whisky to further glaze my eyes. 'I understand he's done some time in a bakery, so he should be able to make bread – if he isn't sea-sick!'

Before we could reflect further on this gloomy prospect, a shout came from the end of the alleyway outside.

'Now then! Where's my willing crew?' bellowed a frenetic voice. Then a moment later a gangling figure sprang into view at the doorway. It was easy to see why Jumping Jeremy was so called; and why he was also referred to as Chicken Head. The most obvious reason was his large, pointed nose, with no chin beneath. His auburn hair was longish at the back, sleeked back behind his ears and overlapping his white polo-necked sweater, but at the front it was cropped short and stuck upwards like a cockerel's comb.

'My God! What have we here then? It looks like an Egyptian casbah. Where's the bosun? Where's Plug?'

None of us had seen the bosun!!

'Oh! Oh! Don't tell me it's Plug McCauly,' muttered Nick.

'Come on then, mi hearties! Sort yerselves out,' roared the mate. 'We'll be letting go shortly. Who's third hand?'

One of the older hands acknowledged.

'Get yourself on the bridge then,' continued Jeremy. 'Three or four of you come for'ard with me and one of you see if the bosun's down below in the cabin.'

'I'll go,' said Nick, and as he had to push me off the end of the seat locker to get out I decided to go with him.

'Why Plug?' I asked as I toddled on behind.

'He chews tobacca,' was the short reply.

The large cabin below the mess-deck is where the officers eat and where most of them slept. I followed Nick down through a hatchway in the alleyway. At the bottom of a short, steep ladder was a vestibule with a small single cabin on either side for the mate and chief engineer. A door led into a large cabin which narrowed into the stern of the vessel, in the centre of which was a large table shaped to fit the space. Around the back of this were leather-cushioned seat lockers which backed on to long cupboards with sliding doors on two levels. These were, in fact, bunks which housed six men: the bosun, second engineer, two firemen, cook and galley boy.

Nick went straight to the first upper cupboard on the starboard side and slid back the two doors to reveal the bosun, a heavily-built man with a round, stubbly face, a thick neck and a bullet head.

Nick shook him violently by the shoulder. 'Joe,' he shouted, 'come on. It's stand by. We're sailing.' He received a grunt and a moan in reply.

'Fuck off,' muttered the bosun, brown spittle dribbling on to his pillow.

'Why, he's as pissed as a newt,' I exclaimed. 'That's brilliant, i'n'it?'

'Don't worry about it. He's not usually like this,' reassured Nick. 'He's a good grafter really. Just drowning his sorrows after signing on a barque like this, I guess.'

'Then why does he do it?'

'Same reason as the rest of us, the money. If you wait for a better ship, you're spending all the time, and Christmas is coming and he's got a lot of kids. You go on. I'll get him out and if not I'll take his place aft. You go for'ard with the mate. He'll want someone with him with a bit of know-how.'

I left Nick to sort things out and went forward to the whaleback. There were already a few swaying figures staggering their way up there.

Jeremy paid small attention to the drunken little rabble around him on the fo'c'sle head after we had cast off. He made his way right forward into the eyes of the ship and stood there proud like a figurehead, looking down at the people on the quay as we moved across the dock and through the lock. I took in the head rope and tried to organise the greenhorns around me to take it down below and coil it under the whaleback.

'Best o' luck, Bob,' a voice called from the lock side, I looked up and saw Benny, the assistant runner, give a slight wave. He was there to see no one jumped off as we left, I guessed. Gibby would be on the other side for the same reason.

'Cheers, Benny.' We're going to need it, I thought, as I watched him slide rapidly astern. I wondered how many times he had said that as he watched ships sail. He would be giving a great sigh of relief that we had departed without problems. Now he could return home. His job was done for today; ours was just starting.

The ship nodded its head to a gentle swell as it moved out into the Humber. Jeremy, the mate, took a quick look around to make sure all was clear, then strode quickly aft across the whaleback. 'You'll need cement to secure that anchor cap, young Dash,' he called, pointing. 'It doesn't fit very well. You'll find some in the bathroom, for'ard.'

So, he knew who I was then! Word gets around when your father is a skipper.

Jeremy didn't wait for an answer. He grabbed the handrails that led down to the fore-deck and slid down them with his back to the ladder, his heels skipping lightly on each rung as he went, 'Don't forget all this spare gear will want stowing before you go below.' With this last remark, directed to no one in particular, he disappeared on to the bridge. I struggled to fit the metal cap round the anchor pipe which ran down to the chain locker, stuffing it with tarpaulin; then I went down to the deck.

Nick had come forward and had taken charge. The bosun was still missing.

'Give us a hand here then, you lot. These wing bobbins want taking for'ard and those hides want shifting, but first we have to get the life-lines up.'

'The mate says the anchor pipe wants cementing,' I offered, as I approached Nick. 'He says the cement is in the bathroom. I didn't know we *had* a bathroom!'

'Well, we have a room with a pump in it, and if there's a clean bucket in there it's a bathroom. Don't worry about the cement, I'll do it. You have to put some soda in it to make it set quick before we get out of the river and she starts taking water. You see to the lifelines.'

I soon found the life-lines and started shackling them up to the rigging. I tried to organise some of the others to help by running them aft, but the old

St. Elstan-class.

St. Apollo.

lass was doing a little nodding and rolling in the increasing swell, so some of those that helped pull the ropes aft didn't reappear. Others who were working forward also started looking a little pale and began retching; then they too disappeared down below. I glanced up at the bridge, but all I could see at the one open window was a squat figure with a balding head and bleary eyes, arms resting on the window ledge with his chin on his hands – the skipper surveying in silence the capabilities of his crew.

We were getting fewer by the minute. By the time Nick came down from the fo'c'sle head, there were practically only him and me to finish off. The wing bobbins were too long and heavy for us to drag them for'ard on our own, so we lashed them up along the rail. The cow hides we managed to jam behind the gallows so they wouldn't move. And what we couldn't move we secured in position with rope yarns until Nick said, 'That's it. We've done our share. If anything shifts now, somebody else can look after it. Come on, Bob. Let's get our heads down until somebody comes looking for us.'

We did go for'ard to the fo'c'sle, but we didn't stay. One look confirmed that the only occupants were three or four of the fresh larkers who had flaked out in their bunks just as they had stood, fully clothed and without moving a scrap of their gear from the fo'c'sle deck. The older hands were all missing.

'There's something on aft, by the looks of it,' muttered Nick, 'and I'm going to see what it is.' He only remained long enough to select himself a bunk and shove in his mattress and pillow; then he was off up the ladder.

I remained a little longer, long enough to dig myself a pair of rubber boots out of my oilskin bag because I could feel we were getting close to the open sea. After donning these, I clumped up the ladder and followed Nick aft.

When I arrived aft there was no one in the mess-deck, just a table littered with empty bottles, a couple of pot mugs with beer dregs in the bottom, a couple of loaves of bread, a big hunk of cheese and some butter. That was obviously the cook's effort for a first meal. There was no one in the galley but I could hear a racket from down below – a lot of giggling and laughing, some cursing and periodically a combined groan coming from the big cabin. I hurried down the ladder and in the vestibule at the bottom found Nick trying to push the door to the cabin open, but it would only give a couple of inches, and with each shove came this loud groan from behind it.

'Give me a hand, Bob,' instructed Nick. 'There's something blocking the door.' Both of us threw our weight against the door and managed to force it open about six inches, but such was the cry of anguish and pain coming from within that we let it go.

'There's a piss-up going on in there and the bastards are trying to shut us out,' Nick snarled. 'Well, they're not going to do that. I know! There's an escape port that comes out on the after-deck. We'll go and have a look through that. Come on.'

We scrambled back up the ladder and along the alleyway out on to the poop-deck. Nick got down on his hands and knees and peered through a large porthole into the cabin. 'Look at that,' he snorted. I got down and peered alongside him. The large cabin table was just below us. The bottles that littered it this time contained plenty of drink, mostly rum and some whisky, but there were also some full bottles of beer still upright on the table. Slumped on a seat locker was Plug, the bosun – conscious now, but incompetent and rolling with laughter at a sight that really opened the eyes. The other half-dozen occupants of the cabin were all laid on the deck in a tangled mass against the cabin door, so drunk that none of them were capable of regaining their feet.

Giggling and groaning, they kicked out feebly with arms and legs in a futile attempt to extricate themselves. They looked not unlike a litter of new-born suckling puppies that had suddenly been abandoned by their mother. I fancied that the tuft of reddish hair I could just see showing through the bodies could well have belonged to our second-in-command. Shocking as it was you couldn't help but grin at their antics. No wonder we couldn't gain entry through the door.

'Look at all that booze,' spluttered Nick. 'They've had enough. We should have some of that before it gets wasted, but how do we get to it?'

Just then a frail young figure staggered out of the alleyway on to the deck to get some air, looking pale and sickly.

'Ellow! Who are you?' exclaimed Nick.

'I'm the galley boy,' replied the waif. 'I want to go to bed, but I can't get in the cabin.'

'Don't worry,' said Nick, his face brightening. 'We'll get you to your bunk, but you'll have to do us a favour if we do.'

'What?' asked the lad.

'Come here,' said Nick, beckoning with his hand. He reached down and pushed open the escape port, which was unclipped. 'Put your legs through here, kid, and we'll lower you down on to the table. But you can pass us up that half-bottle of rum and a couple of beers before you turn in. Don't pay any attention to what anyone says. It'll be alright, OK?

'OK,' was the short reply.

Nick and I quickly grabbed the boy and stuffed him through the port, lowering him down at arm's length until he was standing on the table. Unsteadily he reached down and grasped the required items, passing them up to our outstretched hands. This was observed by some bleary eyes from the floor, but their weak, incoherent protests were ignored by all as we took our booty and scarpered.

Back in the littered mess-deck, Nick and I sat down with a beer each and the rum between us. Nick poured us both a huge dram from the rum bottle; I took a great gulp of mine and felt the raw liquid sear my throat as I surveyed the depressing scene around us, while the ship lurched its way north in the steady swell that ran from that direction. Nick and I chatted for a while and I finished my rum and half the beer. Then Nick decided, having spurned the bread and cheese, to carve himself a steak from the joint of beef that was thawing in the cupboard, and try to grill (burn) it on the stove top. That didn't appeal to me and I decided to leave him to it and make my way for'ard.

Out on the deck, I kept my weather eye on the grey, choppy wave tops as they danced past the scudding ship's rail while I trotted forward. I was almost across the fore-deck, when an agitated voice called from the bridge window, 'Hey, kid! Just a minute, before you turn in.' It was the poor third hand, who was still on the wheel after nearly four hours. He was only supposed to steer the ship down the river under the guidance of the skipper and mate, and here we were well out to sea and he was still up there on his own. 'I'm busting for a crap,' he continued. 'Can you grab hold of her while I slip down for a shit, and I'll grab one of the watch to come up. The mate seems to have gone missing.' I hesitated for a minute, a bit dubious. 'Look sharp pal, I'm messing misself,' he urged.

Maybe I was flattered at being recognised as a fully fledged decky. Anyway, I succumbed and scampered back up into the wheelhouse. I was a bit taken aback at the austere primitiveness of the scene that greeted me. There was much less equipment here than I had been used to in the *Apollo*. The deck gratings were patched and ill-fitting, and there was little polish on the wooden panelling. There were a couple of old Marconi Seagraph depth sounders and a radar unit. The straps were tatty on the drop-down windows, which were already rattling in the moderate wind, and apart from the one engine-room telegraph there was only the steering wheel. This stood at the back of the wheelhouse, instead of the front, and it was huge.

The wheel on the *St Apollo* came up to the waist, but this one was shoulder height, with large hand spokes. A much smaller one was suspended in front of it from the same hub. This was obviously used for quick manoeuvres and it was lashed to the big one with rope. Behind this larger wheel was the third hand, peering over the top at the deck-head compass above him. Pulling impatiently at the massive spokes, he tried to bring the ship back on course before handing over to me.

Jeff, or Chompy, as it turned out he was known, because he had no teeth and was continually chewing his gums, quickly stepped to one side and gave me the course as he handed over. 'North a half west,' he clipped and I repeated it. He also pointed out a couple of small fishermen towards the shore inside us and a large tanker outside; all were passing safely clear.

'Hey! You're not going to be long, are you?' I insisted.

'No!' he reassured me, 'As soon as I've done the business I'll get one of the lads to come and take over. Don't worry.' With that he scurried off the bridge as fast as a ferret.

For the next three hours I never saw a soul or a movement, and I realised I'd been had. I learnt something that day that I never forgot. With most of the crew drunk, and the rest sea-sick, it was now obvious that no one was going to relieve me, but it was getting dark and the drink I'd had was making me sleepy. It was going to take more than *my* eyes to pick out any navigation lights. I considered calling down to the skipper, but I knew that would cause trouble for someone, and I would be blamed. So I decided instead to give a blast on the ship's whistle and see what happened. I stepped to the front of the bridge, grabbed the toggle that hung down from the deck-head and swung on it with all my weight. The hiss of steam and harsh boom that issued from the direction of the funnel made me step back quickly behind the wheel, look all around and listen for the Old Man's footsteps on the stairway from his accommodation. But there were none. In fact, nothing happened.

For the next ten minutes, I kept going to the bridge door and looking aft to see if anyone was coming along the deck or casing, but there was no one. I sagged on the wheel in despair. I knew I couldn't keep this up indefinitely and was considering shouting down to rouse the skipper, when the bridge door was suddenly thrown open and Plug, the bosun, stepped in. He was looking a little the worse for wear, but certainly more sober than when I had last seen him. He was chewing a quid of tobacco and gave me a bleary-eyed, brown-toothed grin. 'Now then!' were his first words. 'You're young Bob Grant, are yeh?'

I confirmed it.

'Well, it's our watch now. Glad to see you're up here early. Where's young Hodgson?'

'I don't know,' I moaned. 'I've been up here all afternoon. I haven't seen anybody for hours.'

'Well, that's tough because you've got another four hours to do. Let's hope someone has called your watchmate.' With that he dropped the window, spewed a mouthful of juice on to the winch below, then looked all around the horizon. Closing the window, he settled against the telegraph and lapsed into silence. Now I was even more despondent. It was obvious that Plug wasn't going to do anything to have me relieved of this wearying job. Pretty soon his head was resting on the window and he dozed off. This was charming. The onus was still on me to keep a lookout, but my eyes too were getting tired and kept closing, and my head was nodding as I struggled to concentrate on the compass. Eventually alcohol exhaustion took over, my head flopped on the wheel and I slept where I stood. How long I slept I do not know, but I was suddenly aroused by Plug, shaking and shouting at me.

'What the devil do you think you're playing at?' he snarled. 'Sleeping on the job! You should be ashamed of yourself. Look, you're two points off course. Get a grip of yourself and pay attention. My God, it's a good thing one of us is watching the job.'

Shamefaced, I roused myself and spun the wheel to bring the ship back on course while Plug continued to berate me. I did consider pointing out that he was the first to bob off, but I realised the bosun wasn't the type of man who would ever admit to that, so I didn't bother. But my lapse did have the desired effect. Plug, with many veiled threats, agreed to take the wheel for five minutes (no longer), while I went for'ard and called out our watchmate. I was very glad when our spell was finally over and I was able to sleep for two complete watches below.

Alec Hodgson, my watchmate, I knew from several previous meetings ashore – not exactly a friend, more a friend of a friend. His position on the ship was similar to mine, in that he was a promoted decky learner. He was a year older than I, though you'd never guess it because he was so naive about life. He had little affinity with fishing and was forced into it by his father, who had been a deck-hand, with aspirations to become a mate or skipper, until a serious chest infection had forced him to retire. Alec's real love was animals, as my one visit to his terraced house revealed.

It was after one of our little drinking bouts, when more than one visit to the off-licence was required. Alec had taken us to his local beer-off for replenishment, which we were able to acquire without hesitation. Then, after consuming more alcohol, myself and one other – Jeff, I think it was – were persuaded to go back to his home nearby.

As soon as we stepped into the living room, straight from the terrace, evidence of animals was everywhere. For a start there was a duck waddling in and out from the back kitchen and a couple of kittens played about on the sofa where I was invited to sit. A canary sang happily from a cage suspended in a corner of the room, out of harm's reach, but perhaps the animal that most took my breath away was the hamster that ran around the teatable picking up scraps. It was even allowed to drink from the milk bottle when Alec was making a cup of tea. When offered a cup I declined apologetically and was offered instead, and accepted, a share of a bottle of Hull Brewery bitter.

The problem was that the booze was starting to take effect and I carelessly spilt some of the beer on the carpet. Of course, I was full of apologies, but Alec's mum and sister just laughed in the same way he did; with eyes narrowed to slits and crow's foot-lines at the corners, they all looked so much alike and were so obviously good-hearted. Alec, still chuckling and with glass in hand, wandered out into the kitchenette, returned with a dried-up floor cloth and tossed it on the floor towards me. I guess I was paying too much attention to my apologies, or my eyes were too glassy and watery, but when I grabbed the little, hard ball of cloth, and was scrubbing vainly in an effort to mop up the beer, there was a shriek from the women, and Sis quickly rescued the baby tortoise from my grasp. After that my only desire was to make a quick exit from this private menagerie.

This then was a profile of my watchmate for the next few weeks.

As the *St Elstan* proceeded northward the weather was as one would expect when approaching Iceland in December. Although it didn't actually blow hard in those first few days, the wind was always fresh, force five to six, with a sea state fishermen referred to as scuffly – a short, choppy sea that regularly lopped over the low rails, making it necessary to wear thigh boots and frocks whenever we were working on deck. Jumping Jeremy and Plug had managed to mould this, mostly inept, motley crew into a reasonable working unit; even Andy, the cook, was producing meals we could eat. Fortunately, his bread, as expected, was very good. If he could manage to fry fish when we started to catch it, then we would survive, and so would he. Already he had learnt how to produce large quantities of bacon for breakfast by baking it in the oven and he was also cooking the eggs in roasting trays.

It is true that stew featured regularly for the evening meal, when he recooked the half-raw dinner joint. But he made up for that when he produced busters (hot cakes) at four in the afternoon.

This weary, old pre-war trawler, however, lacked many of the basic amenities provided by my previous ship. It was difficult to keep oneself clean when there was no bath or washroom for'ard.

There was a room on the port side under the whaleback which was kept fairly clear of spare gear. It had a small, square wooden grating (duckboards) raised from the steel deck, and a hand pump on the bulkhead which would draw cold water from a tank below. This, with two fairly clean buckets jammed in a corner, made up our bathroom. But it took a very hard man to strip off in this unheated area, especially when the ship was pitching and rolling, which was most of the time.

The double toilet on the starboard side I had viewed with misgivings since I had walked aboard, and my fears were proven well founded early on. The steel door had been left open for so long that it was seized and could not be moved, so you could see men squatting there regularly when you passed. I tried to time my own motions when things were quiet, if possible, but one night after tea I had to go. I settled down with an overseas *Daily Mirror* in front of me to act as a shield, when I was suddenly joined by Podgy Fenton off the mate's watch.

Podgy plunged in, unannounced and obviously in a hurry, as he rove his pants down and threw himself on to the metal pan beside me. There followed the most horrendous series of noises and minor explosions, punctuated by gasps and groans, which only paled in their obnoxiousness when overtaken by the smell of a nauseating, gut-wrenching, fruity effluvium of Hull Brewery origin. The fact that the small metal dividing panel between us was only shoulder height meant that this aural and nasal offensive was accompanied by the equally offensive facial contortions of my unwelcome consort. Needless to say, I cut short my own evacuations as soon as possible and fled the scene, with Podgy's plea for me to leave behind just one sheet of my *Daily Mirror* fading in the distance. No wonder he was known to some as Farty Fenton.

The grand old lady we now called home was proving, as promised, to be a fine sea ship, for she seldom took any heavy water, even when the wind puffed up during the night, but it was obvious that she lacked power. The regular beat of the engines one was used to now included a whistle and a clack, a sort of THUMP-WHIT-CLACK, THUMP-WHIT-CLACK, as if everything was not running entirely smoothly down below. She certainly lacked the power of the more modern ships. When she was thrown back on her haunches by a heavy head sea the engine would almost stop, and you could feel her struggling to pick up way again.

Even the chief didn't give you any confidence when he rose from the engine room. He was a dark-skinned man, apparently of Indian origin, and was prone to be excitable, although for the most part he just looked forlorn. He was probably wondering why he had got himself into a set up that would take him into the Arctic Circle, when he was only used to coasting in North and Irish Seas – another promise of a big pay-off by Gibby, no doubt.

There was another unusual feature the *St Elstan* had still to reveal, she had a rat! It was fitting that our pet-lover was the one to discover it. We were approaching Iceland now and our watch had the early evening stint after tea. I was on the wheel and Plug was keeping an eye on the depth sounder, which was running continuously, waiting for us to reach the hundred-fathom line, when he was to call the skipper. Alec was hanging out the window,

playing with a big torch he had bought himself with his hard-earned cash last time home. He claimed it had a 300-ft. beam and he was aiming it at the fore-deck to prove his point. It had been snowing in the afternoon and some had settled in patches on the fore-end. Suddenly, Alec started chattering excitedly.
'Hey, Plug! Have we got a cat on board?' he asked.

Plug turned away from the sounder and looked out the window. 'Not that I know of. What 'ave yuh seen?'

'There, look,' snapped Alec, in a stage whisper, as he endeavoured to keep the torch beam on a creature that was sitting up on its haunches devouring snow.

'That's not a cat. It's a bloody rat,' blurted Plug.

I had stepped up to the window to get a look for myself. What I saw was certainly the size of a full-grown cat, but from there the similarity ended. The shape of its snout and its tail left no doubt.

'Ruddy hell,' I gasped. 'I've never seen one that size before. Where did it come from, Alec?'

'I dunno, from under the fo'c'sle head somewhere. Look, it's off back there now.'

Alec's wiggling of the torch beam had disturbed the monster and it shot back for'ard.

'The lads might not be sleeping so comfy, if they knew that was running around above their heads,' chuckled Plug.

'Aye well, don't forget we'll be sleeping down there next, and I'm not too happy about it either,' I pointed out.

'Well, you can worry about that later. Pay attention to the job right now and make sure she's on course 'cos I'll be calling the Old Man soon. And you stop playing around with that toy and keep a look out,' Plug added to Alec.

The rat was more or less forgotten over the next twenty-four hours. An hour or so later, the skipper was called out when the required depth was reached on the echo sounder and the south coast of Iceland was already on the radar. Soon after that, the heart-sinking order to call all hands to prepare for down trawl signalled the end of the comparatively easy life of steaming.

When the gear was finally down and square on the sea bed, after much screaming and ranting by Jeremy, and grumbling and chuntering by Plug, Bernie, the skipper, just looked on through the bridge window, quite unconcerned, hands stuck in fearnought pockets, and cut down clumpers on his feet, as if he was viewing it all for the first time. The first couple of tows produced only five or ten baskets of good-quality fish, as was expected from what was just a feeler to give the Old Man a chance to see how everything performed. There was more than enough fish to give the cook a good selection; we got the gear aboard and moved on in search of better things.

The skipper decided to steam along the south coast and on to the west side, but the little stoppage and the various engine movements required to shoot and haul the trawl for our two little tows seemed to have disturbed the running of the old triple-expansion steam engine. We had to stop a couple of times for the chief to make repairs or adjustments, which didn't go down very well.

During the time it took us to move around the south coast, the lads all turned in to catch a little sleep, after the few hours' riving and heaving. The cook was left to fillet the fish for tea, for the food stores would have to be supplemented with fish twice a day from now on. After watching him tear the flesh off the bones of the first two fish, one of the watch took pity on him and took over the job of filleting.

'It's obvious by the way yer performing that yer not too used to frying fish,' remarked the decky. 'So I guess yer batter wain't be much kop either. You'd better give 'em summat for pudding that'll sweeten 'em up.'

'What do you suggest?' muttered Andy the cook, biting his lip.

'Depends. What 'ave yer got?'

'Well, I haven't got any pastry made up today. I was giving it a miss for once, but there's plenty of dried fruit,' offered the young cook.

'Naw! That only mecks yer shit,' offered the culinary advisor, as he swept the last fish skeleton into the basket.

'There's also plenty of rice,' Andy went on. 'There's a full sack of rice.'

'Ah! Now yer talking. Rice pudding, that'd be great.'

'But I don't know how to make rice pudding,' moaned Andy.

'There's now't to know,' the seaman pressed on. 'Yer just give the rice a good boiling, for a good while like, then just add sugar and milk.'

'Right!' said Andy. 'I'll go and get the rice.'

Andy soon returned carrying a small sack of rice. 'How much do you think we'll need?'

'I don't naw,' muttered the tenderfoot, losing interest. He hailed from Filey and had spent his little time at sea in inshore boats. 'Yer know what a hungry lot you've got 'ere. A mugful'd fill a dish, I reckon, so put a mugful in for each man.'

'Well, that's twenty men, so twenty mugfuls. I'll need a big pan,' said the cook. 'OK, I'll put it on to simmer for the afternoon. I'm going to turn in for a couple of hours till it's time to get tea ready. Thanks.'

Obviously neither man was aware how rice swells when boiled.

The trouble with steaming between grounds is that you never know how long you're going to be; it could be twelve hours or it could be two. So, if you wake up, the dilemma is whether to get out for a drink or stay put. It's not worth it if you're stopping soon anyway. Others, it seemed, thought the same. When I awoke, all stiff from the hard boards beneath me, I noticed some restless movements in the bunks around me as men moaned and stretched and scratched. One or two were reading; I decided to have a read too until we had some news on what was happening.

Pretty soon I could hear the clump of boots along the deck above as one of the hands came for'ard, followed by a yelp and a curse from the top of the ladder. One of the lads came tumbling down the steep stairway. 'Bloody hell! I've just seen that rat,' he blurted to those awake. 'Have yer seen the size of it. That bastard is gonna do some damage, if we don't get it.'

'What's a matter,' one of the older men sneered. 'Do yer think it's going tuh eat a hole in the ship's side or summat?'

'By the size a' that one it could *kick* a hole in the ship's side,' replied the first, and he began to poke and rake the fire before mending it. He had a bit of a job because the eighteen-inch-high ash pit was full and overflowing. Exasperated, he rounded on Roland, the decky learner, who was lying reading a comic in his bunk directly opposite the stove. But Roland, who at first sight appeared slow, had endured so much criticism and mickey-taking over the last few days that he had developed some back chat of his own.

'Now then, snacker! What's all this then?' snarled the young decky. 'Look at the state of this ash pit. I suppose you know it's your job to empty this, do yer?'

'OK, OK! I will do in time,' replied the learner.

'In time isn't good enough,' snapped his superior. 'This is ready to overflow now.'

'There'd be no harm done if it did,' muttered Roland, referring to the boots and gear littering the deck.

'Oh yeah! So that's the attitude, is it? And what happens when it starts to flow into our bunks?' sneered the decky, raising his voice. 'What then?'

'We'll all just have to move one bunk up, won't we?' drawled the lad, turning the page.

At this stage, the deck-hand was just starting to get nasty when another pair of booted feet descended the ladder. It was Nick, who had just come down from the bridge.

'Right! Stand by your beds,' he announced to all and sundry. 'We'll be stopping in half an hour.'

'Half an hour?' spoke up one. 'What time is it now?'

'Twenty past five,' sang out Nick, searching in his kitbag for a muffler.

'Oh, charming! That means we'll be shooting right on teatime,' said the first, as bodies began to stir.

'Well tea's gonna be late anyhow,' continued Nick, throwing his kitbag into an empty bunk.

'What for?' was the cry.

'The rice pudding's chased the cook out the galley.'

'Are you kidding, Nicko?'

'No! The galley's full of it,' insisted Nick. 'We've had to get the fireman out the engine room with his shovel to trim it,' he added, with a twinkle in his eye.

'I hope he isn't shovelling it back in the pan,' a voice suggested.

'Naw, we haven't found the pan yet,' replied Nick, scampering back up the ladder. 'Come on me hearties, look sharp. Let's earn some money for a change.'

When the ship was stopped and in position, we soon had the gear over the side and lowered in the water. But, when we had lined up on course and were streaming the gear away at full speed, the telegraph suddenly rang stop from the engine room and the engines failed. The ship immediately cruised to a stop. By the time everyone realised what had happened, and the brakes were applied on the warp drums to stop the wire from slacking away, it became obvious that the trawl gear would be foul. The fact that the chief had stopped the engines without permission from the bridge indicated there was a serious problem in the engine room. So, as everyone else was busy on the deck, the skipper despatched the sparks to find out what it was.

Fortunately, the ship swung and settled with the gear on the weather tack. The winch was not affected, so we began the long, slow process of heaving the gear back and trying to unravel it, which took all hands four or five hours. At least the engine room problem was resolved by the time we had finally got everything sorted out, and we were able to shoot away again. The delayed tea that some had worried about at first became irrelevant as no one was allowed to leave the deck to eat it until the gear was on the bottom again, and that didn't happen till very late.

After we had completed two or three hauls successfully, bringing in nothing very exciting – about twenty-five to thirty baskets of mixed fish – it was decided to start the fishing watches, making four watches instead of three. This meant rearranging the existing watches and introducing the daymen into them. Nick was taken off the third hand's watch and promoted to fourth hand, which meant he would take on the responsible job of paying away the warps with the mate and working alongside him on the cod-end when the fish came aboard. It also meant that he would sort of lead the watch which included me and Roland, the snacker who was thrust upon us.

It was about time that the watches were started because with the foul gear and the three tows most of us had been on call for fourteen hours or so already. Bernard, the skipper, had decided to work eighteen and six, that is eighteen hours on deck and six below, so the last watch below would have done thirty-two hours on call.

Nick decided to have an encouraging word in Roland's ear. 'Now then, young'un. I'll bet you're glad to be on watch with two understanding blokes like me and Bob, ain'tcha. All the time yer pull yer weight you won't ave any trouble with us. I sharn't be calling yer four eyes just because of your glasses, see. Now, do as you're told and everything will be fine. You can start by nipping down the fo'c'sle and cleaning it up now, including the ashes, and if you ever consider giving me the sort of slaver I heard you dishing out to young Becksy, then you'll be going down there headfirst. Got it?'

Roland paused for a minute, looking Nick in the eye. Nick gave him a greasy smile. 'Well! Accidents do happen, don't they?' he shrugged.

Roland looked down and kicked away a tab end, then slowly turned and walked for'ard. I didn't get the feeling that Nick had completely tamed him yet.

For the next few hauls, we spent quite a lot of time on deck mending the trawl. As the skipper chased after more fish he must have been skirting the bad ground because we had damage to the gear each haul. It was depressing and demoralising because the winter weather was the usual to be endured off Iceland; a freezing northerly wind whipped snow needles horizontally into your eyes, and the short, choppy seas slapped against the low rails amidships, sending sheets of icy spray across our bare hands as we fumbled with the torn nets on the ever-rolling and lurching decks.

I was pleased, as a decky, to be able to exercise my net-mending skills, at which I was very adept, instead of filling needles, my usual job as a decky learner. But the water on deck constantly swilling the net about was making it difficult, and taking up valuable fishing time. Bernard, the laid-back skipper, seemed able to accept this, but Jeremy, the mate, could not. He tongue-lashed us all on to greater efforts, knowing it was costing him money with the gear laid on the deck.

Stretching my aching back for a moment, I looked up at the decky working nearest to me. It was Alec, I studied his salt-caked face; pale, drawn and pinched. His mouth hung open as he sucked in the cold night air. He looked so weary, struggling to make his frozen hands respond with the twine needle. I flapped my arms around me in an effort to force some blood into my painful hands and called to him. 'Here, Alec! Come and hold up this net for me. It will make it easier for me to work faster and we can get both jobs done that much quicker.'

Alec was glad to drop his net and don a pair of mittens, which he could do if he was only holding up. With the net held up scone (square), and at a comfortable height, I was able to work much faster, which kept the blood flowing into my fingers and made them more flexible. Alec squinted out into the dark and picked out the deck lights of another ship in the distance. Proof, if he needed it, that there were other poor souls suffering like us to wrest a living from the deep.

'Do you think we *will* make it for Christmas, Bob? After such a poor start?' he asked.

'Well, it's still early yet,' I responded, 'and you know what this lark is like. Three or four days' heavy fishing and you've caught your trip, and that can happen at Iceland any time.'

'I hope so,' mused Alec. 'It's just that I was hoping to buy my sister a puppy for Christmas, if we get home in time. I thought it might cheer things up.'

Well, it'll certainly liven things up, I thought, when the pup gets among the kittens, the duck and the hamster. Soon after that we were putting the gear over the side again and fishing was resumed.

Our own pet rat featured again in the next couple of nights. During the quiet periods, it was observed from the bridge, scuttling across the foredeck into the pounds for scraps. And on one occasion the giant rodent was seen dragging an abandoned codling out of the scuppers back under the fo'c'sle head, much to the consternation of those that slept for'ard. Rats were unusual aboard a trawler and were most undesirable; they were regarded as unlucky, apart from anything else – and this situation was soon to come to a head.

Over the next couple of days we fished much better. Bernard, the skipper, had been forced to slip off the edge of Eldey Bank and scrape around The Blinders, a submerged reef. This was a dangerous area because the reef was miles off the land, and it was difficult to keep a check on our position while hauling because of the strong tide that flowed there. Nor, of course, could it be seen beneath the water. But, as we were catching enough fish to keep us on deck from haul to haul, he persevered.

Nick, Roland and I – on the fourth hand's watch – were lucky enough to

Deck scene on St. Elstan-class vessel.

St. Apollo-class working port side gear.

have the watch below after tea, 18.30 to 00.30 hrs. This meant that we could stuff our pokes with the evening meal, and then turn in till midnight and sleep it off. Not the best watch below but certainly the second best.

We were all getting weary now and turning out was a struggle after such a short sleep, even though we were called half an hour before we were due on deck. Nick kept an eye on us and made sure we turned out on time, especially Roland. One night, when we had been called at midnight, with fish waiting for us on deck, Nick nagged us to roll out in good time and get our warm gear on, almost physically dragging Roland out to make sure he didn't sleep in after we had left, as he was inclined to do. When the snacker had finally donned his obb-wool stockings and boots, he practically pushed the sleepy-headed youngster towards the fo'c'sle ladder.

'Come on, Rollo! Get a move on or we won't have time for a drink,' Nick remonstrated.

Roland slowly ascended the narrow ladder with Nick close behind until his top half disappeared into the hoodway above. Then he came to an abrupt stop halfway up. Nick, a couple of steps behind, suddenly found his way blocked by Roland's bottom. 'Now then, what have yuh stopped for?' shouted the irate decky. 'Don't fall asleep here of all places,' and he gave him a poke in the rear end. Roland uttered not a sound but gave two or three feeble little kicks downward, in an apparent effort to retrace his steps. Nick was not inclined to let him do this, with time running out, and he made an extra effort to force him up.

What Nick didn't know was the sight that confronted the now-wide-awake Roland at the top of the steps. With the fo'c'sle stove set alongside the ladder, the stovepipe ran up by the side of it, through the narrow platform inside the entrance, and up the side of the doorway out on to the whaleback top. Squatting upright, and snuggling close to the lagged pipe for extra warmth, with its swollen, pregnant belly protruding, was the now huge rodent. Its large, sneering incisor teeth were not more than eighteen inches from, and on a level with, the pale, twitching face of our unfortunate decky learner. Behind the teeth and rigid whiskers of this grey monster were a pair of black, beady, glaring eyes which never left Roland's.

I think everyone knows how aggressive an animal can be when protecting its young, especially when threatened, and that was an impression that the bespectacled youngster was desperate not to give. Another shout from down below and a determined shove had Roland nearly head-butting the creature and the lad freaked out. Letting go of everything, he dropped like a stone right on top of Nick, and both finished up rolling on the fo'c'sle floor with shouts and curses. Entertaining as this was for me, the timing was not right, so I decided to mount the stairway as quickly as possible and get aft to make a drink before it was too late. Fortunately, when Roland and Nick took their dive, the noise was enough to scare the rat, so it was no longer visible when I climbed out the forecastle, making it more difficult for Roland to explain himself later.

Roland's story was confirmed pretty quickly, however, as the rat continued to visit the spot whenever it was quiet, and only vacated it at the last moment, leaping over the weather step and across the feet of anyone poised to descend, and causing a few deckies to get nervous about calling out or turning in. It was regarded as a problem that had to be solved soon, before the critter had its young and we were infested. The trouble was we were kept so busy on deck that no one had the time to root the creature out and find its nest. However, things were soon to change.

Although we were doing alright, the skipper was not happy about working the reef without a reliable engine. He had a report that some ships had found a good bag of codling on top of the bank, working near the limit line, and he decided instead to join them. When we hauled next time, with the usual amount of damage to the trawl, Bernard made his move. The order came down to heave up the trawl doors and lift the ends, and one of the watch to the wheel. Our watch was on duty and, as Roland was not allowed to take the wheel and Nick was doing a special job on the cod-ends, it was left to me to go to the bridge.

With my waterproofs off and the rest of the crew still working on deck, I welcomed the warmth and comparative comfort of the wheelhouse, as I took over the wheel from the skipper and repeated the course. Over the next thirty to forty minutes, Bernard busied himself between the radar, the depth sounder and the chart room, as he plotted our position and adjusted the course for the reported position of the fish. Then he settled down to watch the sounder as we gradually made our way up the bank. But the skipper had barely settled himself, and there had been no chance of any conversation, before a loud hissing of steam could be heard from behind the wheelhouse, and a sudden great plume of black smoke wafted from the funnel and climbed many feet into the air. At the same time the engine slowed and once again the telegraph rang as we gradually came to a stop.

Bernard was furious and made it clear that he thought half the trouble was due to the inexperience of the chief with this type of engine. Then he lapsed into silence as he lounged against the telegraph, his arms folded and his head down deep in thought, imagining, no doubt, what he was going to say to the gaffer when we got home.

I remained behind the wheel and watched the compass aimlessly while the ship fell off against the wind. A shout from the mate on the deck was ignored by the skipper. He remained in a solemn trance, staring at nothing, lost in thought. A few moments passed, then the wireless operator entered the bridge from the wireless room. He gave me a wink and a wry smile in passing, then thrust a telegram pad under the skipper's nose. Bernard refocused and read what was on the pad; then he blurted in exasperation, 'So the fishing is improving?' He looked up at the sparks for confirmation and received a nod. 'Well, that's a bastard. And here we are laid idle, while they're scooping it up.' At that point, the starboard bridge door opened and the mate stepped in, removing his sou'wester.

'What's up, Skipper! We're not shooting here, are we?'

'No we're not!' snarled the skipper. 'And if the chief doesn't sort out this engine room soon I doubt if we'll be shooting anywhere.'

'Why? What's wrong?' asked the mate.

Before anyone could answer, we heard the clumping of leather boots on the veranda. On the far side of the wheelhouse, the port side door was flung open and the wild-eyed little chief engineer stumbled onto the bridge. His perspiring face was soot-streaked and his skin as red as a boiled lobster. 'Skipper,' he babbled, 'I think the furnace crowns are coming down, and I can't shut the fuel off. We're going up, we're going up!' and he waved his hands upwards like an orchestra conductor asking for a crescendo.

There were a few moments of stunned silence, then all eyes turned to the skipper. Bernard was still leaning on the telegraph, arms folded and tight-lipped, staring with disbelief at the distraught little chief.

The sparks was the first to break the silence. 'Do you want me to get hold of someone to stand by us, Skipper?' he asked.

Bernard just twisted his mouth and shook his head, still staring.

Jumping Jeremy could stand the inaction no longer. 'I'll tell the lads to get their life jackets out,' he said, turning towards the door.

'STAY WHERE YOU ARE,' shouted the skipper. 'You heard what he said. WE'RE GOING UP. According to him, we don't want fucking life jackets, we want parachutes.' Before anyone could react to this cynical remark, he addressed the chief. 'Have you called the second out?' he snapped.

'I told the cook to call him when I dashed up here,' he replied.

'Well, get down there and get him to give you a hand to shut her down. And when you've done that get the second to report to me while you check round.' To the sparks he continued, 'Get in touch with our nearest ship and tell them we've a bit of a problem and may need some help. Then give them our position, which I'll let you have shortly.' Finally, he said to the mate, 'Go down and get the fish off the deck next, while we've still got a donkey pump to wash'em. Then finish off the trawl, have one watch clear and loosen the gripes on the lifeboats and make sure everything is running clear.' Then, apparently noticing me, he added, 'You can do that, Bob. It'll keep you handy on the boat-deck, in case I need you.'

Greasing the slip hooks on the lifeboats without any grease could be a tricky job. But it looked like that was my task because the only grease available was down the engine room, and I didn't think I would be welcome down there at that moment, with the pressure on everybody in a potentially dangerous situation. Anyway, I wasn't keen to go down there myself when I thought of the chief's words. I just took a crocodile spanner and worked on the lifeboat bottle screws for a while, keeping a wary eye on the engine-room skylight nearby. I also chipped at the slip hooks to clear them and shipped up the davit handles.

All this time the ship laid dormant, rolling in a lazy swell with snow swirling round us and settling on the upper structures. There was plenty of shouting and clattering echoing up from the engine room, and a lot of coming and going to the bridge. After some time, I decided to return to the bridge and ask the skipper if he wanted the boat covers removing. 'No, not yet,' the skipper instructed. 'If you've cleared the rest, leave it for now and report back to the mate.'

When I got back to the fore-deck, the fish had been cleared and put below, and the crew were putting the finishing touches to the trawl. I spotted the bosun in the waist of the ship, trying to finish off a hole in the top wing, but the net was swilling about in the duck pond, as we called the area where the water continually washed in through the main scupper port. I decided to help by holding up the net where he was working, as this allowed him to stretch his back. Plug said nothing, but continued to let me perform this simple task, instead of sending me packing to a heavier job.

For a while I studied Plug's tobacco-stained, bewhiskered face as he chewed his quid, while his hands worked the needle expertly. He leaned into the constant roll of the dormant ship without being aware of it. A sharp rap on the back of my knuckles from the net needle, the usual silent indication that I was allowing the net to sag down, brought me back to the job in hand.

'If we do have to go in, do you think that'll mess us up for Christmas?' I finally blurted.

Plug paused long enough to spurt a gob of tobacco juice at a screeching seagull standing on the rail alongside us, causing it to launch itself into the biting wind, before replying.

'Christmas was never on the cards, kid. So don't worry yourself about that. My wife will already have borrowed money to buy the kids their presents. My main concern is earning enough to repay that at the end of this trip. So, whatever happens, it will be up to Breakdown Bernie up there to scoop fish aboard as quick as he can.'

Suddenly there was a yelp, followed by excited shouting from the lads working under the fo'c'sle head. They had uncovered the rat while moving some net. It shot out from under the whaleback on to the fore-deck, and most of the deckies had dropped what they were doing to give chase. Grabbing large croc spanners, hatch battens or crowbars, they lashed about at the massive rodent as it zig-zagged around the deck, chased by a decky with the hose pipe. Among the hunters was Alec, the animal lover, half-heartedly waving a spanner about, until the panic-stricken rat shot straight at his legs and he instinctively brought his weapon down to pin it, smacking it right in the middle of its back and apparently breaking it. The rat let out an awful shriek and scurried away on front legs only, dragging its useless back legs behind it into the shelter of a pile of old net.

Alec was distraught because he had delivered the fatal blow; dropping the spanner and clasping his hands to his cheeks, his glaring eyes focused on the spot where the crippled rat had disappeared. The men around him were quick to spot this weakness in their shipmate and lost no time in harassing him with cries of 'Shame', 'Disgusting' and 'Heartless sod.' Whether this was to tough it out of him or just for their own amusement is hard to say, but the effect was to crumple Alec. His head sagged forward and, chin on his chest, he sobbed. This stopped most of the cat-calling. The men just stared with disbelief and disgust, but there were a couple of calls of 'Dry up and pull yourself together, you pansy,' from one or two of the harder old salts as they turned away.

After some hours of hard work by the engineers, and much consultation with the insurers ashore, we were allowed to proceed at slow speed, on two fires, into Reykjavik, the capital of Iceland. This journey ashore made everyone depressed. International law required all the fishing gear to be stowed and secured before entering port, and we all knew it would be some time before it was used again and we could earn some money.

Some of us who had never been into Reykjavik were excited, but if we thought it was going to be more comfortable there than on the cold Arctic Ocean, we were in for a surprise. The outermost arm of the outer harbour, where we tied up, was covered deep in snow and ice, as was most of the town, making it less inviting for a walk ashore. Things got worse when the shore-based engineers came aboard to work on the boilers and immediately shut down the stokehold fires. This killed off most of the heat that was generated aboard the ship, leaving only the fo'c'sle fire for'ard and the cabin and galley stoves aft. The bridge and centre of the ship was perishing.

Fishermen and trawlers were meant to fish. When they're not fishing there is little else for them to do, and idle hands are mischievous hands. Bernie, the skipper, knew this; and he also knew that strenuous work kept men warm. So he hit on the idea of a boat drill. In order to get our lifesavers running free, he ordered us to lower them in the water – not an easy task in an old vessel, where the davits and running blocks have not been used for many a year. It took up most of the day to get both boats in the water but eventually they were floating free. Lowering boats into the water was one thing, but these were not really designed to be brought back, certainly not without power. The only power available to us was steam, which on this occasion was unavailable – much to the skippers embarrassment – so the boats had to remain over the side.

It was inevitable that, in spite of the conditions, some of us would want to walk into town, so we prevailed on the skipper to organise a sub, or loan from the agent, out of our earnings. The skipper was naturally reluctant to do this, as we hadn't really earned anything yet, so he fobbed us off by saying he would have to get the owner's permission first.

The next day was Sunday and, as there was nothing to do apart from a little cleaning in the morning, five of us decided we would take one of the lifeboats for a row around the harbour, with Nick steering and four of us to do the rowing. Of course, as the lifeboats had spent most of their lives in the lee of a smoking funnel, the gear in the boat was pretty sooty, and we must have looked a pretty sight with our gear and faces caked in black. Our trip round the harbour was rather erratic, with much splashing and rocking, as neither Roland or Alec were very adept at rowing, but eventually we got it together and rowed out of the harbour into the fjord to show our prowess to the Sunday walkers promenading along the quay.

These gathered in numbers towards the end of the quay, with some show of amusement as we turned around and headed back inside. The reason for their excitement became obvious when we rounded the end of the jetty. An enemy vessel shot out from behind it, in the shape of the other lifeboat, manned by the older members of the crew who proceeded to give us a broadside of snowballs. In disarray, we backwatered and, under the orders of Admiral Nick, swung round and rowed to the outside of the jetty. Three of our members clambered up on to it and began throwing down snow cannonballs for us to stack up, much to the amusement of the gathering crowd.

Presumably our opponents were doing the same for they did not attempt to follow us. Once loaded, we set off again to enter the harbour, only to be met again by the same challenge; our antagonists had been tipped off by the crowd above. There then followed the great battle of Reykjavik Harbour, as the two boats crossed and re-crossed, delivering broadside after broadside with much colliding and oar fouling and splashing. Twice more we re-armed, with the crowd tossing fresh snowballs down to us to save us disembarking. Finally, we decided that we were cold enough, wet enough and tired enough to pack it all in and return to ship, having saved a fair proportion of the inhabitants from a boring Sunday afternoon.

It was obvious we were going to spend a few days in port, so it was inevitable that the skipper would have to get us a sub. It wasn't much but was probably enough to give us one afternoon and night ashore if handled sparingly. As soon as the Icelandic kronur were in our hands, we organised ourselves and departed at intervals in little groups.

Bearing in mind that hot water was at a premium aboard the ship – there was no way to get it without boiling a bucket on the stove – that no one had any shore gear warm enough to combat the elements, and that the only footwear we had to cope with the snow and slush were sea boots, it was no wonder that people ashore kept their distance. I went ashore with Nick, Alec and Becksy, the young decky who had the argument with Roland. We admired the town, which was after all the capital of Iceland. It wasn't greatly developed but appeared a bit Americanised, with its suspended traffic lights and American cars, due to the air base the Yanks had close by at Keflavik.

Most of the young girls we spotted were very pretty, but they were largely taken up by the American forces, probably for the goodies they could provide. There were no pubs like we have at home. Most of the drinking was done in hotel bars, which we didn't have the nerve to use, dressed as we were. So that left us with a poor choice of cheap cafes for refreshment, mostly containing workmen. Nick did manage to strike up a rapport with the girl who served our strong coffee, but she was too busy to be any more than just pleasant.

We did get a beer in one of the dockside cafes, but the few females we saw in such places were middle-aged and pretty rough. We soon lost heart and set off back to the ship, but there was little waiting for us there except for a game of cards in a cold mess-deck. Nick and I decided to have a game of crib while Alec looked on. Becksy sloped off to the fo'c'sle to have a read.

The most interesting part of our card game was watching the ingenious ways that Nick tried to fiddle the points when we were counting up at the end of each play, but Becksy soon skipped back into the mess-deck with something more interesting. His face was flushed with excitement as he threw himself down on the first seat inside the doorway. In a loud stage whisper he revealed,

'Hey! Chompy's knocking off a tart in the fo'c'sle.'

'How do yuh know?' asked Nick sceptically.

'I saw 'em,' hissed Becksy.

'What, in full view?' gasped Alec.

'Naw, they're in his bunk. There's no one else down there.'

'Are you sure?' I queried doubtfully.

'Course I am. His curtain doesn't reach right across his bunk. You could see her legs and his bare arse going like a fiddler's elbow.'

'Well, well!' mused Nick. 'And how could he afford that, do you think?'

'He rounded up some cash doing deals with some of the lads who weren't interested in spending ashore. He sold a nice Ronson lighter to Roland, the snacker, and I know he did a deal with one of the firemen.' Becksy seemed to know it all.

'Well, it's disgusting,' announced Nick, with mock distaste, 'and he shouldn't be allowed to get away with it when young men are looking to retire to their boudoir. We will have to discreetly disturb them.'

Nick jumped up from the table and set off for'ard, with the rest of us in safari behind him. As we approached the whaleback, Nick put an erect finger to his lips and proceeded to tread lightly under the fo'c'sle head. Glancing down the fo'c'sle ladder as we passed, he moved right forward where some of the spare gear was stowed and spotted some alloy-metal globe floats, hung up over one of the net-pounds.

'Here! Climb up and pass me those five bogs down,' he whispered to Alec.

Alec obeyed quietly. Nick thrust them at me. 'Hold these while I cut them free,' he muttered.

Once they were separated, he gathered them in his arms and moved towards the fo'c'sle companionway. A quick glance to make sure all was clear below, then he dropped the metal balls one after the other down the steps. The racket they made as each one hit nearly every step and bounced up against the companionway side or hit the coal stove near the bottom was enough to cause near panic in the female below. She let out a shriek and curling her legs up lashed out with knees and shins, catapulting Chompy clean out of the bunk among the rolling metal balls.

We four culprits crowded into the hoodway entrance to see the effect and were rewarded with a glimpse of bare boobs and bum, as the woman searched for her clothes and before Chompy recovered enough to look for the perpetrators. A quick exit was called for and the sabotage team scurried aft before Chompy could spot someone on whom to exact his revenge.

It took five days before repairs were completed, including one day to flash up the boiler and raise steam. These extra five days would be added to the expenses of the trip, which would then be deducted before the skipper and mate received their share of the profits. Also to be taken into account was the fish we had already caught. This affected us all. It was now five days older and we still had most of the cargo to catch – that is if we wanted this voyage to pay. No wonder Bernard and Jeremy looked strained when we left the port to face the rigours of the Icelandic waters; the pressure was on. The Icelandic grounds are prolific and yield a lot of fish if you are in the right place at the right time. But there are also two elements that will frustrate you most of the time – bad weather and rough grounds. Bernard decided he would have to try to ignore both if he was to catch up on time.

We moved up north to the Isafjord Gully and North Cape area. This time of year there was always plenty of fish somewhere in the vicinity, but the conditions were usually extreme with black frost and severe north-easterly gales to contend with. As we searched around the different grounds – sometimes on the shoals, sometimes in the deep of the gully – working in scuffly weather, about force four to five, we often picked up hauls of fifty to sixty baskets of codling or haddock, with some flats. These would be considered a good living if we had our normal fishing time, but we had lost so much time this trip that Bernard was desperate to find bigger hauls to try to make up.

We eventually found what we wanted in the very deep water off the western edge of the Continental Shelf, a place known as the Hindenburg Line. Here we found two or three bags of good, solid, jumping, fighting cod; they were difficult to handle when gutting, but would pay well if we could get enough of them. But this steep edge was difficult to fish. The ground was bad with many snags and patches of soft mud; the currents out here were strong and, in bad weather, made the swell very steep, causing the seas to sweep the deck regularly. Handling the ship must have been difficult, particularly when the gear came fast on the bottom and especially with so much towing warp out. The fish was coming aboard quickly, but we had to fight for it as the weather was deteriorating rapidly. The short, sharp seas constantly hit the rails and broke inboard. How I wished for the higher bulwark rails of the *St Apollo* because the men were knocked down regularly. But Bernard knew he had to press on while the fish were there. So much for being laid back.

The wind continued to increase, and once again our gear came fast on the bottom. We started to haul; the seas tossed the ship around and slapped against the bow, preventing it from coming round, and all the time the winch was steadily heaving the wire in. The tidal current was also pushing against the ship and the wires began to sing. Suddenly there was a loud bang and one of the warps sagged slightly. We had obviously parted a wire on the gear somewhere and would now have to recover our expensive gear on one warp. The skipper gradually worked the ship back towards the trawl, trying to get over the top of it, but the strong wind – now force six, verging on seven – pushed the ship away. The strain on the wire prevented her from rolling or lifting, causing even more water to slop aboard among the fish left from the previous haul, swilling it around the deck as the poor old lass wallowed in this salty stew pot.

Eventually there was a jump on the remaining wire and the ship came lively again. She had let go from the bottom and we quickly brought the gear to the surface. But, of course, we could only bring one end alongside, the rest of the gear swilled away to windward. With our workshop now bouncing and rolling, we had to try to grapple on to another part of the trawl with the Gilson hook to heave it up and alongside and then try again further along.

As it was the fore-end that had parted, we had to grapple with the after-derrick Gilson to get the hook on to some other part of the gear. The mate constantly threw the heavy hook to windward without success, but eventually it fastened on to the head-line and we began to heave steadily, lifting the trawl partly out of the water and towards the ship.

The derrick Gilson was not a wire designed to lift a full set of gear out of a sea which was swirling, boiling, peaking and sucking at everything within it, and when the ship rolled the strain was too much. With another loud bang, the Gilson wire parted just two metres from the winch, and everyone ducked to avoid the recoil. All that is, except the man at the winch whipping drum, pulling back on the wire. This happened to be Chompy; he had no chance and the steel six-strand wire whiplashed straight into his face. Chompy's head was jerked backwards and he was thrown on to the swirling fore-deck.

The mate raised both hands to cease all operations, as the nearest men to our stricken shipmate rushed forward to lift him out of the water. We all knew this was going to be serious. Four men stumbled aft on the rolling ship, carrying the semi-conscious decky between them. His sou'wester framed a bloody mess where his face should have been. It would have been impossible to get him up the vertical ladders to the bridge, so he was hurried aft into the mess-deck and laid on the mess table as he was, boots and all.

It was apparent that when the wire whipped across Chompy's face it had slashed an inverted V-cut from one jawline, up across the bridge of his nose and down to the other jawline – a cut so deep that all the flesh above his mouth had dropped down to reveal a gaping hole down to the skull.

At first Chompy was laid on his back, with his head propped up, but he started spluttering and spitting and blowing the blood that poured off his top lip away from his mouth – the only orifice left for him to breath through – and so he was turned on to his side. He did not attempt to speak while all this was going on. Only his eyes, still visible above this horrific, gory tear, searched the faces of his helpers for some indication of how serious his condition was.

The skipper came tumbling down the ladder from the boat-deck, carrying a first-aid box with field dressings. As he pushed his way into the mess, Alec, who had been one of the carriers, staggered out and vomited in the alleyway.

The skipper reeled when he saw the state of Chompy's face. His intention was to stop the flow of blood; he was reluctant to apply dressings to such open, raw flesh, but there was no alternative.

He did the best he could, placing sterile wads here and there. When this was done, he gave orders to those around to remove Chompy's boots and cut his oilskin off, and then to help him down the companion stairwell to the main cabin below while he was still conscious. 'I'll go back for some more stuff from the medicine chest,' he snapped. He knew he would need some morphine before the pain and shock set in. As he stepped out into the alleyway, he came face to face with Jeremy, the mate, who had not seen the state of Chompy close up. He had been trying to secure the deck temporarily with the few remaining men.

'How is he, Skipper?' asked the mate.

'He's bad. We're going to have to take him in,' said the skipper, with clipped words.

'Oh, no! We're not going in again, are we?' pleaded Jeremy. 'Can't you patch him up?'

'Jesus Christ,' spat out the skipper. 'I can't patch that up. He'll be lucky if the hospital can. I'm going to take him in to Isafjord, but first I need some advice from the radio doctor. I want you to get that gear aboard within half an hour. Dump it on the deck anyway you can. If you think you can't do it, then we'll have to chop it away. Now, look sharp! Get the non-combatants to look after Chompy till I get back.' With that he spun round and shot up the steel ladder to the boat-deck above.

By non-combatants the skipper meant all those who did not work on deck.

With all the deck-hands working, including the watch who had been below, we threw hooks into everything, whether it tore the net or not, and hove the trawl alongside to be lifted on board with the big tackle block. Everything was dumped in a great heap on the fore-deck. It was going to take hours to sort out, but everything was on board in the required time and we were able to make way full speed for Iceland.

Chompy was put in the mate's berth, just off the main cabin, away from prying eyes. Jeremy wasn't going to need it anyway. Like the rest of us, he was going to be on deck until we reached port and back, trying to unravel the great mound of bobbins, wire, net and fish which covered the fore-deck.

An estate-car-type ambulance was waiting for Chompy, ready to whisk him off to the little local hospital, as soon as we arrived, and when the skipper had sorted his belongings and everything with the agent, we left. We heard later that one of the young nurses who received him fainted when she saw his face, and as soon as he was stabilised he was flown down to the big hospital in Reykjavik for microsurgery.

Once again we returned to the job of trying to catch a trip which would clear expenses – this time with a man short and a very weary crew. No one knew how far away Christmas was and no one could be bothered to work it out. The only thing we were looking forward to now was the end of fishing and the journey home.

At last, the skipper finally called it a day and told us to stow the gear. Food was getting low, but the real reason was the fuel oil and *we had* managed to scrape 2,000 kits together, though how much of that was still saleable was anyone's guess.

It wasn't a case of queuing up for a bath after we had clewed up this time because, of course, there wasn't one. This time the chase was on for hot water and a bucket to carry it in. None of us had been able to wash for at least a week, but we all had been soaked in sea water many times, and had been forced to work on sometimes and let our clothes dry on us, so it was imperative to rinse the salt and sweat off our skin to rid ourselves of saltwater boils. Washing your whole body down out of a bucket is not easy, but we all managed it in the first twenty-four hours of our homeward journey and were able to settle down on our first evening steaming for a game of cards, content in the thought that the gear was stowed and everything washed down.

It was less than two days before Christmas, which was on a Saturday, and we were expected to dock the day after and land our catch on the Monday. It was obvious we would not have anything to celebrate the great day with, but we knew we could celebrate it later with our families.

Our little group from the Reykjavik escapade were reflecting on this while we played our game of solo. 'Poor old Chompy,' mused Alec. 'The trip has been hard enough for us all, without him having to suffer that horror, a married man an' all.'

'Well, maybe that's the point!' retorted Becksy. 'Maybe it was punishment for messing about in Reykjavik?'

'Nonsense,' snapped Nick. 'You might as well argue he did right to take his chance while he could, being in a job like this. He'll be lucky if any woman takes a second look at him now, I reckon.'

Just then one of the watch came down from the bridge. It was Podgy Fenton. 'I've just heard some great news that'll amuse you lads.' he smirked. He received no response from any of us, though he had our full attention. He pressed on. 'The Old Man has just been on with the office and they've told him to shoot again for twenty-four hours!' He finished with clenched lips and his head tilted back as he looked down his nose to see the effect of his words.

'Who do you think you're kidding?' sneered Nick. 'You're not winding me up with that. Think of another one, Podgy.'

'It's true,' the tubby decky snapped. 'Because Christmas Day's on a Saturday, they're counting the Monday as Boxing Day and there's no market for us to land. The gaffer says he's not having one of his ships laid about in dock doing nothing for an extra day, so he wants us to shoot on the rising ground north of Scotland . . . and if you don't believe me smell o' my drawers.' He finished with one of his own well-worn cliches – always enough to make the stomach turn over.

There was a long silence while we all reflected on what this meant. Chopping down the trawl from its stowed position, shackling up the wires again, lowering derricks, shipping up deck boards, and heaving out the trawl doors again – not to mention more fish to gut.

As the old ship lifted and lurched and creaked, while it thrust and thumped its way south-east, I studied my raw hands, which had started to dry out, with the skin cracking at the joints, and shuddered at what was to come.

'But what's the point?' snarled Nick at length. 'All yer gunna catch on the rising ground are coley or dogfish. And they won't fetch much.'

Podgy shrugged. 'Well, that's the score,' he muttered.

Becksy suddenly jumped up and threw his cards to the table. 'Well, they can all go and get fucked if they think I'm shooting again,' he screamed. 'I've had enough. They can stuff it and keep any money due to me if they want.' He stormed out of the mess-deck and made his way for'ard to his bunk just in case.

We all felt the same way, as would most of the others, but we knew it would be to no avail. To refuse a legitimate order at sea was recognised as unlawful disobedience, tantamount to mutiny, and that's the way it would be seen in the courts, where we would surely finish up, if we attempted to strike or anything like it. So we all quickly made our way forward to our bunks; rest was essential if you didn't know when you would be called or for how long.

As expected, all hands were called in the early hours of Christmas morning, two to three hours before we were due to arrive at the new fishing grounds, in order to prepare everything for shooting again. There was much to do and the crew were very slow to turn to, only turning out in dribs and drabs, with plenty of grumbling and cursing. But eventually the officers managed to get them organised and we shot away the trawl on our new venture. To make matters worse, when we hauled again, the trawl laid out on the water to reveal at least three bags of thrashing, twitching, large coley, which was hauled aboard on to the fore-deck and the trawl was shot away again.

The poor cook was particularly nervous at this because he knew a lot of the crew's frustration would be turned towards him come mealtimes, especially as he was finding it difficult to provide any meals that didn't consist entirely of fish. Fortunately, he had saved a large piece of pork that had been purchased from Reykjavik for the main meal. But what would Icelandic pork taste like when cooked?

Fine drizzle descended on us when we climbed into the pounds to gut the big black fish, and we had been told that there would be no watches below. They would be too difficult to work for the sake of twenty-four hours. Coalfish, or coley, are a particularly bloody fish, and the gore oozed out of them when we slit them open and removed the intestines. The blood continued to flow when we threw the carcasses across the deck, as was apparent when the bosun, with a great swing of the arm, threw a particularly large fish which plastered the face of Podgy Fenton, who was facing him across the pounds. There was no apology, just a cheery 'Merry Christmas, Podgy!'

'Bollocks,' was the terse reply.

Chapter 10

THE FINAL INITIATIONS

During that day's fishing we put down another 380 kits of fish. At the end we were all falling about like drunks and tripping over everything down to a matchstalk, until the skipper finally had mercy on us and we hauled for the last time. As we headed towards the Pentland Firth, we had to clear up the decks once again and stow everything before we could rest. Clewing up this time took so much longer because everyone was exhausted, having been up for thirty hours plus. Eventually the decks were clear and that just left the stowing of the for'ard derrick. One poor soul would have to climb the rigging to the crosstrees to shackle up the wire used to heave up the derrick; not much fun on a rolling ship when you're feeling so weak.

I was sent on to the fo'c'sle head, the whaleback, to unshackle the derrick stay from the ring bolt on the breakwater. It was while I was bent down unshackling the wire that the bridge window went down with a crash and the mate's head shot out. With his arm pointing straight at, or beyond, me, he screamed, 'Bob! The Merry Men of May! Get down off there!'

The Merry Men of what? I puzzled. Was this another joke? Then I remembered having heard of the tide rips that ran across the western entrance to the Pentland Firth when a strong wind was in the right direction. Against a spring tide, they built up a series of steep waves and rollers for a distance of a hundred and fifty yards or so, like a bubbling stewpot. This had been nicknamed 'The Merry Men of May'. All this took only seconds to recall, but when I swung round and looked ahead I saw a wall of water, followed by a Grand National course of waves, less than thirty yards away.

I knew I wouldn't make it across the slippery steel deck to the ladder, so I grabbed the only handhold available, the ring bolt against my feet. Of course, the trough came before the sea. The ship's head dropped into it and ploughed into the following peak, scooping up tens of tons of angry water, which dropped with a crunch onto the fo'c'sle head, sweeping all before it. When it hit me, I was picked up and tossed into the air, spinning and tumbling in blinding white foam until something hit the palm of my right hand. I clasped it with superhuman strength, thus arresting my flight. As the water drained away, I found I was swinging from the handrail that surrounds the whaleback, but I was outboard and the ship was still ducking and diving. Amazingly, it was not the top handrail that I was holding but the middle handrail, which meant my eyes were level with the fo'c'sle deck. As I swung, I was able to grab the rail with my second hand in another vice-like grip until the ship came through the turmoil and steadied itself.

From the bridge, it looked as though I had gone clean over the side because my body was below the level of the fo'c'sle head. The lads on the fore-deck, who had naturally ducked for cover when the seas hit, also searched for a sight of me in the water. Strangely, it was Alec, being the handiest, who was the first to clamber on to the fo'c'sle and stagger towards the rail. His first sight of me was of my eyes, peering wildly above the edge. Filled with shock and relief, he pointed at me, shouting, 'HE'S HERE. HE'S STILL HERE!' Then instead of trying to help me, he just started shrieking with laughter. He said later it was at the look on my face, but it was obviously shock.

Fatigue was overcoming me and I couldn't wait any longer, so I shuffled my hands along the rail towards the corner of the whaleback, where grateful hands grabbed me and pulled me inboard. As my feet touched the deck, my knees gave way and I slid down in a bit of a heap in the corner of the fore-deck. The lads crowded forward laughing, slapping me on the shoulder with smart remarks: 'You nearly left the ship without permission,' and 'Your double somersault with pike only received four points.'

Then I saw Nick grinning down at me. 'You alright?' he muttered.

'I thought I was a goner then,' I gasped.

'Well, you wasn't. So don't worry about it. Just regard it as an initiation. You aren't a real fisherman until you've been outboard at least once.' Then he pulled me to my feet and the work continued.

That night was the last before docking and we had the evening watch on the bridge. All was calm and relaxed, the ship's radio was tuned to Luxembourg, Kay Starr was singing 'Wheel of Fortune,' and our thoughts turned to romance. We had missed Christmas but I for one was determined to make up for it when we got home.

We were in luck when we settled. The market was good as predicted after the festivities. We had landed over 2,400 kits; and, although a little was unfit, the trip still made over £8,000 and paid us well – though most of us signed off and looked forward to a week off and a chance to celebrate the New Year. The *St Apollo* was still under repair for another ten days and I had been promised I could sign on when she was ready, so I looked forward to the chance to enjoy myself with plenty of money in my pocket. Over the next few days, I circulated with some of my new-found shipmates, and sometimes bumped into old ones, as we did the pubs and the occasional dance, jumping into taxis all the while. Everyone seemed to be at home at this time.

One afternoon Becksy and I were drinking with some other fisherlads in one of the quieter pubs, when it was decided to find some life elsewhere. We all charged out, I was ushered into the inevitable taxi to save drinking time, and we shot off to another pub, the Paragon. This pub was notorious for the prostitutes that frequented it, as I quickly realised when we entered the large smoke room. It was divided into large cubicles made of five-foot high, dark-stained wood, each housing a large, polished table that could seat about eight people. In two of these sat a couple of heavily made-up women in their late twenties or early thirties, showing a fair amount of their ample bosoms, accompanied by two or three well-sozzled males. In a third sat three garishly dressed women; two were middle-aged, the other was younger and not unattractive. They were alone. On their table were two half-glasses of Guinness and a gin glass with a little in it. At the large bar on the left of the room lounged three men talking to the man behind it. Meanwhile a speaker blasted out 'How Much Is That Doggie in the Window'.

As we walked in, the largest of the three women shouted to us, 'Hi, Lads! Come on in! You're just in time to buy us a drink.'

One of the guys we were with recognised her immediately and turning to us he chuckled, 'Christ, it's Big Gill. We should be alright here for a bit of a giggle. Come on.' We ordered drinks all round and squeezed in around the women, with Becksy and I perched dubiously on the end of each seat. Then followed a load of bawdy banter. Big Gill knew a lot of dirty jokes and was quite amusing at times, but I wasn't comfortable and was looking for a chance to dip out.

Before long the swing doors pushed open and two very attractive girls walked in. The first was a brunette with straight, silky hair, bright red lips and flashing eyes; the second was quite different, with bushy, light-auburn hair, waved and curled. Her face was pale and delicate; she wore a pale-pink lipstick on well-shaped lips; and her eyes seemed to show amusement at everything she saw. She looked quite innocent and tended to hang back while her friend went to the bar to inquire about someone they were looking for. She only looked about seventeen and I wondered if she knew the type of establishment her friend had brought her into.

Becksy had tapped my foot to draw my attention when they walked in and then told me in a low voice that he vaguely knew the first girl; she was the sister of a chap he had sailed with. As they moved towards the bar, he jerked his head sideways and, picking up our glasses, we moved over to them. The second girl had half-perched herself on the end stool and, as Becksy engaged her friend in conversation, I moved towards her. She smiled encouragingly and I asked if they were staying long.

'Only a few minutes, I think,' she answered, glancing at her colleague.

'Well, can I buy you a drink while you're here?' I asked.

'Thank you. I think I'll have a port and lemon.' She smiled sweetly.

'Port and lemon?' I repeated quizzically.

She giggled. 'It's my mum's drink. She got me on to them,' she explained.

Becksy had already asked the first girl, and we'd already decided to have another one, so the drinks were soon sorted.

'What's your name?' My next question was obvious.

'Penelope,' she said, with a twinkle in her eyes.

'Penelope?' Once again I repeated what she had said. 'Gosh, that's posh. Are you kidding me?'

This time she laughed outright. 'No, that's my real name, but everyone calls me Penny. And *her* name is Sheila.' She indicated her friend who was now in deep conversation with Becksy.

'Ah well, Penny! Now that's a pretty name to suit a pretty girl. I think I'll call you Penny.'

'Feel free,' she said, with a cock of the head and a smile.

'Do you have a job?' was my next question.

'Well, I work at Metal Box,' she replied, dropping her eyes.

'Oh! You've got the afternoon off then?'

'No, I work part-time. I only go in certain days when they have a special order. It keeps me in touch with my mates.'

The conversation with Penny flowed easily. I was really getting to like this girl. She had a ready wit and a carefree attitude and she seemed to like me, but the call of time from the barman brought things to a close. Three o'clock already, I couldn't believe how time had flown. Then Big Gill called from their cubicle. 'Come on, lads! If you want to carry on drinking, you can all come back to my place.'

Penny visibly shrank on her stool. Crouching down behind me, she whispered, 'You don't want to go with them. If you want to carry on drinking, you can bring a drink back to my sister's. She won't mind. Sheila and I often go back there for a drink after we've been in town.'

Becksy was quick to react 'That's fine, then,' he said. 'We'll get half a dozen beers. What'll you girls want to drink?'

Sheila chipped in, 'Get us a few Babychams, that'll do.'

'Right.' Becksy ordered the drinks to take out and a taxi.

In the taxi, the driver reluctantly allowed us all to squeeze in the back and Penny sat on my knee. She had to keep her head down, so she rested it on my shoulder. Maybe she wasn't quite as innocent as she looked. The taxi was directed to a street off Hessle Road and, during the ride, while the other two were preoccupied, Penny and I whispered suggestive little things to each other. This just made her giggle and snuggle closer. I had my arm around Penny's waist and the other hand on her thigh, and eventually I turned my head and planted a long kiss on those lovely, expressive lips. When I withdrew, Penny continued to suck at my bottom lip until she lost contact, like a kitten suckling at its departing mother. The numerous drinks we'd had made me lose my inhibitions, and we were just warming up when the taxi pulled up at the end of a terrace and we piled out behind Penny into a small two-up and two-down house.

Penny's sister received us without any qualms and cheerily invited us in. We stepped straight from the street into a small living room, which just managed to house a sofa, two easy chairs and a radiogram, tucked in a corner alongside the chimney breast. On the mantlepiece were a couple of photographs and some flashy trinkets. Penny's sister had a small baby, which took up most of her time, and they occupied the easy chair alongside the fireplace. Becksy and Sheila claimed the sofa and continued to make best use of it, which left the other well-worn easy chair for me.

Penny produced a small table for the drinks from a back kitchen which, thanks to a flimsy extension, was larger than most and, I had noticed, contained a ceiling pulley for drying clothes. When Penny had fixed us all up with drinks, including Sis, she came and joined me on the easy chair, sitting once again on my lap. Sis started the gramophone going with a Donald Peers LP that was already on the turntable. It was a bit out of date, but no one minded as it suited the mood.

There was only occasional chat, but plenty of kissing and fumbling as hands sneaked surreptitiously inside clothing, hinted at only by the odd squeak or moan. I was getting aroused and Penny knew it. She acknowledged it with another giggle, and when Sis took the baby out into the kitchen to attend to it, and the other two were completely preoccupied, she took my hand and led me to the stairs opposite the front door. We went up to the floor above and into what Penny called the second bedroom. Although only small it managed to contain a three-quarter-size bed pushed against one wall, a bedside table and little else except for a clothes basket. Once inside, Penny closed and latched the door; then she turned towards me and, moving close, thrust her crotch close to mine. Her eyes glanced up at me with a twinkle as she wrapped her arms around my waist, and pulling my shirt up at the back she slipped her hands in and raked her nails down my bare skin.

'Come on then, Big Boy,' she murmured. 'Let's get into bed.' With a quick peck on the lips, she turned towards the bedside table and started to undress. As I peeled off my shirt, I watched her slip off first the little jacket of the smart two-piece suit she was wearing, then the white, see-through blouse, followed by her skirt and stockings, and then surprisingly her little panties, leaving her bra until last. She stood sideways on to me and I was in awe at her beautiful body – the tight round buttocks, the flat stomach and the gentle protruding curve of her lower abdomen, arcing down from her navel, and then the extra swell of the bushy mound of Venus before it was lost behind the curve of her thigh. All this I drank in intoxicatingly as her hands doubled behind her back to undo her bra. Then came the final release of those voluptuous, up-tilted breasts with the bright pink rosebud nipples.

Penny, aware she was under observation, scampered into bed, pulling the covers over and trapping them under her arms as she sat upright and twinkled back at me with a huge grin. After a moment, sensing a hesitation on my part, she laid back and flinging the covers right back again she revealed once more her lovely, curvy, inviting body with its gingery, curly bush hiding the ultimate prize. Shocked into action I pulled down my trousers and underpants. My rigid member sprang free, extracting a gleeful little shriek from Penny as I scrambled alongside her over the foot of the bed, stopping halfway to fasten my lips on the pinnacle of her creamy breast. My hand rested on the silky skin of her thigh and after a few moments I moved on up to kiss her lips. My hand moved up one thigh, with the thumb trailing up the inside leg, and perky Peter slid up along the other, eliciting another squeak before I fastened my eager lips on to her beckoning mouth.

Over the next ten minutes, the submission, acceptance and finally the encouragement and desire of my partner when our bodies were completely linked had me trembling in ecstasy. Her low moans, grunts and gasps were a compliment, and our perspiring bodies a testimony, to my efforts. I couldn't get enough of Penny; I wanted to envelope her, to consume her and for her to consume me.

Eventually we were spent and could bask in the knowledge that we had pleased each other to the ultimate. We continued to show our mutual appreciation with whispered words and caresses. Then, as Penny continued to show her gratitude with kisses and suggestive body movements, I was aroused again. When I had finished, Penny's panting and gasping showed how hard she had worked to please me, but after satisfaction comes exhaustion, and with exhaustion came the pangs of guilt. What right had I to do this to this girl? True, she was a willing partner but was she aware, were *we* aware of the possible consequences?

The front door banging downstairs brought me back to the reality of the situation. How long had we been up here? Were the others aware of what we had been doing?

For some inexplicable reason, I thought that if we hurried out of bed, dressed quickly and tip-toed downstairs we might not have been missed. And that is what I did. As I donned my pants, shirt, trousers and shoes (I hadn't removed my socks), I noticed that Penny was in no such hurry. She sat in her panties on the edge of the bed, carefully smoothing on her stockings. She spoke, 'Well now, you were a greedy boy doing it twice, so that'll cost you five pounds and a pound for the room'

'What!' I looked at her in amazement. 'You mean you're on the game?'

'Well, what else? You didn't think it would be that easy, did you? And I'll have you know I'm very particular who I go with.'

'"But at your age – that is – how old are you anyway?'

'I'm twenty-six.'

'*Twenty-six!* You can't be. You only look about seventeen.'

'Thank you. That's all the more reason why you should be happy to pay, unless you want me to cause trouble.' With this last remark she turned and gave me a pointed stare.

Without another word I drew a wad of notes out of my back pocket, threw six on the bed and then scampered down the stairs. I heard Penny in the background. 'Thanks. You can come again sometime, if you know what I mean,' Then came that giggle.

The living room was only occupied by Sis, still fussing with the baby. She looked up and smiled.

'Where's Becksy and Sheila,' I enquired, taking my coat from the back of the easy chair.

'I don't know if they went to a club or back to her place,' she replied indifferently.

'Thanks. Well, I'd better be going now,' I said, moving towards the door. Once outside I looked self-consciously from left to right. The only person visible in the little terrace was a woman sat in the doorway of the bottom corner house facing inward. She was braiding net hung from a wooden bar fixed across the entrance. Earning herself a few extra shillings, no doubt. I made sure she was not looking in my direction – before hurrying away.

I was full of remorse. Hell! I had finally lost my virginity proper and it was with a prostitute. I couldn't tell this to anybody.

New Year's Eve was fast approaching, and I knew I would be going away soon after, so I continued to enjoy myself as much as possible. There were plenty of dances on the go at this time and I went to one or two with my pal Jeff, who was one of the few of my friends who didn't go to sea. Some of the small dance halls like the Newington and the Majestic were OK, but they didn't serve alcohol. The most popular venue was the Scala on Anlaby Road because it had two bars and also featured some of the better local bands, like Tommy Fisher's. It was also popular with the outgoing girls.

Unfortunately, it had a bad name for fighting and violence, usually outside after the dance. Jeff and I went to the Scala on a Thursday night, which was always busy, and it was packed. Of course, neither of us could really dance; the only things we could do were the 'Polly Glide,' which you did linked up in lines, or 'Balling the Jack,' where you formed circles and danced around on your own, miming the words. Neither allowed you to talk to a girl much, although Jeff could stagger around a little doing the waltz. We spent a lot of time going in and out of the two bars, where I met up with plenty of old shipmates and other fisherlads with their girlfriends. Jeff and I had an understanding that if either one of us linked up with a girl the other would back off and allow the friendship to develop.

I must admit there was a lot of merriment and fun with the lads in the bars, telling jokes and recounting funny incidents that happened at sea. We all had a skipper, mate or other shipmate in common who we knew or had sailed with and could tell a funny story about. It was also a good laugh daring each other to ask a girl to dance and then watch the shambles that resulted. It was during one of our visits to the bar, when the band was resting, that we, that is the crowd that I was with, met up with some Norwegian seamen. We were pleased to welcome them to our city and hoped they were enjoying their time at the dance. Of course, the spirits were flowing by this time, while we all sat round a small table in a corner of the bar. The Norwegian lads had taken as much drink as any of us and were a little bit sloshed, as were most of our gang, and it was at this point that a very unfortunate incident took place.

Among our group were a couple of guys with a bit of a reputation. One was a thick-set kid with blond hair swept back in an accentuated quiff. He had a pale face and a square jaw and would have been good-looking if it wasn't for the pock scars that lined his features. He was known as Blondie Warboys. The other was more sinister; his reputation suggested he had his own graveyard. He was tall, slim and square-shouldered, with a chiselled jaw and close-cropped, borstal-style hair. I noticed he had a tattoo on each earlobe, but it was his steely grey eyes that really menaced, slashing you to pieces with darting glances.

His name was Ricky Bashby, and he was probably the oldest of our group, in his early twenties. Ricky, it seemed, was often out of a ship and appeared to get most of his cash by hovelling ex-shipmates. His humour relied on demeaning jokes and put-downs. Nevertheless, he had managed to get himself a regular girl of sorts and she was at the dance with her friends. Mel, for that was her name, short for Melanie, looked pretty common. Her untidy hair, loose mouth, poorly applied make-up and regular use of bad language suggested that her aspirations had not been set too high. She had joined us briefly once or twice with a couple of gum-chewing mates.

The conversation with the Norwegian lads progressed nicely until we asked them if they were enjoying the dance, when they said they were disappointed that none of the nice girls wanted to dance with them. Then Mel and her friends drifted by. Ricky magnanimously suggested, 'Mel will dance with you, if *I* asked her,' and pointed her out as she passed.

To which their spokesman replied, 'No tak! Not dat type, we want decent girls.'

This shocked all the lads – even me. I was surprised at the speed of the assessment, but things turned ugly when Blondie declared, 'Hey! That's Ricky's girl you're talking about.' The boys started abusing the foreigners, calling them scrobs and threatening them. The Norwegians, for their part, realised their mistake; they immediately stood up from their stools, leaving their drinks, and backed away with a slight lift of the hands, which clearly said sorry and goodbye, as they left the bar to lose themselves in the crowded dancehall.

But the lads weren't going to leave it there. They discussed and re-discussed the import of the remark, constantly lubricating their throats with more drink until they finally decided the statement was not only a slur on Ricky's charming girlfriend but an insult to all of British womanhood, and the perpetrators should be punished in full. None of my attempts to pacify them was accepted, although I had to admit it was an arrogant remark to make for a visitor. The boys decided to teach the Norwegians a lesson when they left the dance, and proceeded to seek them out and keep an eye on them. I had lost Jeff. He had found himself a girl, so I drifted around on the periphery of this militant little group, trying to restore their good humour, but they continued to close with the Nosks and exchange insults and threats. There was plenty of pushing and shoving going on each time.

Eventually the Norwegians decided to leave early and, as soon as they had some space, they slipped out without being spotted by the gang. But there were plenty of others to see them leave and pass the message on. I watched our mob arming themselves with bottles and glasses and decided to slip out ahead to warn the intended victims to make tracks fast. I left the dancehall quickly with glazed eyes and strode out on unsteady legs. Soon I spotted the merchantmen ambling along ahead of me on the side of the road, hoping to catch a taxi. I closed with them quickly and implored them to make a run for it, warning them that my colleagues were intent on doing serious damage. But they said they were not inclined to run from anyone, and certainly not from any snivelling Englishmen. Then they crossed the road to the other side.

They were adamant and sneering in their remarks and, as there were four of them, I decided that they could look after themselves. Then I tottered on, as the street where I lived was not far away.

A little further along the road was a level crossing and as I approached it the gates swung closed, holding us all up. As we waited for the train to pass, I noticed an amorous couple close by who had no concern for the rest of the world. A hefty black boy had his girlfriend backed up against an advertising hoarding and he completely enveloped her as they kissed and fondled each other. On the other side of the road, two of the Norwegians had entered a public urinal. The other two were standing talking, when I noticed one of them glance back down the road. I looked back towards the canopied entrance of the dancehall.

Sure enough, I saw Blondie and Ricky had left and were running towards us, with the others straggling behind. Ricky's hand held a glass tumbler; Blondie's, a bottle. The two Norwegians on hand were unable to run, even if they had wanted to, because of the crossing gates behind them, so they braced themselves for the onslaught to come.

Once again, I felt it my duty to intervene and crossed the road to intercept the two drunken fishermen. I moved towards Ricky, my arms extended in an effort to restrain him. I shouted at him to at least get rid of the potential weapon he carried. Without taking his eyes off his intended victims, he lashed out and pushed me in the chest, snarling, 'Fuck off, you interfering bastard or you'll get it first.' As he brushed past me – his eyes never leaving his prey – he stooped and I was mesmerised at the delicate, practised way he lightly tapped the glass on the ground, just hard enough to shatter the rim. The largest of the two merchantmen – their companions had not yet left the toilet – took off his coat and wrapped it round his hand and arm as a shield. Then he too advanced.

It was futile for me to interfere any longer. I moved away back across the road, with a final shout for the stupid cunts to come to their senses, as Blondie also moved in, bottle raised. The big Norwegian lunged forward with his padded arm, trying to dislodge the glass from Ricky's hand, but Ricky easily parried the blow, ducking under it and sweeping upwards with the jagged incisor into the big lad's face. His head jerked back, flinging a snot of blood from a sweeping gash around the corner of the eye and across cheek and lip. Beyond, I saw Blondie lash down with his bottle at the other youth's head. The two remaining Norwegians rushed from the toilet in support as more fisherlads ran up to join the fray. The passing train had drowned out the noise of the mayhem at first, but now as it rumbled clear the cursing and shouting was attracting attention, as people leaving the dance realised what was going on.

I turned away from the sickening sight and hurried away across the railway lines, intending to put as much distance as possible between me and this shameful scene, but before the noise had even subsided police and ambulance bells could be heard arriving. I hadn't covered much more ground when an ambulance hurried past me, and I wondered how many had been hurt and how many had been arrested. In my befuddled state, I couldn't resist returning to find out the damage.

When I arrived back at the scene, very few people remained on the street. I could see patches of blood and broken glass in the area of the fight, but all around was quiet. Then, to my surprise, I spotted the same couple, still huddled against the hoarding. Nothing, it seemed, could disturb them, but I decided to try. So busy were they smooching, as they had been all the time, that they didn't appear to see me until I was quite close. I decided to take the innocent line.

'Excuse me!' I addressed the back of the black guy's head. 'But has there been a disturbance here?'

He broke away just enough to glance at me over his shoulder and said, rather disdainfully, 'You should know, you were one of the gang that started it.' Then, without another word, he returned to the matter in hand.

I was so shocked, not only because he had seen so much, but also that he should include me among the aggressors. Speechless, I turned away again. I was deeply troubled that if he, who had probably seen it all, considered me part of the gang, then others, including the police, would see it that way as well. It was a lesson learned and a wary introduction to the violent side of fishing life.

Chapter 11

TOTAL COMMITMENT – THE FUTURE IS SET

The Christmas break had been great but now money was sparse. I had a little bank balance which I had drawn on, but I didn't like doing it. After all, I was working hard to build it up. My shipmates had often talked about a decky needing a fair amount of money, if he intended to sit for any tickets – that is, if he was to sit his exams for promotion – because that could take eight to ten weeks at least, and you would need to support yourself for that time. Anyway, money was scarce and I needed to get back to sea. I was looking forward to going back in the *St Apollo,* so I started to get myself down the dock in the mornings. Jack Gibby told me that, if I wanted to go back in the bigger and better ship, I would have to go back as decky learner because there were so many men wanting to sign on, especially at this time of year – after the break and when markets and fishing would be good, despite the winter weather.

After some deliberation I accepted and Gibby signed me on articles immediately, even though there were still three days before she was due to sail. I was happy because I knew Gibby was only signing selected men so early. As I left his office, I was advised to say nothing to the dozens of men crowding around the entrance to the company offices, so I left quickly, pushing through the crowd of expectant deckies and engineers, only smiling and nodding at those I knew and hoping they wouldn't ask me directly if I'd signed.

Back home I told the family what I had done; although it was obvious they had mixed feelings, they did their best to show some enthusiasm on my behalf.

In the evening of that same day some bad news emerged. The *St Leander,* sister ship to the *St Apollo,* identical and built at the same time, had been in a serious collision with another trawler as she was returning home, less than half a mile from the dock. Further information the next day revealed that the *Leander* had healed over and sunk. The crew, most of whom had scrambled out on to the hull of the ship before jumping into the water, were all saved thanks to the quick thinking of the skipper of an oil barge, who left the jetty and headed straight for the area and was able to rescue every man. Of course, this accident caused turmoil at home, but fortunately no lives were lost, something Hull families constantly feared in an industry that suffers more fatalities than any other.

I was glad to be back at sea. The pressure over the last couple of days for me to change my job had been a strain; it came not only from my family but also from friends and acquaintances, all shore-based of course, who commented that two sister ships had both been in a collision within weeks of each other and considered this a bad omen. Superstition always crept in at such times and I was glad to be out of it. It was great to be back aboard my old ship on a new venture, with Tommy Nighty still in charge, and I had come to realise now that I didn't want anything to interfere with my chosen profession. The extra experience I had gained on my previous trip meant I was more confident and, with the skipper's support, able to take on more of the full-fledged deckies' jobs and work alongside them. With the ship's enforced stay in dock, the owners had decided to give her a full survey, and everything was painted up and spick and span, which helped to brighten the severe January days.

It was Norwegian coast season, when there was plenty of fish and good markets, although the deep water and strong tides there made it difficult for all. It was particularly hard for the skippers because of the hundreds of ships there at this time of year, but Tommy came up trumps on this traditional ground. Nighty managed to catch us a couple of good trips of good fish which paid well, so at last we were in the money and life was good. The company had built two new ships the previous year and were in the process of building two more. These ships were larger than the *St Apollo* and had an extra level of accommodation below the wheelhouse; they were commonly referred to as double-bridgers. This extra level of accommodation and their greater size meant that all the crew could sleep aft. The advantages of this were considerable and the *St Britwin* and *St Alcuin* became the envy of all the deckies in the firm.

Nighty continued to do well over the next few trips. As two more new ships were due to be brought in to service, promotions all round were expected, and Tommy was offered the *St Alcuin*. Although some of the crew of the *Alcuin* were to remain, Nighty was allowed to take part of the *Apollo's* crew with him, and he asked me if I would like to be one of them. Of course, I was flattered that he was taking me into the larger ship, but it was still only as decky learner. Promotion, it seemed, was still not on offer, but the facilities would be so much better.

The deck crew in the new ship slept aft in two large, eight-man cabins, one on deck level and one down below. There would be no more running across the fore-deck in all weathers when changing watches or going to meals; the galley and mess-deck were just down the alleyway, and the bridge could be accessed through the top of the engine room. We also had a proper bathroom with showers as well as a bath. The officers, down to bosun, had cabins amidships, beneath the captain's accommodation, which itself was more spacious.

The deck fittings and working were just the same, of course, except we had a fish-washer, but that new invention, designed by a skipper, had also been fitted in the *St Apollo* before we left. All in all things were much more comfortable, at least when we were off the deck. Tommy was enthralled with his new ship and stood grinning at us from his exalted position through the open bridge window as we steamed down the river. He joked and shouted, 'What's a'tween decks', as he enjoyed the extra elevation.

Bigger ships mean bigger fittings, higher rails and heavier gear. As a tall person I had an advantage over smaller, more experienced men. I thrived in the *St Alcuin* and became accepted as one of the best decky learners in the company, but still promotion was not forthcoming. I looked, and was, a fresh-faced kid. Then one of the older men I had sailed with quite a lot had a quiet word with me. 'You've got to realise, Bob,' he said, 'that Nighty's happy to keep you as you are. With you as one of the decky learners he has, in effect, got an extra decky. You're still very young, so if you want to get early promotion you've got to be prepared to go in one of the old ships where it's harder to get good crews.' I realised he was right. It would be hard to leave the comparative comforts of the high-flying *St Alcuin*, but if I wanted to progress it had to be. I decided to have a word along these lines with Jack Gibby.

At the end of each trip, when we had to go to the runner's office, I would broach this subject with the wily old ship's runner, but he usually fobbed me of with a joke and suggested I was doing very well where I was. I was impatient to make progress, so I persisted each trip with the argument that I was ready, as many of my shipmates agreed, but still Jack seemed reluctant. Eventually he pondered, scratched his head and said, 'Yuh see, Bob. You might have a fair amount of experience but you started early – under age, in fact, if you remember. The recognised age for a decky, or spare hand as it ap

'Well, you managed it before, Jack,' I insisted.

'Yes, well, the circumstances were different then. At the moment even the old ships are well-manned in the summer. It's during winter when men are more scarce.'

We left it at that. Jack was quite sympathetic, promising to keep me in mind if an opportunity arose, and next thing I was back at sea again for

St. Alcuin

another three weeks. Back aboard the ship, I told my friend and mentor what had happened. His reply was short and to the point. 'Huh! Opportunities are no good if you're not there to take advantage. You need to stop ashore, Bob.'

I decided as autumn was approaching that I would take a trip off. I needed a rest and I was able to organise a week in the sun with my friend Jeff – the first time we had ever flown. Majorca, a sparse but sunny place, had only just become available to ordinary workers like us, but afterwards I would have to walk the dock every day like all the other out-of-work fishermen.

Back from holiday, I was tanned, well-rested and eager for work again, but I insisted to Gibby that I wanted a spare hand's job. Two or three weeks passed by and ships, old and new, came and went. Each time one was landing, I was down on the dock early, but still no offer of a deck-hand's place. With two new ships entering service, it thinned out the regular men a bit, but still no chance of getting promotion, though it was hinted that I could have a job as decky learner in one of the new ones. This was very tempting, but I resisted and stuck to my guns.

Then, one morning, I went to the office, when no ships were landing, to have a quiet word with Gibby while there were no men around. I no sooner entered the runner's office when Jack beat me to it. Welcoming me cheerily, he said, 'I've got a chance for you at last, young Bob. There's the *St Nectan* just coming off survey with a couple of spare hand places to fill. You can sign on her if you like.'

My beaming smile faded a little when I heard the name. 'The *Nectan?* But she's a coal-burner, isn't she?'

'Yer-rs,' Jack emphasised. 'She's the last of 'em. They didn't convert her. They'd probably sell or scrap her before they spent that money, but she's just been overhauled and she's in tip-top condition, so do you want the job or not?' He thrust out his chin towards me.

I knew I had to make the breakthrough and this was probably the only chance. I also knew from tales well-told that a coal-burning trawler was a big step back in discomfort and grime. 'Yes, of course I want the job, Jack,' I beamed, 'until something better comes along, eh!'

Jack ignored this last remark, turned to the ship's log and pencilled in my name. 'Right,' he said, with finality. 'Just get yourself down here the day after tomorrow, when we're signing up. OK?'

I left the Fish Dock with mixed feelings – elation and trepidation. It was certainly a move up the scale because I was there for as long as I pulled my weight, but I remembered the discomforts of the *St Elstan*. This was a similar ship but it being a coal-burner made things worse. Coal was dirty and got into everything; it had to be trimmed from bunkers and fed into furnaces, and the ashes had to be removed. There was also never enough bunker space, and some coal had to be carried in the fishroom, which needed washing out afterwards, of course, usually during fishing. All in all a lot more work. Still I was a spare hand.

Over the next forty-eight hours I swaggered a bit more as I informed my friends of my step up and revelled in the thought that my weekly wage would increase to five pounds, let alone that my poundage would be even more if we made a trip of any sort. So it was with a spring in my step that I walked down to the office on signing day, passing some of the decky learners I knew who were standing outside other companies. I wouldn't tell them of my move up until I was on my way off the dock, just in case.

I swept into the office past a few odd-bods who were hanging around. Jack stood at his high desk writing, one foot crossed over the other. As I approached, he turned his head and glanced at me through his glasses. 'Oh hello, Bob!' he said casually. Then, with a wave of his pen in a direction across the dock, he continued, 'You better get to the doctor before you sign on. She's going to Greenland.'

'WHAT!' I spluttered. 'GREENLAND! A coal burner? Why?'

There was a deliberate pause. 'Because there's no fish anywhere else, and they're catching plenty at Greenland,' was the weary reply.

'But can she carry enough coal to get us that far, right across the Atlantic and beyond?'

'Don't you worry about that. Let the powers that be sort that one out for yer. You just go and see if you're fit enough to go.' Jack turned away, the matter closed.

On my way to the doctor, I pondered. Head down, I never even saw my learner friends, who were still outside the other companies. Anyway, I decided, what did I know about coal-burners? All my fears were based on what other deckies had talked about while at sea. Well now I'd better try it for myself. But I decided not to tell Mum we were going to Greenland. She already knew I was going in a coal-burner, but I would avoid telling her where we were going. After all, she need never know, need she?

The taxi driver had found out where the ship was laid while I was in the clothing store and now he swung the car off the darkened, cobbled dockside road on to the wooden sleepers that formed a track across the rail lines, past some empty coal trucks, and into a quayside space amid some heavy trawl spares. The vessel that confronted us was not an old coal-burner. She had the graceful lines of another of the company ships that had been purchased recently and was standing high in the water.

'This isn't the *Nectan*, pal,' I addressed the taxi driver. 'This is one of our other ships.'

'I know that, sunshine,' he drawled. 'But if you look close there's a lot of smoke belching into the sky amidships. That's your ship the other side of this one, a lot lower in the water by the looks of it.'

I peered out of the taxi window and could see what he meant. The smoke belching into the sky was not coming from the streamlined funnel of the ship in front of us but from behind it, and looking closer I could see there appeared to be a silhouette of the masts behind also. The two ships were laid side by side perfectly in line, but although there was little difference in the tonnage the *Nectan* was almost completely hidden.

The cabby helped me out with my gear, and I thanked him and paid him. Then with my new thigh boots over one shoulder, my kitbag over the other and the rest of my new gear clutched to my chest, I ascended the gangway (a rare facility) on to the deck of the first ship. When I crossed to the other rail and looked over and down I could barely see the deck of my ship in the dark and gloom of the early morning. I dropped my boots in to the waist of the *Nectan*, but it seemed a long way down; I lowered my kitbag to the full extent of the lanyard, but still had to drop it the last two feet. Swinging my body over the rail, I had to lower myself right down on to my elbows before I made contact with the *Nectan's* rail.

Having negotiated the transfer successfully, I eventually collected my belongings and strode forward; but, when I stepped down at the break of the deck onto the fore-deck, I splashed nearly ankle deep in water in the duck pond. I stared down in the darkness at the scupper port to see if it was blocked and holding the water, but it was clear. In fact, it was through here that the water was lapping in. I recoiled a little and stepped back in surprise. God! I thought. If she's taking water on deck while she's still in dock, what will she be like when we get out into the North Atlantic?

Turning away, I strode forward to the usual fo'c'sle accommodation below deck and dropped my gear down the steep, long ladder into the dingy, windowless room below. When I descended into the fo'c'sle it appeared empty at first, and I thought I was the first to arrive, but then I heard snoring coming from a bunk foreside which had a makeshift curtain across it. Obviously, someone had beaten me to it and was probably sleeping off a hectic night, although I wondered what sort of person was prepared to spend an extra night in a floating dungeon like this.

I collected my gear off the floor and moved to the opposite side of the room from the snorer; as one of the first aboard after a survey, I had the choice of position. As usual in this class of trawler, the bunks were three high to take full advantage of the limited space. I chose a middle bunk; the bottom bunks had the disadvantage of the seats alongside them, which meant that there was always someone plonking themselves beside you to pull on their boots or whatever. My mattress and heavy gear had been put on board by a bag carrier, so when I found them I was able to make my bed up. I had just done so when some more of the crew stumbled down the ladder, cursing already.

'Fucking hell!' snorted the first guy, as he descended the last step and turned to survey me and the rest of the scene. 'My feet are soaked. What's all that fucking water doing on the deck?'

Before I could answer, another member of the crew followed him down the steps with his own complaint. 'Jesus Christ! She seems bloody deep in the water. Fancy tying us up outside of a survey ship'

He was implying the ship inside us was being overhauled and thus empty of all gear, and that was the reason why she was riding so much higher than our ship.

As other members of the crew arrived – some I knew and some I didn't – they all had the same impression that the ship inside was surveying, but as the tot glass was being passed around quite freely no one was really paying it much attention. Then the last couple of men came aboard and confirmed that the other ship was not a light ship, for there were crew on her deck and she was sailing also. This caused some consternation among the lads when they realised that we might be overloaded. But, too late, the order had already been given to stand by for letting go. The mate was for'ard on the fo'c'sle head, demanding some men to come and cast off the ropes. Now the law of the sea, which is bred into most true sailors and makes them obey the last order, prevailed. So, with much chuntering and complaining, the crew turned to and we sailed.

One of the men who joined me on the whaleback was Alec, my old shipmate from the *St Elstan*. It figured that he would be on this trip for the same reason as me. As we passed through the lock pit on our way out into the river, we took stock of the little mate who had only recently joined the company and was standing right for'ard on the stem. He was standing so straight, stretching his five feet seven inches to its maximum, as proud as a peacock. Wally Peach was his name, but it seemed so strange – mates were usually big chaps in our experience. Neither of us knew him, but it appeared some of the older chaps did, judging by some of their chiding and wisecracks, suggesting he was a Wally by name and a Wally by nature. It indicated he maybe didn't have the respect that a mate usually received.

As the first light appeared in the dawn sky, we slid through the lock and said our goodbyes to Gibby and Benny, each stationed as usual on either side of the entrance. Then the mate turned and selecting Alec and I as two of the most gullible started to chase us up to store the ropes while the rest of the men left the fo'c'sle head. The mate, too, descended onto the fore-deck and, to indicate his lack of confidence, was overheard asking some of the older hands what the Old Man was like, before he went on to the bridge to join him.

Our skipper was a tall man, slightly scruffy and loose-limbed. Although heavy in chest and shoulder, he was rather gawky and had a long neck. His name was Richard Swan, but Dicky Swan seemed a contradiction in terms; he was known as 'Swan Neck' around the company. Dick never wore his false teeth at sea and used to greet you with a gummy grin. He had a crude sense of humour and laughed at his own jokes, but he also had a temper. This, however, did not strike fear into the men who knew him. The trouble was that Dick wasn't particularly successful at catching fish, which is what the average crew admired. But, as an ex-Hull Trinity House boy, he was well-educated and he was very good at navigation, and that is probably why he got this job of taking us across the Atlantic to Greenland because a lot of the waters around there were still uncharted territory.

When Alec and I had finished securing the mooring ropes, we went down into the fo'c'sle to unpack our kitbags and change into our sea gear. It was while we were doing this that one of the crew came down and told us the watches had been set and we were both on watch with the mate. This surprised me because I thought he would have wanted at least one experienced man on watch with him. What I hadn't realised was that Wally wanted two young guys who would rive and tear with blind obedience and wouldn't question his decisions.

Our watch didn't start until we had left the river. The skipper, mate and third hand were charged with taking the ship down the dangerous river Humber, and then the first watch would take over. We continued to prepare ourselves for the trip ahead and to get to know our shipmates, when a change in the motion of the ship told us we were entering the North Sea. Sure enough, a call came down the ladder for the watch on the bridge. I was first on deck in time to see the Spurn lightship receding on the port quarter and I made my way up to the wheelhouse.

The bridge on the *Nectan* was pretty much identical to the *St Elstan*, with its loose, drop-down windows and large wheel near the back bulkhead. I took the wheel off the third hand, who gratefully handed over – giving me the course, which I repeated – and scuttled off the bridge. The mate was in the port corner, having to stretch himself to see out of the window; he was still in his shore gear, with an open raincoat slung around his shoulders. The Old Man was on the other side, moving restlessly from window to window, where he had to stoop slightly to see out of them. The mate turned to me as I took over and unnecessarily instructed me to keep her straight. It was meant to show the skipper how efficient he was. I responded with an 'Aye-aye'. You wouldn't say the atmosphere was strained, but it certainly was not relaxed, so it seemed that the mate's over-eager efforts to woo the Old Man had failed up to now. He tried once or twice more with a few sexy quips about his time at home, but only got a slightly bored response from Big Dick.

Eventually, the Old Man, satisfied that all was clear, decided to see if the sparks had cleared us with the local radio and logged on to the next station. He turned, and stooping, entered the narrow six-foot-long alleyway immediately to my right that led to the wireless room at the back of the bridge. As he did so, Alec entered the bridge with three pots of tea. 'Ahh!' said the mate, a little more relaxed now that the skipper was not in the immediate vicinity. 'Just what the doctor ordered. I suppose it's the next best thing to a pint of beer.'

For the next fifteen or twenty minutes, the mate chatted to us, trying to get the measure of his watchmates. It appeared he had been made aware that my father was one of the bosses and he was at pains to assure me it would make no difference to him. He obviously didn't realise my father and I had little to do with each other away from home. After a while he returned to his concern that he wasn't making much impression on the skipper.

'I understood he was a chap that liked a joke,' he moaned.

'So he does,' I assured him, though I hadn't actually sailed with Swan Neck before. 'He's always been known to like a bit of fun and a giggle.'

Wally turned away and took a good look around the horizon. He moved across to the other side of the bridge where he could lean on the telegraph and peep down the alleyway into the wireless room. The Old Man seemed happy enough at the moment, as we could hear him chortling with the sparks at something they heard on the radio. Wally looked on with what appeared to be a little envy that the sparks was enjoying the captain's favour. I concentrated on my steering, not wanting to attract criticism from any direction. Likewise Alec was keeping a good lookout. The next thing, Wally stuck his hand in his raincoat pocket and pulled out what looked like a jumping cracker.

'Well, look at that,' he chuckled. 'That's left over from some fireworks I bought the lad for Guy Fawkes Night.' Then, with a gleam in his eye, he said, 'Do you think I should let it off and liven things up a bit?'

I was a bit taken aback at such a stupid remark because Wally seemed to be serious, but then the devil in me took over and I found myself saying, 'Why not! It'll probably set the Old Man off skylarking.'

'Naw,' Wally hesitated. 'Maybe I shouldn't.'

'Go on, sure you should,' said an alien voice from within me. 'Nothing ventured, nothing gained.'

Then, with a sudden rush of blood, Wally said, 'OK, I will.' He pulled a lighter out of his other pocket and lit the touchpaper; but, instead of throwing it harmlessly into a corner, he threw it into the entrance of the narrow alleyway. For half a minute nothing happened as the fuse burnt down, and the interminable delay had Wally biting at his lip. Then I saw a look of horror gradually sweep over his face as a shadow appeared in the light from the wireless room; the Old Man was coming out.

The timing could not have been better or worse, whichever. Big Dick had got right into the middle of the alleyway when – BANG, CRACK, WALLOP – the jumping cracker was flying around Dick's ankles, causing him to do a war dance of exceptionally energetic proportions, accompanied by yelping and hollering as he banged his head, elbows and knees on the side of the narrow passage. I was not privileged to have a direct view of this startling performance, but it showed clearly in the terrified glance that Alec shot over his shoulder, before turning and pressing his nose to the bridge window in a show of enthusiastic lookout-ing, and the look of excruciating pain on Wally's face as he flinched with every snapping explosion before the skipper shot out on to the bridge.

Dick's eyes were bulging and he was foaming at the mouth. The spittle flew as he roared, 'Who was the fucking bastard maniac who did that?' Then immediately spotting Wally's face he continued, 'Was it you, you demented, bird-brained little cretin? What were you trying to do? Set the fucking ship on fire?' With that he made a lunge at the terrified little mate, who ducked under his arm and shot out the bridge door onto the veranda, with Dick screaming after him. All this I witnessed out of the corner of my eye as I paid unwavering attention to the compass above my head. The screeching and whining we could hear suggested the skipper must have caught up with the perceived terrorist, but I guess he must have got away in the end as the Old Man returned empty-handed.

The skipper, although still upset, didn't show any malice towards we two obviously innocent parties, but I was expecting the mate to have a go at me for aiding and abetting when he returned. However the mate didn't return entirely; he just kept peeping in the bridge door to see if the Old Man had turned in. He, in turn, kept hanging around because the mate wasn't present. So the watch was completed without any retribution towards Alec and I.

But this incident was pretty soon forgotten when it became obvious that we had our hands full getting the old lass across the Atlantic safely.

The weather began to turn nasty as we were negotiating the tricky tide rips of the Pentland Firth. Once we were clear of the narrow channel, the wind began to increase from the west; by the time the ship had reached Cape Wrath and opened up the Minch, it was screeching at force eight to nine. We were back on watch, and negotiating the fore-deck to reach the bridge had been almost suicidal. The poor old *Nectan* with her bellyful of coal was struggling. Even with her engines thrusting as hard as they could, she was just wallowing in the turmoil. Each time the old girl managed to climb over the peak of an onrushing sea, she would drop, like a flagstone in a pond, into the trough between waves; then the sea would just fold in on her fore-deck, which would appear to submerge for an interminable time, until eventually she would drag herself back to the surface from the sucking waters.

Whichever of us was at the wheel had a constant struggle to keep the ship head on into the angry swell, watched constantly by the skipper, who puffed nervously on one cig after another. The others could do nothing but watch the struggle, with noses pressed against the bridge windows, stepping back when heavy water was thrown at the bridge front. The water spewed in round the loose-fitting windows and drained away through the deck gratings, hissing and steaming when it reached the steam pipes running beneath. Many times I looked at the shore light of the aptly named Cape Wrath flashing at us through the port side window, hoping to see it slide aft as we made progress, but it didn't seem to move at all.

After an eternity of lurching and jolting and slamming, the bridge clock ticked round to watch time, but the conditions were still so violent that we couldn't get for'ard to call out, and the skipper daren't ease down to allow it because we needed full power to keep the ship into the weather. Eventually the wind did ease, to draw breath it seemed, and one of us was able to scramble across the fore-deck to get the next watch out, all be it forty minutes late. Shortly after we got for'ard we could hear the wind screaming again, but fitful sleep did come and the next two watches passed all too quickly as we were called to the bridge again. Some of the anger had gone out of the storm and the wind had veered more southerly; we seemed to be making some progress at last, and although the light of Cape Wrath could still be seen, it was fading away on the port quarter.

It was during my spell off the wheel that I decided to go aft to make sure the big kettle was on the stove, ready for making a drink. I went out the lee door on to the lurching veranda and was backing down the short ladder on to the engine room casing, when I backed into someone struggling with a rope on the spray-lashed casing top. It was Hughie the second engineer, dressed only in jeans and a coal-and-grease-streaked T-shirt, which was stuck to his back with spray. He was pulling back on a rope which ran through a pulley and down inside the big stoke-hold vent. I had never seen this before, but there was actually a sliding door in the side of the ventilator which allowed him to do this.

'What are you doing?' I shouted in his ear, above the noise of wind and water around us.

'Pulling up the ashes from the furnaces,' he shouted over his shoulder. With that a tall, narrow bucket appeared in the doorway and he held the weight with one hand as he reached in and grabbed it with the other. The doorway was just big enough to allow him to waggle it through out on to the casing top.

'I didn't think it was your job as second engineer to do that,' I said.

'It isn't,' he replied. 'It's the fireman's job really, but my mate has sprained his wrist and can't grip the rope properly, so I said I'd do it for him.' Sweat and salt spray dripped down his face.

This was typical of Hughie. I had sailed with him before on the *St Apollo* when he was just a fireman. Things were much more comfortable for him there in an oil-burner. But he was always prepared to help people when he could. I guess Hughie had done the same as some of us and joined the coal-burner to get promotion to second engineer, even though he'd held the ticket for a while.

'What next?' I shouted.

'I've got to tip this over the side,' said Hughie, dragging the bucket towards the casing ladder. 'They won't let you tip it on the deck because the clinker would jam the scupper ports.'

I looked down at the deck, five feet below us, awash with the seas constantly breaking over it, then looked at Hughie's unlaced stoke-hold boots and grabbed his arm. 'OK, Hughie. I'll do that for you. I'm rigged for it, I've got thigh boots on.' Hughie gratefully stepped to one side as I climbed down and took the bucket on my shoulder. Then waiting for the roll, when the decks would clear a bit, I took two or three strides, banged the bucket on the rail and tipped the ashes over. I returned the can to Hughie. 'How many more?' I asked.

'About four or five,' he replied, letting the rope slide through his hand as the bucket descended to the stoke-hold plates again. 'But it will take Jack a while to fill them with his dicky wrist, I expect.'

I thought about that for a moment. If it was a struggle for him to fill a bucket, then how does he manage to fling a shovelful of coal to the back of a furnace through a small door? No prizes for guessing who does that for him as well. I looked at Hughie while we were waiting for the next bucket – his sandy hair and pale complexion, which would have had freckles if it ever saw any sun, the twinkle in his eyes, and the smile lines ever visible at the corners of his mouth. He was a good shipmate, full of fun, with a good sense of humour and a fondness for playing pranks on people, if he could get away with it. There were some good people doing this job you were proud to sail with and Hughie was one of them.

Four more times I took the can from him and only got caught by the water once, when it rushed round my legs and slapped my bottom, but my oily fearnoughts repelled most of it better than Hughie's dungarees would have done. Soon he slid the door shut and declared, 'That's it. Thanks, Bob. I won't forget this. Better get down there now. I'll see yer.' He clattered off along the casing in his hobnailed boots, and I dashed back to the bridge, having been too long already.

When I stepped back on the bridge, the mate gave me a glare and enquired about the tea. 'I didn't have time.' I said. 'I had to get back to relieve the wheelman,' and I explained what I'd been doing. The mate mumbled something about not doing engineer's jobs and concentrating more on my own; then he dispatched Alec to go and tell the galley boy to make the tea. Not long after Alec returned, the galley boy stumbled on to the bridge, carrying a small, brown enamel teapot by its makeshift rope handle. I had to admire the resilience of these young Hessle Road lads. It was only his first trip, and to protect himself from the sprays he was wearing a short, showerproof mac with a hood he had brought from home. This was probably the farthest he'd been from the galley since we left, but it didn't faze him. He staggered unsteadily across the swaying bridge to the pot racks; then discovering that our three mugs all had some cold tea in them, he threw the contents one after the other through the deck gratings at his feet. This incensed the mate, who had just returned from the chart room. 'What do you think you're doing?' he snapped.

'What's up?' enquired the startled kid.

'Well, do you do that at home?'

'No.'

'Then don't do it here.'

'Well, what should I do?'

'Empty them out of the window.'

'But I don't do that at home either.'

'Get off the bridge, you cheeky little bastard.'

We were more than halfway across the pond before the weather eased enough for us to get on the deck, start to put the trawl alongside, and prepare wires, derricks and other gear ready for shooting. We had two days at this; but, as stated before, the mountains of Greenland are so high that on a clear day you can see them from sixty miles away, and the range at Cape Farewell was peeping above the horizon long before we were ready. This wouldn't have bothered us normally because we would round the Cape and steam another day or two up the west side before starting to fish on the Greenland banks. But, on this occasion, a group of Hull ships were catching a lot of fish close in at the Cape; so, of course, we were going to try our luck with them.

Many times before, ships had tried to fish on the edge of the shoal at Cape Farewell, which only just extended beyond the three-mile limit, but the ground was so bad they couldn't tow. Skippers had seen on their sounders as they passed that there were oodles of fish swimming there; but, as soon as they put their gear down, the trawl came fast on the bottom within minutes and was torn to shreds.

Previous ships I'd been on had tried it with the same result, so it was with some trepidation that we approached the area now. The lads were moaning that it would be a trip of mending and replacing gear if we attempted to remain here. They thought it was a treacherous place because of the other threat posed by this area – *the icefields*.

You can and will encounter heavy ice anywhere in the waters surrounding Greenland, but at Cape Farewell the icefields were constantly flowing past, brought down by the predominant southerly flow that carries ice down from the glaciers further up the east coast, then round the Cape and up the west side. There were clear periods, but they only lasted for a day or so before the next batch came sweeping down. As we steamed in close and began to weave through the loose ice on the edge of the fields, the mountains seemed to tower above us; but still the ships were not visible, although we could here them clearly on the radio. Then the skipper spotted them through the binoculars; their masts and funnels were just visible at the very foot of the mountains. God, these guys were close in. They were not just inside the three-mile limit. It turned out that at times they were fishing nearly inside the baseline of the limits, only cables away from the rocks!

Fishing inside the limit didn't pose much of a problem from the authorities. A Danish possession, Greenland was too vast for them to police properly at this time. There was only one gunboat and it was stationed at the capital, Godthab, some 500 miles or so up the west side. True, they also had a seaplane stationed further south, and that was a threat occasionally when they could afford to launch it. What had deterred poaching in the past was the thought of the bad ground and strong currents, but now the trawlers had found the ground was better close in.

That, however, did not suit Dickie, our skipper. As an ex-Trinity House boy, he had been taught to obey the rules, and fishing illegally was not something he was happy with. Nevertheless, he could not ignore the amounts of fish his competitors, in effect, were catching. After gleaning some information from friends, he settled down on a tow they called the bicycle track, which meant keeping two miles off the larger islands by radar. This appeased Dickie's conscience a little; thinking that he was only a mile inside the line didn't make him as bad as some of the others.

This plan was enough to provide us with a good living. We were catching two or three bags of fine cod for a relatively short tow, and keeping clear of damage most of the time. Fish was coming aboard faster than normal, but this in itself caused a problem after a few days, as we were running short of space. It must be remembered that we had two days of steaming coal still unused in the after fishroom. Normally after three days of fishing the after fishroom would have been clear of coal and all hands would have washed it out so we could fill it with fish. But, having stopped to fish two days sooner, this coal was still unused, while the forward fishroom was full already. This dilemma worried the skipper and mate constantly. It didn't matter if some of the other ships were catching nearly double what we were, if we were not clearing space fast enough to take it.

These were extra problems caused by us being a coal-burner. This was not very common in these waters at this time, although there was one other coal-burner in the vicinity, a ship called the *Roman*.

The skipper and mate considered dumping coal but were reluctant to do so. If the fish were to take off completely in this area, which often happened, then we might need that coal to steam round to the other side of Greenland.

Eventually it was decided to wash out those pounds in the fore-end of the after fishroom that were already empty, which meant clearing coal from the centre of the fishroom to allow the water to run away. So a couple of men were sent down to help to clear the coal by half-filling the tunnel that connected the fishroom to the stoke-hold. This left us short-handed on deck, but when the job was done they were able to clear the slushwell that would pump away the water when we washed out the empty pounds.

This manoeuvre allowed us to carry on fishing for another couple of days. By this time, the rest of the coal had been used and we were able to wash out completely and transfer ice from the ice box in the very fore-end of the fish-hold. It had been a very difficult way of working, which had worn out the crew, but we realised that we already had the makings of a very good trip on board. If this fish would hang on a little bit longer, we would be in for big money. But that was the problem. Good fishing – or rather the best fishing – never does hang on. But, if you're patient. . . .

However, some skippers aren't always patient, particularly if the competition around you is keen, and you know there are big pickings close by. Our hauls had slacked off a little, and it was obvious the fish were moving. Dicky, our skipper, extended the tow a bit and this improved results. But when he tried to vary it more we began to do damage and had to lay for the next couple of hauls, mending the net and thus wasting time. So Dicky decided to stay with our regular tow and keep the fish coming in steady for the rest of our time. This took the pressure off everyone and, as the weather was reasonable made for fairly comfortable working. Even the bosun seemed pretty relaxed as he joined us in the gutting pounds, shouting. 'Don't forget your hearts, clots and curtains,' the usual cry of all bosuns to remind their crews to make sure they removed all the innards cleanly. It proved that he was already thinking of our chances on the fish market when we got home.

Our competitors closer in, some of whom had steamed down from the north-west, were not content to accept a moderate return for their efforts; they began searching around, but then they too began to do damage. Those that moved out found themselves worse off. Then, skirting the rocks, one ship moved even closer in and came up with a massive haul, which began a free-for-all as the others closed in. More and more of the group were towing around and between rocks which were mostly awash; this was a very dangerous practice, as these inner waters had not been surveyed and were not charted. In fact, the only rock that was shown on the chart inside the baseline, apart from the main islands, was a large one that rose to a height of 175 feet. It was marked on the chart as 175 and was referred to as that by all when used as a datum point. As more and more large hauls were reported by those that ventured closer, a sort of madness overtook most skippers in the vicinity. Spurred on by greed and the need to compete, they moved in closer than prudence demanded.

These lucrative hauls were banded about on air and must have been driving Dicky mad, when you considered that *our* voyage was nearly over. He had been patient and kept fish coming aboard at a steady pace, and had not dodged about and experimented like the others, so we had more or less competed up to now, but these big hauls would make a difference. The trouble was, we had not been inside at all, so Dick had not familiarised himself with the area, and to try to do so now would put him at a big disadvantage. Anyway, things were getting more tricky now, even on this tow, as the loose ice and growlers were increasing around us, making it more difficult to keep on the narrow strip we were working.

The banter and stories from inside became more frantic as one skipper reported that he had passed over such a shoal patch on the bottom that his warps nearly came out of the water; yet another big haul was the result. Then something happened which made up Dicky's mind; the visibility started to drop as the fog came in.

Visibility grew less and less as the white ice floes began to fade in the grey mist. The difficulty of picking them out for the men on the bridge became more obvious when we started to have some near misses; some of the ice floes and large growlers were bumping and scraping down the ship's side, a sound that the men in the engine room certainly didn't like. Dick called the mate to the bridge and, after a confab, the mate went straight down the fishroom. It was obvious that the skipper had asked for an accurate tally of the fish on board.

We soon heard that Dick had decided to go for an earlier market and cut the voyage down by a day, which would improve the expense sheet and beat all the other big-hitters from this area. Before we knew it, we were making our last haul and everyone on board was cock-a-hoop, especially as we discovered we had more fish than we had thought. The old lass really had done us proud.

The fog was coming in quite thick now, as we took the gear on board and turned away for our long haul back across the North Atlantic. Dick called up some of the skippers in among the melee and told them we were going. They thanked him and wished us well but had no time to talk as things were getting fraught.

Happy as we were, knowing that the ship was finally heading home, it's surprising how weary everyone becomes when the sense of urgency falls away once the fishing process is complete. There was still a lot of work to be done to secure the trawl and clear up the deck, which was completely littered with working gear and deck boards and such. It was going to take all hands four to five hours at least to clear it and make us safe for the crossing. Meanwhile the ship gradually eased its way through the fog, clear of the icefields, before coming to full speed.

We tired deckies were stumbling around the deck, humping the heavy gear away. Through the windows of the bridge, which were open, of course, because of the poor visibility, we could hear excited voices over the radio from the ships we were leaving behind. Over time they began to fade a little, as we put more distance between us and them. It must have been more difficult for them now picking out ships on the radar from the ice and rocks.

We had nearly finished squaring up the deck, when we detected some consternation and then panic in the voices coming over the air. The people on the bridge also appeared to be disturbed. Then we heard the news.

Someone had piled up on the rocks; it was the *Roman*. Everyone's heart beat a little faster. Some of what happened next we heard ourselves, and some was relayed by the bosun, who was one of the look-outs. The *Roman*, which was one of those close in, had come fast with its gear on the bottom, causing the ship to stop in the water; then, while she was out of control, the current had swept her on to one of the rocks nearby. The story we were told claimed the skipper had alerted the ships nearby that his ship was pushed right up on to one of the rocks next to the 175. They were trying to get a boat away, but the current was so strong it was almost rolling the ship over. Then the transmission went dead.

Ships round about immediately hauled their gear and tried to get in position to help. But, of course, the fog was still thick, and manoeuvring among the flowing ice still very dangerous.

We were nearly fifty miles away by now, but our skipper said he was turning around and coming back to help. However, some of the most experienced skippers among those at the scene said that he shouldn't. There were about ten ships in the area already; it would take us about five to six hours at least to get back through the ice, and they figured we would be more of a hindrance than a help in the present conditions. They added that the people ashore had been informed, and already some small inshore fishing boats and Eskimo skiffs were putting out from the nearby fjords. Later there was a report that an aeroplane was being launched with a lifeboat on board from a US Air base in Greenland.

Reluctantly, Dick was persuaded to continue on the homeward journey. Tired as we were, most of us were sorry we were not going to be able to render some assistance to the stricken vessel. But when exhausted bodies turn towards their bunks oblivion results, accompanied by a complete release from the cruelties that fate delivers, until the vigorous shaking of a watchkeeper's hand brings you back to the call of duty and the dire realisation of what had transpired.

Every watch that manned the bridge was hungry for information, and it wasn't long before we heard the dreaded news that several bodies had been picked up by a Hull trawler. As more news eventually filtered through, it was mentioned that some of the bodies had been savaged by seagulls and their eyes pecked out, but it was difficult to know the truth when information had been passed from mouth to mouth. Then came some better news that one man had been rescued alive from one of the rocks by a small boat and put aboard a foreign ship, but he was the only survivor.

Normally the run home from any fishing trip is happy and relaxed if the weather is fine, with feelings of satisfaction and anticipation, but this trip everyone felt empty and sad with a strange sense of guilt. We had survived without hurt or injury, going home to family and friends, with the prospect of two days of spending and partying, if we were up to it. But those men in the *Roman* and their families would get nothing, except what we survivors and the fishing fraternity collected for them. They didn't deserve this end; like us, they were only trying to earn a good living for themselves and their loved ones, obeying orders and working hard. Why should fate treat them so?

Each evening after tea on a homeward journey, when the off-watch crew would gather in the mess-deck to socialise and play cards or dominoes, the air was usually rife with jibes and dirty stories. But not this time, this time it was different. Oh yes, we still gathered in the mess-deck and went through the motions because life goes on and you can't let the sadness of the affair or fears for the future consume you. But the atmosphere was muted and the men were quiet with only an occasional quip at the state of play. On one occasion, when I was ambling forward on the bouncing deck as the ship rode the sweeping rollers on a scuffly sea, I was suddenly aware that it was only the waist-high rail that was keeping me safe from these sometimes vicious waters. In the past I had thought it was my common sense, my awareness, my nimbleness that was helping me to cheat the sea, but now I realised that this restless ocean could claim any one of us if it wanted to. That, I knew, would depend on God.

We came home to St Andrews Dock on an afternoon tide, and as we approached the quay we could see that there were more people than usual to watch us in. Apart from family and loved ones, who seemed even more delighted and relieved to see us back safe and sound, there appeared to be a number of observers from the local community off Hessle Road, who had come to see the first ship back from the location of the tragedy. Probably some of them were connected to the families of those who had been lost, hoping to glean some extra information of how theirs had come to pay the ultimate price.

As the little tug pulled us through the dock to our discharging berth, the many workers around the dock stopped and turned to stare in curiosity at the group of us lining the fo'c'sle head. There was even a *Mail* photographer snapping us, not only because we were the first ship back from the treacherous Cape, but also because we were the only other coal-burner present at Greenland and were similar to the *Roman*. So much for trying to keep that quiet from Mum.

We made a decent trip, as we had hoped. Although I'd had enough of coal-burning, I did go back for another three trips, though not to Greenland. At least it took us away from the lamentation and hysteria when the bodies came back, and the inevitable pressure there would have been from my mum and sisters to quit the job, had I been home.

Chapter 12

THE DRIVE TOWARDS THE ULTIMATE GOAL

I had wanted to get out of the *Nectan* from the first trip; but, if I also wanted to sit for my tickets the first thing was to get enough sea time. The amount of actual sea time required to sit for a mate's or bosun's ticket was four years. But I had heard from one of the teachers when I was sitting for my decky learner's ticket that, with a special recommendation, one could sit for a bosun's ticket after only three years, and I was well on my way to accruing that. I had this dream of getting my skipper's ticket by the time I was twenty-one, if I could only stay in a ship. That's why I had been in no hurry to sign off and risk losing time at home waiting for another vacancy in a better ship. Then I heard that recently there had been frequent changes in my old ship, the *Apollo*, which was skippered now by a hard case known as Lugs Larsen, who apparently drove his crews very hard. As it happened, I knew Larsen, whose real name was Leif. But his large ears, which didn't stick out but ran nearly the length of his head, meant that he was known by all as Lugs.

Leif Larsen was a Dane who had only been in the firm for a year or so. He had spent most of his fifteen years at sea in small North Sea fishing vessels, and had come across to England to try his luck at deep-sea trawling. Leif had tried a couple of firms before coming to us as a mate, but his workrate and drive had been so impressive that he had been given a chance as skipper. Despite his lack of knowledge of our traditional fishing grounds, he was making a go of it, thanks mainly to his crews, who he pushed to the limit.

My knowledge of Leif was social. He made a friend of my father, who was in fact his boss and belonged to the same club. He was very kind to my mother, who was now nearly bed-ridden, and brought her flowers and little presents. His wife was also very supportive of her and often visited.

That was when I met their only daughter, Christina, a real Scandinavian-type blonde beauty of nymph-like attributes. When Christina's beautiful blue eyes settled on me, they let it be known that they liked what they saw. This precocious young girl was advanced in every way and looked like a mature seventeen-year-old, but she was actually only fifteen. So I stood off – or tried to.

Leif seemed like a good guy when you met him ashore; he was full of fun and laughed a lot. He liked a good drink and could consume plenty. He certainly had an eye for the girls, and often went missing for the odd couple of hours, much to his wife's consternation. I also noted he often got his laughs at someone else's expense.

When I'd completed my fourth trip in the *Nectan*, I signed off and let it be known that I wanted another spare hand's job, even if it meant signing on the *Apollo*, if there was a chance. There had been some good reports from the skipper and mate of the *Nectan*, where I'd made quick progress for my age, due probably to the lack of competition. I had been doing the fourth hand's job, which meant working alongside the mate on deck, where I was able to learn and make an impact due to his lack of height. One trip I was made deputy fishroom man; both were selective jobs reserved for the more competent decky, so I was good enough now for a better class of ship. Gibby seemed to accept that and said we had better see what happened when the *Apollo* got home in a few days' time.

I spent the first couple of days at home, as usual, out on the town with my friends, as usual, going to dances and visiting the big pubs that had concert nights. These were sort of singalong nights where anyone could get behind the mike and make a fool of themselves. These were great nights for picking up the girls if you were cheeky enough. I spent the days looking for books and training manuals that would help me with my job. I had been using an old *Fisherman's Handy Billy* my father had given me. This was a book that told you a little of everything, from knots and splices to the sailing articles and navigation lights; it even told you how to put out a kedge anchor – all information that a skipper or mate would need to know. I was keen to learn and had set my sights on quick promotion, whatever it cost.

The *St Apollo* was back- Lugs Larsen was back.

I was among the crowd of men at the entrance to the company yard when the ship was settling. With me was my pal Charlie and around us were most of the crew of the *Apollo,* waiting to be called up to the pay office to settle their account and receive their share of the trip; it had been a reasonably good one. Also among the crew were other hopefuls like ourselves wanting to sign on in the runner's office at the inner end of the yard. It was obvious to listen to the crew that it had been a hard trip and the skipper, according to them, had been a bastard, so some were signing off. Charlie, like me, had done some time in an old rustbucket to get his start as a decky and was now looking for a better ship. He was feeling confident because he had been very friendly with the runner lately and had spent an afternoon with him in one of the working men's clubs, plying him with drinks.

Lugs Larsen suddenly turned up in his flash car and parked it in a reserved space opposite the offices. When he had alighted and locked the car, he smiled at the crowd and said good morning as he strode across to the stairs, nodding to some of those he knew and displaying the deceptive charm typical of most skippers when they were ashore. Those who were going back responded, but there were a few who just turned their backs when he passed.

Also among the little gathering were two well-known characters, Billy Fudge and Gerry Grey. Both had a reputation as hard men; they had been in plenty of fights and for the most part had come off best. But they also had a reputation for being strong and powerful workers. These were naughty boys, but they were mostly mischievous rather than nasty; and they were not partners, more like competitors.

Billy Fudge was a heftily built man, a little above average height, about five ten, with powerful shoulders and a barrel chest. He had a short, thick neck and a strong jaw with wide jowls and high cheekbones, a broad aquiline nose, black, bushy eyebrows, and black, longish, greasy hair. But Tommy's twinkling eyes looked sincere, and the flash of white teeth when he smiled made you want to smile too. Gerry Grey was a taller man, over six feet; he too had broad shoulders and a big chest, but was narrower in the hip. He had a much fresher complexion and was losing his sandy hair – something he was very sensitive about. He had a prominent, well-shaped nose and jaw, but his eyes looked more calculating. Gerry was a very jocular man, but he had the habit of shoving whoever was next to him with his forearm to provoke the desired response whenever he cracked a joke.

These two stalwarts held court among the group who were waiting, verbally sparring with each other to amuse the little crowd.

Charlie and I watched the antics of these two jokers with some amusement.

'Bloody 'ell,' remarked Charlie pensively. 'There'll be some fun aboard if one of them gets signed on.'

Pretty soon Jack Gibby came scuttling down the stairs from the offices above and made his way to his own office down the yard. He called to the group in general, 'The pay office is ready to settle with the first two now, if you go up.'

The first two men, who had been waiting longest, scampered up the stairs; the rest began to shuffle about, now things were buzzing. A noise from the inner end of the yard had the group turning, men from the riggers' shed next to the runner's office were dragging out some wires to be loaded on a handcart for delivery to the newly returned ship. At the same time, net and ropes were being dropped down from the net-loft above. At last Gibby emerged from his office and called, 'Gerry! Would you like to come in and sign?'

As Gerry Grey hastily pushed his way through the crowd, Charlie looked towards me silently and raised his eyebrows. Shortly after, Gerry emerged from the office, followed by the runner, who shouted, 'Come on then, Billy. Let's have yer.'

'Suck back!' muttered Charlie, 'He's signed them both.'

After Billy Fudge came out, there was a bit of a pause before Gibby appeared again and called, 'Bob, can yuh come in a minute?'

There was just that little hesitation on my part before I moved down the yard and entered Gibby's office.

'Now then,' said Jack, lounging with one elbow on the desk, pen in hand. 'Are you still happy to sign?'

'Sure Jack, I'm ready,' I said, but there was a hollow in the pit of my stomach.

Jack neatly blotted my signature on the log as I turned away. 'OK. Be on board at noon, day after tommorer,' was all he said.

My mind was juggling with so many thoughts as I walked out of the office and down the yard, but I started to calm a little when I heard Jack calling Charlie into the office. Things shouldn't be so bad if we could support each other in this next venture.

The next day, I went out in the morning to get some toiletries and a few last things to pack into my kitbag, and had a couple of beers with Charlie to celebrate our sailing together. We made light of the forthcoming trip and joked about it a lot with friends who, in turn, tried to pile on the gloomy side. I returned home in the afternoon to find Leif Larsen and his wife in our front room, visiting my mum. When I entered Dad turned to me and said, 'Ah, Rob lad! Just in time to save my legs. Get a couple of G and Ts for Leif and Jean, please.'

Mum was wrapped up in an easy chair, face flushed, and delighted to have some company. I was happy to do the honours.

A couple of drinks later, the conversation was jovial but naturally often touched on fishing. Then Leif said, 'I unterstand Bob's signed on witt us – so I'll have to watch my Ps and my Qs dis trip witt der gaffer's lad on board.'

Dad seized on this immediately. 'Don't you pay no mind to that, Leif. I don't want you to show him any favour. You work him as hard as anybody.' This I agreed with, but I was going to regret my father giving him such licence in the days to come.

I was glad to be back aboard my old ship. Sailing just after noon meant that most of the crew were half-sloshed, but the work got done anyway. Strangely enough, Billy Fudge and Gerry Grey were not too bad, although both had rosy eyes and were tiddly enough to start messing about. It was obviously their first trip with Lugs Larsen and this amused them; they were continually shouting at each other, cupping their ears, and saying such things as, 'Speak up! *I* don't have any ear trumpets.'

Maybe the skipper was too busy on the bridge as we were navigating down the river, or whatever, as he didn't appear to hear them; but we were sailing in dangerous waters if this sort of thing continued.

After a couple of days, Lugs Larsen indicated what his attitude towards me was going to be. I was on the bosun's watch with Billy Fudge, who wasn't as bad a watchmate as I'd expected, although he was always looking to have fun or be mischievous. He was in the habit of playing silly pranks or cracking childish jokes, but on the whole he pulled his weight, which was considerable. We were into the third day steaming, and our early morning watch was just coming to an end before breakfast, when the fore mast-head light blew just as the skipper came on to the bridge for the first time that day.

'Dat'll have to be replaced, Buster,' he said to the bosun, Jerry Keaton, whose nickname was Buster, for obvious reasons. As it was my spell on the wheel, this job fell to Billy.

We had cleared the Orkneys and were crossing the west Norwegian Sea towards Iceland with a following sea on the starboard quarter, which was causing the ship to roll quickly. Not much water was coming aboard, but the rapid swinging of the mast-head didn't make any trip up there very attractive. Billy's bulk and heavy build made him ideal for lifting and pulling, but he was not very nimble. I guessed he would be OK to the top of the rigging, but this job went beyond that.

Billy spoke up quickly. 'I don't think I could manage it up there while she's performing like this, skipper,' he said, shaking his head. 'My arms aren't long enough to reach up to the crosstrees.' This surprised me; that a man of his experience and reputation should admit there was any job that he couldn't cope with.

The bosun was just about to press him, pointing out that it had to be done, when Lugs interrupted. 'Don't worry, Buster. If dis chap is too heafy to climb up there, young Dasher can do it, can't you, Dash? If he grabs the wheel from you?'

I was not very pleased with this suggestion. The spell on the wheel was supposed to be a safe job during a watch. I wasn't keen to climb the mast either in these vigorous conditions, but I could hardly refuse after Fudgey had reneged. He, too, was miffed at the skipper's reference to 'this chap.' He thought everyone knew his name, but he quickly stepped forward to take the wheel off me.

Armed with a small shifter to open the lantern case and a new bulb tucked up my jersey, I began to climb the port rigging. The ship was still rolling violently and the mast-head above me was describing an arc of about twelve to fifteen feet overall. The risk of the lively ship flinging me over the side was not so great while I was negotiating the first twenty-five feet, where the rigging was fairly wide, but the three shrouds closed together and linked into the same shackle on the mast. Over the last four feet it was impossible to get my rubber boots onto the rat-lines. I had to wrap my legs around the closing shrouds and hitch my way up until I could reach the crosstree with my hand and get my foot onto the single metal rung that was welded to the mast at this point.

The crosstree was a narrow steel platform which extended three feet out on either side of the mast; it supported the lifting blocks for the Gilson wires and I had to get around this to reach the mast-head lantern just above it. The single step rung helped me to hitch my chest onto the crosstree, but at this point I lost my footing, which left the bottom half of my body swinging with every lurch of the mast. For a few moments I clung terrified to the cold steel of the crosstree, draped across it and looking down at the wallowing deck below. It looked staggeringly small from this height, barely forty feet above it; too small, it seemed, to support this mass of steel to which I now clung.

I could see the intent face of the bosun at the bridge window, staring up at me, his mouth hanging open. There was no sign of the skipper. The mast swung rapidly back and forth, shaking me like a terrier shakes a rat. Every effort I made to get my knee up and on to the platform was thwarted by the violent movement. My hands were cold and, with my chest taking all of the weight of my body, the spare bulb was now pushed up against my throat; I was getting short of breath. After a few moments of squirming, I managed to get a footing, with one foot on the steel rung and the other on the shackle that held the rigging shrouds. These precarious footholds now gave me enough support to stretch up and reach the top of the mast-head lantern.

I decided to try and work from this position; with only one hand clutching hold of the little platform, I managed to unscrew two of the butterfly nuts securing the lantern lid, but I could not shift the third with my rapidly numbing fingers. Reaching into my fearnought trousers, I extracted the small shifter and was able to loosen the last nut. Flinging open the top, I could just reach the bulb with my fingertips and was able to remove it and fling it vigorously over my shoulder, where I knew it would find its way into the turbulent waves below. I now retrieved the spare bulb through the neck of my jumper and pressed it into place, giving the thumbs up sign to the watching bosun below. He disappeared from the window and a moment later I was pleased to see the light come on inside the lantern. I hastily slammed the lid down and secured the nuts. The most difficult part was still to come as I lowered myself down from my swinging perch, with trembling, weary arms at full stretch, to the comparative safety of the rigging beneath. As I scrambled down the rat-lines on shaky legs, I noted that nobody was watching my final descent. The bosun had disappeared again, presumably to fill in the log.

The extra work needed on this ship was apparent from the start, with the extra nets that had to be fixed while we were running off. Usually a ship would use one trawl per trip. If you were lucky, a trawl might last two trips, although it may require constant repair. If you were unlucky, then two trawls might be needed. In this case, three trawls and all the spare net we carried was new and had to be prepared. It showed how the skipper was constantly getting into bad grounds and doing damage. So the days spent steaming were full days, and the daymen and the watches were on deck from first minute till last, working furiously with needle and twine, which was making hands sore before we even began fishing. Sometimes the evening and morning watches had to help out setting up or putting gear away, instead of keeping a lookout.

Even so the mood in the fo'c'sle was good and cheery, due mainly to the antics of Gerry and Billy, who were constantly ribbing each other, each claiming to be the more handsome and owner of the better physique. Each in turn would pose in front of the small mirror in the fo'c'sle doorway, pull in his stomach, flex his muscles and swagger around in an exaggerated way, claiming he had the bigger chest, which left the rest of us in fits of laughter. Meanwhile the other would just sneer at such a scrawny figure.

Charlie and I also added to the fun by challenging each other, and some of our shipmates, to do tricks and compete against our buddies. One of the tricks I had learnt involved throwing a bight or loop of a heaving line over a bar some feet above and passing it round the back of the head. By tilting the head backwards it was possible to pull down on the other ends and lift yourself off the floor and up towards the bar – something that all were keen to do. What they didn't realise was that lifting oneself wasn't such a problem, it was lowering oneself down again that was almost impossible, as Charlie soon found out when he tried it.

After pulling himself no more than two feet off the deck, he realised he couldn't take the weight off his hands without jerking his neck, and was left suspended there to the amusement of all. As Charlie was left swinging to the roll of the ship, someone spotted a tin of grease that had been left for'ard by one of the engineers and, sneaking up to him, dropped the flap of his fearnoughts and smeared his privates with it. Charlie, of course, with his head tilted back, was unable to identify the culprit, and could do little about it until he was lifted down by sympathetic mates.

This game travelled round the ship, and when it was introduced to the second engineer, who was a fat man weighing seventeen stone plus, he took it on and proved that even he could lift his weight using the back of his head. With the rope passed over a pipe above, he pulled himself over three feet off the engine-room plates; but, of course, he found he couldn't lower himself down again. He was left suspended in the middle of the engine room while the rest of us pretended to walk away and leave him. But when I looked back from my hiding place and saw the way his neck was stretching, with that massive body swinging on it, I was frightened he was going to pull his head off, so I was the first back to help him down. Although he rubbed his neck a lot and thought his tendons were stretched, he took it all in good part and laughed along with the rest of us when the lads suggested he was a foot taller. They decided that, in future, instead of calling him Gerald or Gerry, as he was known, they would call him Gerr-affe. The spirit in the fo'c'sle was good, but the working practices were wearing.

When we did start fishing, the skipper chose an awkward way of working. Normally, if a lot of damage was expected, it was the practice to put a trawl on both sides of the ship. When one was too badly damaged for quick repair, you could change over and shoot away the other trawl, which was ready on the opposite side. Lugs, however, was not confident of shooting the port trawl without fouling it; instead of rigging a complete set of gear on that side, he only let us put the net along the rail as a standby. So when the net we were using was badly damaged, we had to chop it off the bobbins, heave it across the deck and drop it in a heap, while we took the other standby trawl back across the deck and stitched it in its place. Once we had shot away, it meant the damaged trawl had to be unravelled and spread out before we could even begin to repair it; and very often before we had done that the new trawl had been hauled and was damaged again, so it was non-stop repairing. It gave the crew little chance to get at the fish, which was the real money-earner.

This led to long, difficult, hard-working days, with only moderate amounts of fish coming aboard, and was clearly due to Lugs Larsen's limited knowledge of the complex and difficult grounds at Iceland. At the end of each eighteen-hour spell on deck, I was only too glad to throw my aching, though now much hardier, body into the sanctuary of my bunk for four or five hours. But then there was another problem; Billy Fudge, my watchmate and the only other occupant of the fo'c'sle during our watch below, would constantly call to me from his bunk to ask if I was asleep. This, of course, kept disturbing me; but, when I pointed out that I *would* be asleep if he would only keep quiet, he pleaded with me not to sleep before he did, as he would be at a disadvantage. Infuriating as this was, there was little I could do to shut him up. Bill was a simple-minded fellow, and too big a hunk for me to threaten, so I just had to wait till exhaustion took over.

Lugs Larsen was not averse to fishing in bad weather either, and he pushed it to the limit when everyone else had quit, in order to catch up. Iceland is noted for bad weather during the winter, so most of our repairs had to be made while seas were slopping over the rail and the net was sloshing around the deck. This, of course, slowed the job down and made it more difficult than ever when we were heaving net around the deck, as Larsen wanted, instead of changing over, and he started tongue-lashing us for more effort. Considering the difficult conditions, this angered the men, who were giving it their best efforts, and they snarled and grumbled at the constant berating from the skipper through the bridge window. But Fudgey and Gerry had more to say.

'WE WOULDN'T HAVE SO MUCH FUCKING MENDING,' shouted Gerry, without looking up from his work, 'IF WE DIDN'T HAVE SUCH A MICKEY MOUSE SKIPPER CAUSING IT.'

'YEH!' added Billy. 'A MICKEY MOUSE SKIPPER, WITH MICKY MOUSE EARS.'

This had some of the lads snickering, and achieved the desired result, as the bridge window slammed shut. But I guessed that we would pay for those remarks and, sure enough, after we had shot away, we did.

While we were gutting, the mate came off the bridge and told the bosun that whenever we hauled with damage, we had to call out the watch below immediately to help with the mending.

This was demoralising news. Sleep and rest at a premium already. After eighteen hours hard and intensive work on deck, we each had only six hours off to clean up, eat and sort out any problems with saturated gear, before climbing into our bunks, leaving only four to four and a half hours for actual rest. Calling us out in the middle of that, apart from chopping up our short sleep periods, meant that when the job was done the watch affected was still entitled to go back to bed and claim the rest of their time, even if there was only an hour due to them. This, of course, set watch times back, and if the next watch was called out as well it compounded the problem. Chaos was the result and morale plummeted.

With the weather deteriorating, the next couple of days carried on with constant interruptions to the watches, and the effect on the crew was clear to see as they staggered around the deck and tripped over everything. The wind continued to freshen and had reached force six to seven, with seas of ten to fifteen feet running at the ship and sometimes crashing aboard, amidships and aft side, scattering the men and knocking the slower ones down. Smaller ships around us were beginning to lay with their gear aboard, but we continued to fish, as Larsen pushed for those extra hauls. This was the situation as the gear was paid away again for another attempt. But, as we heaved the cod-ends out on the derrick Gilson and released them into the raging waves, someone noticed a shackle on the forward end of the head-line was nearly undone, and it was held aboard while one man rushed aft for one of the crocodile spanners that was stowed around the deck. As he passed the winch, he ran over some net that was still inboard and caught his foot in one of the meshes. He went down, but as he did so the net outboard pulled tight and dragged more of the trawl *and him* over the rail. He let out a strangled shriek as it did so.

Billy Fudge and Gerry Grey, who were nearest, courageously threw themselves on the piece of net that remained inboard, and their combined weight managed to hold up its flow over the side. The rest of us, realising that this was only a temporary delay before the turbulent, sucking seas dragged the rest of the net over the dipping, tossing ship's rail, and them with it, ran to get something to heave the net back. A twenty-foot hook rope, used normally to heave on the after-quarter rope, was laying behind the winch, and this was quickly hooked into the fore salvage of the net and taken to the winch barrel.

Thanks to the quick action of Gerry and Billy, our stricken shipmate was suspended clinging to the net outboard, halfway between ship's rail and normal water level, with the rolling seas washing over him. The hook rope's hold on the trawl was precarious, but by heaving steadily we were able to bring the trembling decky close enough to the rail to get his hands over it. Other deckies jumped on to the remaining net, clinging on to it to try and hold it inboard while the mate scrambled half over the rail. With one man holding on to his legs, he reached down as far as he could, and with seas now washing over both of them he managed to slash with his knife and clear the meshes fouling the luckless decky's boot.

All this time, the foaming, thrashing seas raged and sucked at the net, trying to claim their victim. Meanwhile the seagulls swooped and dived low, shrieking, it seemed, in excitement that so many men had been put in jeopardy.

Our man was retrieved safely, although the net had twisted his foot badly, and he had to be helped aft. The trawl had been released over the side and was billowing away from the ship in the surging swell. Even though the wind was increasing, the trawl was lowered away, probably because temporarily it was the easiest option, till the men had regrouped and rested. We shot away with difficulty, but thankfully the trawl did not foul and was square when it reached the bottom. We were towing again.

The men trooped aft and flopped in the mess-deck, still dripping in their wet gear, each grabbing a pot of hot, sweet tea to rejuvenate them. Removing only their sou'westers, they slumped in their seats awaiting the next orders. The mate came in only long enough to get his tea and take it to the bridge to report to the skipper. The mood was subdued in the mess as we sat, with only an occasional remark, listening to the wind rush and howl through the deck fittings outside, while the ship jumped and lurched, struggling to drag the gear through the mounting seas. We had all seen and suffered similar conditions before, but we had been able to take heart in the knowledge that our turn would come to take a break at a specific time and go below. This time, we were not even assured of that and it was leaving its mark.

With seas coming aboard continuously, even while we were towing, it would be impossible to mend the spare trawl which was still laying on the deck. This was confirmed when the mate came down and instructed us to get out on deck, secure the spare trawl and lash it up along the rail to prevent it going over the side or fouling the scupper ports. Then we had to clear the fish as quickly as possible before we hauled the gear back and took it on board. With the weather still deteriorating, it was imperative that this was done immediately, but the tired crew were slow to move. This rebellious attitude was stirred up a little by remarks, mainly from Billy and Gerry, that this should have been done earlier before conditions had got so bad, and that the skipper should be made to stew in his own juice. Eventually, after some chivvying by the mate and the bosun, the more rational members started to make a move, saying we had better get it done before things got completely out of hand.

It was at times like these that my pal Charlie and I tended to stick together; our mutual familiarity often helped when working in difficult situations. Out on deck there was plenty of water slopping over the rail, but by working as a team the men soon had the net lashed up and secured; then we turned to the fish, which was on the weather side. By now the wind was screaming, with plenty of heavy water thrown aboard amidships and aft side; but where we were on the fore-deck the rail was higher and the ship more buoyant, so only the tips of the waves were lapping over. Yet this was still enough to slop the fish and us around. The amount of spray flying around was making the eyes sting and the nose run, and you constantly blew and spat the saltwater from your lips as it drained from the face. Non-stop, inventive cursing of the sea, the place and the job helped us complete the task, until the last fish was below and we could fasten the hatches and scamper off deck for another brief rest.

Gutting gloves were changed for mittens, ready to take the trawl on board again, but the order didn't come immediately, as the ship was performing violently and we figured that the skipper was waiting for a lull in the weather to give us the chance to haul the trawl back safely.

On the bridge, Larsen was wrestling with the wheel and watching both the weather and the sounder, trying to keep the ship on good ground until there was a break in the raging wind. To come fast with the gear on the bottom now would be treacherous. The mate joined the skipper on the bridge in case help was needed, and both scanned the sky to wind'ard, looking for a sign of a break that would give us a chance to scramble the gear aboard. But there was no such encouragement. In fact, the wind screamed harder and Larsen was getting very worried. Reports from other ships, which were laid and dodging further round the coast, suggested that there was worse to come.

'We can't carry on like this,' he said to the mate, as he momentarily clung to the rolling bar beneath the bridge window and stared beseechingly out at the maelstrom before him. 'We'll have to try and get the gear aboard somehow.' But the wind was so strong now that it was tearing at anything that was movable. The stays and wires from the mast were singing, dragged tight as bowstrings by the snarling rush of air.

The ship was listing permanently to one side, pushed over by the force of the wind. Then a phenomenon started to develop which none of us had ever seen before. The weight of the wind was so great that it actually forced the swell down; the waves were flattened and only a turbulent white spume covered the sea. The mate and skipper looked around in sceptical disbelief. Although the wind was still buffeting the windows with frightening ferocity and threatening to push them in, and the ship was laid over a little, there were no seas running and crashing aboard, just this white foam whipping across the water. As this continued for more than five or ten minutes, the skipper must have thought that his prayers had been answered, but not in the way he had hoped.

'This might be our chance,' roared Larsen. 'Get the boys out there quick and start hauling.' With that, he reached over and rang the telegraph for stand by. As the mate grabbed his sou'wester and turned to leave, the skipper added, 'Be extra careful out there. You've got extra men, use them.' The mate nodded and dashed from the bridge.

When the men in the mess-deck heard the telegraph ring in the engine room, everyone's heart missed a beat. OK, this is it.

The winchman for this haul got to his feet to don his sou'wester and mittens, and his watchmate prepared to stand by the towing block, as the first step to hauling back the gear. Just then, the mate burst into the mess and, bearing in mind what the skipper had said, he warned the men what to expect.

'Right, there's no swell much at the moment. But the wind is powerful and it will take charge of you if you're not prepared. That's why I want two of you to go to the winch. Someone else can go to the block. You can get down the leeside. Be careful.'

The two men left the mess-deck and the mate's eyes settled on Charlie, for no other reason than that he was the nearest. 'You can knock out, Charlie,' he said, 'and again take someone with you.'

Charlie glanced at me, but I was already preparing to follow him. We waited a minute to give the other men chance to get to the winch, and then we moved out down the alleyway. As we approached the open doorway at the end, there was a constant howl or moan from the entrance, and we could almost see the wind rushing past it. Charlie stepped out with care, keeping a hold on the edge of the entrance, and it was a good job he did, as the wind snatched at his oilskins and nearly dragged him away, until he was able to brace himself better and lean further into the wind. He opened his mouth to say something, then gasped and closed it immediately. When I – better prepared – stepped out, I could see why he didn't speak. You could not face the wind; it just blew the air out of your lungs. You had to turn at least sideways on and dip your head into the blast in order to breathe.

The hundreds of metres of warp that pulled the gear along the seabed passed through a towing block that hung over the ship's rail aft, thus allowing the ship manoeuvrability. When the winchman shipped up (connected it to the warps), a man aft would lever open the block allowing the gear to be hauled back. This was Charlie's job.

The order to knock out normally comes from the skipper, but in these conditions a pop on the ship's whistle was the sign. On hearing the whistle, Charlie moved towards the ship's rail, still leaning into the wind. He carried a crowbar to lever open the block; but, as both hands were needed to handle the crowbar, he couldn't hold his position on the little platform inside the bulwarks. This was where I came in. Putting my shoulder against his buttocks, I held him up to the rail, supporting him against the incline of the listing ship and the force of the weather. Such was the weight against the ship that the warps were leading out at a sharp angle from the rail, pulling the block out nearly horizontal.

We knew that this was dangerous; there had been cases in the past when the strain had been so great that the block and chain were thrown inboard on release, on one occasion smashing into the face of the decky releasing it. Charlie and I tried to protect ourselves by part-sheltering behind a boat-deck stanchion when the safety pin was withdrawn. Then, with a heavy tug from Charlie, the block flew open with a bang, slamming itself downward against the ship's side, as the warps sprang out into the frothing sea and the men at the winch began heaving the gear back to the surface.

Heaving the trawl up would take ten minutes, so Charlie and I scuttled back into the companionway, gasping for breath. The other men came out of the mess-deck into the passageway, wrapping mufflers around the neck and lower face and donning sou'westers, preparing for battle. 'What's the fucking score out there then?' we were asked.

'Fucking pollute,' panted Charlie. 'There's no heavy water coming aboard yet, but you can still hardly stand with the bastard wind throwing yer about. You'll soon be knackered working in these conditions, I can tell yer.'

'And you're gonna need your muffler over your nose,' I added, 'because this wind sucks the air out of your lungs as soon as you step outside.'

'Brilliant!' blurted Gerry Grey. 'This is going to be some fucking pantomime getting the gear aboard this time. That's if we can do it.' Then, with a sag of resignation, he continued, 'Come on then, let's get at it. And watch yourselves. Don't take any chances for this cunt.'

Making our way along the deck was difficult. We had to hang on to every handhold and drag ourselves along. Continuing sheets of spray were sweeping across the deck, filling the air and slashing the eyes, making it difficult even to see as far as the fo'c'sle head. I tried to look to wind'ard, but I could only manage quick glimpses, and then I'd have to turn away to catch my breath. How we were going to get the gear aboard working like this was a mystery.

The warps were stretched out taut at right angles to the ship; and the trawl doors, each weighing over three-quarters of a ton, broke the surface of the sea at least thirty yards from the ship, spinning and swaying with the strain from the dragging net and bobbins behind. I could just make out sou'westered heads tilted into the wind, peeping out round the corner of the casing side behind the winch as they tried to control the ascent of the swinging doors towards the gallows sheaves. This was achieved with difficulty, but even when the doors were tight up it was impossible to get the hanging chain through their brackets because they were being dragged out at such a high angle.

Men tried to climb up the gallows frames to reach the heavy chains, but they were just being blown off; many attempts to support or help were frustrated as men fell to the deck gasping and exhausted. The noise was terrific as the wind still raged around us and we tried to work out a way to secure the doors – essential before we could retrieve the rest of the gear. Eventually, weary of trying to communicate in the difficult conditions, the men scrambled off the deck into the accommodation to regroup and catch their breath.

Larsen, on the bridge, was horrified at seeing his men leave the deck with the gear still suspended and the ship in a vulnerable position. From the comparative comfort of the bridge, he had been trying to give orders through the intercom, which had speakers for'ard aft and behind the winch, but the howl of the wind and the hiss of the spray made it difficult to hear them unless you were close by. Now he was reduced to popping on the ship's whistle to attract the mate onto the bridge.

The men stumbled into the mess, spluttering and blowing the draining salt water from their lips. No one removed a single item of their dripping waterproofs, as they just stood catching their breath and casting guilty looks at each other. It was against their code of practice to leave the deck with the job incomplete or without permission.

Eventually Gerry spoke, trying to justify our action. 'Fuck that for a lark,' he snarled. 'I don't mind being swilled about. You expect it at this game, but trying to work in these conditions is ridiculous. Lugs has pushed it too far this time. He's gonna lose someone at this rate. We've already had one man over the side. He just keeps shooting away in bad weather when everyone else is laid and dodging, then he leaves it to us to pick up the pieces...' No one replied to this statement. They knew it was true but it didn't help to dwell on it.

Just then the bosun stumbled into the alleyway and pushed past the few men who were lingering there. He had remained on deck trying to secure some of the wires that were swilling about and now he spoke. 'What are we larking at?' he snapped. 'What are you all doing in here? We can't leave the gear hung out like this. We've got to get those doors unclipped so we can get the trawl aboard.'

'Oh, yeh!' retorted Gerry. 'You tell us how. We can't even reach the doors with them stretched out from the ship like they are.'

'We'll have to try and pass a wire through the bottom gallus sheave, hook it on to the back strop of the door, and heave it down towards the rail so we can get the chain in. That's the only way,' the bosun explained.

'Do you realise the strain there'll be on the links?' responded Gerry. 'That'll be very dangerous.'

'It's all very dangerous. We knew that when we came out here,' he sneered in reply.

Before there could be any further exchanges, the mate pushed his way into the mess-deck, carrying a bottle of rum in one hand and a large tot glass in the other. 'The Old Man has sent you all a dram to give you a boost and says if you can get the gear aboard he'll send another down after.' With this, he started dishing large tots around to all hands.

'Oh, that's typical!' snorted Billy Fudge. 'The usual skippers' ploy. If there's a dirty or dangerous job to be done, they think they can soften you up with booze, but that don't impress me.' Still he took his glassful and downed it in one.

'Righto, me lads!' chirped the mate, as he was dishing out the last couple of drams. 'The wind's definitely easing now, so let's get this gear aboard and we might get a bit o' kip while it fines away. Let's get on with it now.'

The warming effect of the rum in our stomachs did the trick and once again we trooped out on to the screaming deck.

It was true the wind had eased just a little; it was still blowing hard, but it didn't swipe the breath out of our lungs so much when we faced it, and that made things bearable. We were able to secure the doors and heave the rest of the gear alongside; but, as the wind began to ease, the swell started to get up and the mounting rollers began to sweep aboard. As each swept towards the ship, the men working aftside watched them with a wary eye, dashing to and from the rail as the occasional one crashed aboard and caused them to leap for the comparative safety of the engine-room casing.

Three times the heavy bobbins were dropped aboard, but the fury of the swell dragged them back over the side. No one wanted to take the risk of securing them because that part of the deck was the most dangerous. Further aft you could leap for the casing top, further for'ard you could dash behind the winch, but in that position beneath the bridge veranda there was nowhere to run. I was among those working aft and I watched the frustration of the officers and others as the bobbins kept pulling out, holding up proceedings. Taking a chance, I suddenly saw an opportunity between seas to dash out and throw a chain around the bobbins when they dropped aboard for the fourth time. Some may say it was taking the initiative; others would say it was the stupidity of youth. All would agree it was a big risk; and I paid for it because, as I had to stoop to make the final hitch, I didn't see the fluid express flying towards the rail where I was working until there was a cry of 'WATER!' from my shipmates.

I leaped for the handrail on the accommodation side to prevent being swept away. That's where the huge wave caught up with me as it poured aboard, picking me up and smashing my chest against a roller sheave on the casing side, and breaking my vice-like grip on the handrail. Completely submerged in water for half a minute, I was swilled about like a strand of seaweed in the surging brine, until the water subsided through the rolling scuppers.

My shipmates aft, who had managed to leap onto the casing top above the water level, watched anxiously as I disappeared beneath the broiling waters. They were relieved to see my bedraggled body still remained when the waters subsided and jumped down to help me to my feet. The intense pain in my chest told me I had probably cracked a couple of ribs, and my arm was tender where the water had wrenched at it, trying to drag me clear, but the adrenaline was flowing so much that the pain was bearable. However, as I moved towards the rail with the other men to wrestle with the trawl, another sharp stab of pain made me hesitate and step back till I caught my breath. Immediately, there was a shout from the open bridge window directly above me. 'Come on, Dasher. Get stuck in. There isn't much time.' Good to tell the weather had eased if we could hear our tormentor again, and trust Lugs to pick me out. One of the deckies next to me, who realised the unjustness of this remark, shouted for him to get his head in, but the words were lost in the hurly burly of the action.

Men were being swilled about and knocked down all over the deck, some sustaining minor injuries, but this was no time to be nursing our wounds, as we rushed to scramble the net together, pulling with our hands until we could take the first heave on the bellies. Soon, in spite of the conditions, we were heaving the small amount of fish aboard, and the skipper could move his engines to bring the ship into the wind and under control.

When the fish was finally clear and the deck secure, and we could scramble out of the swilling water into the sanctuary of the messroom once more, we were able to remove our oilskin frocks and top gear and grab some much needed supper. The weather outside had turned squally, the wind easing for a few minutes and then screaming again with driving rain. The skipper, we guessed, was dodging the ship in towards the land for a lee until the forecast indicated better.

Now that we had eaten and could relax round the mess table till the next orders, my ribs were giving me a lot of pain. So I laid on my side to get some relief and in no time I was asleep.

Shortly after, Lugs Larsen came into the mess with the promised bottle, presumably as a peace offering. Although others were sagging across the tables, he spotted me laid out and sneered, 'What's wrong with him? Is he knackered?'

'No,' replied one of the lads. 'He's hurt his ribs, I think.'

'Well, he's never reported it to me,' continued the skipper. 'He'll get over it. Leave him where he is. The rest of yer can have a dram and then get turned in for a couple of hours till the weather improves.'

When he had left, the boys roused me and told me to get for'ard to my bunk with the rest of them for a well-earned break.

The trip wore on with plenty more incidents of foul or damaged gear, and Lugs continued to work me the hardest. I knew what he was doing. He was trying to regain his credibility by proving he had no favourites, and the manager's son meant nothing to him. But I knew he would be entirely different when we were ashore. Meanwhile the strain was beginning to tell on me, but I was getting close to my target so I was going to stick it out.

During the last day's fishing, while we were hauling, there was a loud bang and a gush of steam from the winch that brought it to a halt. Nothing could be done until the chief arrived on deck. He soon identified that the starboard cylinder had split. There was nothing he could do about it, so there would be no more fishing that trip. He blanked it off so we could get the rest of the gear aboard on one cylinder. That was a struggle, but the crew were pleased that we were going home.

During the homeward journey, the chief indicated that we would get extra days in dock this time because the winch job was a big one, even for the shore gang. This suited me fine because the extra time meant I stood a better chance of a full recovery.

Chapter 13

DISTRACTIONS AND DANGER ZONES

Although I was glad to be home, of course, things were looking pretty dull and quiet because none of my friends were around to have fun with. My sea-going pals were all away and even the shore-based buddies were away for various reasons – some on holidays, others on work-study courses.

So, apart from having the usual drink in one of the pubs with my shipmates after settling, I was left to mooch around on my own. Charlie had agreed to go with his father to visit his brother in Fleetwood, so I was happy to accept Dad's invitation to join him and Mum for a night out and a meal at a country club which was popular with both trawler skippers and fish merchants. What I didn't realise till we got there was that we would be joining Lugs Larsen and his wife and daughter at their table to celebrate his daughter's sixteenth birthday. We were also joined by a fish merchant and his wife, who were long standing friends of the family, thus making a table of eight.

We celebrated Christina's so-called coming of age with a drink at the bar. As usual Leif was gushingly cheerful and friendly with me, but I had no problem with that, as it was the same with most skippers when they were ashore.

Christina was vivacious, and flashed her eyes at me as I took my seat at the table, diagonally across from her. She preened herself and made sure her off-the-shoulder dress was a little more off the shoulder as she settled herself. There seemed to be a little smile of triumph playing about her lips as she hitched herself up alongside her mother, I didn't know why. Perhaps she was aware of the impression she was making, with her silky blonde hair flowing to her bare shoulders and that inward curl framing an angelic face. The dress she was wearing was a pale, peachy colour with a frilly top and a decorated bodice, gathered tightly round a ridiculously narrow waist, and a knee-length skirt with a bit of a flare to it. Christina didn't have a large bosom but it was very prominent; her breasts stuck out like two mini-pyramids and were probably unfettered – so sharp that I thought she could skewer the bread roll on her side plate if she leant far enough forward.

As the meal was served, the wine flowed freely and the conversation was cheerful and animated. Leif couldn't resist telling a couple of sexy jokes, and as the final course came along the cabaret started. This was a guitar-playing singer who also told a few jokes; some of these were a bit near the bone, but by this time no one cared anyway.

As soon as the act was finished, the resident band took over and a few people got up and took to the floor. With a glance at me, Christina announced that she would like to dance. Without hesitation, Christina's mum and my parents prevailed on me to accommodate her. A waltz was playing. Fortunately, my many boozy visits to various dancehalls had eventually taught me both this and the foxtrot, so I allowed myself to be pushed off my seat and towards the floor, where the lovely Christina joined me. I must admit my desire to get my arm around that tiny waist overcame any trepidation I might have had about my dancing. Christina, too, showed enthusiasm; as soon as I took her right hand and slid my arm under her left she moved in close to my body with a bump, as if a magnet had drawn her. My partner might have had a tiny waist, but it gave way to well-rounded hips, firm buttocks and shapely thighs, which were well entwined with my own as we moved around the floor.

Christina was soaking it up as we swayed together. She allowed her forehead to rest against my jawline, and her hair smelt so fresh in my nostrils it made me catch my breath. I had to speak to break the spell.

'Well now!' I murmured. 'Sixteen, eh! I guess that makes you a young woman now then?' Christina lifted back her head and looked up at me. I was transfixed by the lovely Cupid's bow of her slightly pouting lips. Those eyes were still smirking.

'It means I've reached the age of consent, if that's what you're getting at.' The smirk increased as she returned her head to my cheek.

The way our bodies moved against each other was now becoming so suggestive that I had to cut the dance floor in half and work the half furthest away from the prying eyes of our parents. Someone once said that ballroom dancing was a navel engagement without loss of semen.

I was thinking that if Christina continued to rub the swell of her lower abdomen against my upper thigh whilst massaging my crotch with her right hip, then I would prove that statement wrong.

A foxtrot followed two waltzes; I had never been so long on a dancefloor with the same partner. Then they announced a quickstep. For one reason or another, I was already breathing heavily, so I suggested to Christina that we sat that one out. Reluctantly, she agreed, though I think she would have preferred more time to rub up against me to better determine the firmness of my desire.

When we returned to the table, three or four of our group were engaged elsewhere, so Christina took the opportunity to sit alongside me. We joked and I teased her that she was becoming a seductress when she slid her arm in mine and offered a gentle kiss on my cheek.

'Not at all,' she countered. 'Just a thank you for a very enjoyable and interesting twenty minutes!'

Christina made it clear that she wanted to see me again soon. She was at college and had a day off the next day, though in the evening her family were entertaining some relatives from out of town. She asked if she could visit me at home. Chris knew that she had to move quickly as my time ashore was limited. I wasn't so keen for our families to see us so closely associated, as a pair that is. I wasn't sure why. Maybe because she was a bit young, though there was little more than two years between us. Or maybe because Lugs Larsen was her father, and if he thought we were dating he might use or hold this against me.

Anyway, I tried to discourage her a little, saying that I was going to be busy on the dock in the morning, while in the afternoon I was going to take my dog for a long walk, as I had promised to do at least once between trips.

We lived on the edge of town now and I loved to take Rex rambling over the fields. Christina also lived on the edge of town and not too far away. She offered to cycle over and join me for the walk. I figured that would be OK, and we left it at that.

The rest of the group came back to the table and Christina returned to her seat.

The next morning I decided to go to the Nautical School and see my old tutor Mr Glanville, who had taken me through my decky learner's ticket, and subsequently my first-class net-mending ticket, and had given me such encouragement to press on and sit for my officers' tickets. Now I had some considerable sea time under my belt, I intended to ask him how best to proceed. He was extremely pleased to see me and advised me to go to the pool office to get my official sea time accumulated, then on to the company office to see if they were prepared to give me the special recommendation which would allow me to sit for my bosun's ticket one year early. I thanked him and promised to keep him informed of my progress, then I proceeded to the Fish Dock.

The fishermen's pool was set up by the trawler owners to register the number of days each fisherman spent at sea in order to gauge holiday entitlement. Every trip on any ship with the number of days at sea was recorded for each seaman, and they were easily able to tell me the number of days I had accumulated in total. When they presented me with the information, I was delighted to see that I needed only ten more days to complete the three years I required. One more trip would be more than sufficient.

I was cock-a-hoop that I had got my time in so quickly, but now I had to see if the firm would back me.

I moved on down the dock towards the company offices. I had decided not to involve my father in any way and would approach the enquiry window for advice like any other employee, even though most of the staff knew me.

It was near the end of the week, when there were usually few landings and things were relatively quiet; but, as I passed the offices of a smaller trawling company, somebody stepped out into the road and approached me with hand extended and a smile on his face. I viewed him with a suspicious eye. I knew him alright, though we had only sailed together for one trip. His name was Teddy Turner, known as Tacky Turner, and he was a fireman who never seemed to hold down a job for more than one trip. I had sailed with him on my second trip in the *Apollo*. He'd had a few kind words for me when I was finding things a bit tough, but I had been paying for it ever since.

Hovelling, as it was known, was a widespread practice on the dock among fishermen. A crewman who had recently landed would often give a backhander to an old shipmate who was less fortunate, and Teddy had taken his share out of me over the years. As he was nearly always out of a ship, he had managed to catch me every two or three trips on the strength of that one trip we had sailed together.

I had given in to him because I didn't want to appear aloof in any way in view of my father's position, and here he was again trying his luck with me. He greeted me enthusiastically.

'Now then, young Dash. You're looking good. Have yer just landed?'

'Oh hiya, Teddy,' I said, taking his hand. 'No, we landed early in the week but we're in for a few days with a winch job.'

'Well, that's good,' continued the smiling cadger. 'Did yer make a good trip?'

'Well, not bad as things go. Nothing special, but you earn it with Lugs Larsen.'

'Oh, fucking 'ell! Are you with 'im?' Teddy tossed his head in sympathy. 'I'm surprised that *you* chose to go with Lugs.' Again that suggestion that I could choose. 'Mind you, he may be a bit mad, and he does work you hard, but you usually make a krone or two, if you can stick it. Now I've had it tough since I last saw you, I've been ashore for seven weeks.' Teddy let this last, sad remark sink in. 'You haven't got the price of a drink yuh could let me have, have yer? You know I'd do the same for you if you was out of a ship.'

Although I knew the chance of that happening was as remote as hitting an iceberg in the Humber, I gave in to him and slipped him a ten-bob note just to get rid of him. I didn't want anything to delay my intention to progress my future today.

Teddy soon took off when he had got what he wanted. Wishing me luck, he departed and I proceeded to the office. When I arrived I didn't even approach Gibby's office. I went straight upstairs to the cashier's office and knocked on the enquiry window. One of the cashiers answered and recognised me immediately.

'Oh hello, Bob! What can I do for you?' he smiled.

'Hi, John! I was wondering if you could help me. I've got a fair amount of sea time in now and I was hoping to sit for my bosun's ticket early, which I can do if I can get a letter of special recommendation from the company. Can you tell me how I might do that?'

John smiled even more broadly. 'Well, if you've got good reports of conduct in your discharge book, and you've sailed for this company most of your time, which I know you have, and you're sure you have enough sea time, then you must write to Mr Price, the company secretary, and ask him if he will recommend you. I'm sure he will, if you write it properly.'

So that was it. I thanked him and departed.

I vowed to put the letter together as soon as I got home, but could I submit it before I completed my time? That was the question. I figured that Mr Price would not bother to check on my time; he would be more interested in checking my discharge-book reports. As good old Tommy Nighty had given me excellent reports while I was with him, I thought they would be satisfactory, so I decided to put the letter in just before we sailed. Maybe then it would be ready for me when we came back.

That afternoon was fine and sunny, a lovely day. Father was out at work and my sister was cleaning the house and fussing around Mother. I had told them I would be taking the dog for a walk later and I busied myself tidying up the garden until I saw Christina dismounting at the gate. She greeted me with a lovely smile and she looked so fresh and pretty. She was wearing a white blouse with a short pleated grey skirt, a bit like a gymslip, and she had short white ankle socks and sandshoes on her feet. I took her bike and put it behind the garage. Then I called Rex, who was playing with a ball, and we set off down the country road.

I strode out steadily downhill, throwing the ball occasionally for Rex to chase. Christina was happy and gay, sometimes skipping alongside me like a little girl, throwing her arms about and flicking her skirt up, sort of accidentally, to show a fine, shapely leg. Sometimes she swung on my arm, clutching it to her chest, and causing her low-buttoned blouse to billow out and show that she wasn't wearing a bra. She giggled when she saw my eyes flick downwards at the extra flesh exposed.

'Oh, Bob! Isn't it lovely to get out in the countryside, where it's so quiet and peaceful. Where you can take in the fresh air and feel the sun on your skin,' she cooed.

'Well, the sun seems to be getting to plenty of your skin,' I quipped, 'but it certainly is warm.'

'No wonder. You've got too many clothes on,' she giggled again. 'You should take them all off.'

'Oh yeah! Fine, I'd soon get arrested,' I replied in mock shock, 'walking along the road in the nude.'

'Well, let's get off the road,' she retorted.

'We will do shortly,' I said, 'but I won't be taking my clothes off.'

'Maybe not,' she countered, 'but you can take your shirt off and get some sun.'

'Maybe,' I murmured dreamily.

At the bottom of the hill, we crossed a slightly busier road and picked up a bridle path that climbed up another hill past an open pig farm. There was a large field with numerous little, round corrugated-tin sheds, and outside nearly every one was a sow with a litter of piglets fussing round or feeding.

'By! Look at that lot,' I remarked. 'There must be hundreds of 'em. What a life having to cope with those little devils all day.'

'Not a bad job for the hogs though,' chuckled Chris. 'They'll have been hard at work as well. Must be this country air that makes them frisky,' she added, with a cheeky sideways glance at me.

We climbed on up to the top of the hill; the bridle path curved away to the right, but ahead of us was a break in the hedge with a stile into the meadow beyond.

'Well, give me your hand then and help me, like a gentleman,' said Chris, as we moved towards it.

I took her hand as she stepped up on to the platform; then she turned towards me as she brought her knee up and lifted her foot over the fence, giving me a lovely flash of her inner thigh, almost to the top. Christina jumped down on the other side and swaggered away without waiting for me, knowing she had caught my interest again.

As I followed her, I observed the confident swing of her hips and was intrigued at the constant change in her as she moved from girl to woman and next minute back to girl again. I watched the light breeze rippling her blonde hair, caught the slimness of that waist again and the shapely legs. Christina was lovely; she knew it and exploited it, but it was good for a girl to know she was pretty sometimes.

This meadow was a large one which swept down the other side of the hill towards another road, before it started to climb gently again across the more manicured land of a stately home. Down at the bottom left-hand corner of the meadow were some horses near a gate and a water trough close by. We walked to the right, along the top of the meadow where there was a small copse of trees a quarter of the way down. I threw the ball for Rex past Christina and then chased after it with him. He got to it first and chased away with it before bringing it back to me. Then I threw it again, still walking on. Christina tiptoed up behind me and pulled my shirt right up from the waist

'Come on. Let's have this shirt off and let the sun get to that pale skin,' she admonished.

'Hey, Cheeky!' I cried in mock outrage. 'How would you like me to do that to you?' I made a lunge at her, and she skipped away with a shriek,

'Don't do that. I've got nothing on underneath,' she giggled.

'I know,' I said with a leer, 'but neither have I.'

'Ooh – risque!' she taunted with a rise of the eyebrows.

I chased after her, but she was too quick for me, and as my shirt was flapping I undid the buttons and peeled it off. It's true that the last three years in the Arctic had left my skin rather pale, but the constant hard labour had firmed up the muscles in my body, and Christina had to comment.

'Hmmm – not bad!' she viewed me with a critical eye. 'That's if you like alabaster figures.'

I chased her again, looking for retribution, and as she ran from me she tripped and fell down on the edge of a grassy hollow. I threw myself down on her and pretended to pin her down but she just threw me off and rolled away, expecting me to follow. Instead I just laid on one elbow and admired her as she laid back with her blouse billowing and her skirt halfway up her thighs. She made no attempt to adjust her dress and just laid there with a devilish twinkle in her eye, assessing her next move. I pretended to lose interest and started juggling with Rex's ball.

Then we started a game played by courting couples all over the world – 'wrestle for the ball'.

Christina lurched forward and tried to pinch the ball, which I held away from her. Then, as she lunged again, reaching for my arm, she plonked her supporting hand right into my groin. I let out an 'Oouf!' of surprise. She must have been studying it because she scored a bull's eye and gave a little squeeze before withdrawing. Was she sampling the goods? A glance at her showed a big grin, with her tongue just playing on her top teeth. Resuming the game, I continued to toss the ball up. Christina snatched at it, but didn't connect properly and knocked it away; it fell just beyond our feet down the slope. As I scrambled for it, she suddenly slid a little way down the slope and kicked the ball away. This caused her skirt to ride up, revealing some thin white panties stretched tightly over a fascinating bulge at the top of her thighs. There was just a hint of a dark shadow around a tell-tale crease at the bottom. I let my eyes feast on this for a few moments before looking up at Chris. She was not embarrassed at all. The twinkling eyes were challenging this time, the pouting lips were parted, then she gave a defiant little thrust of her pelvis.

That was it; I could resist no longer. There was no one around and the chances were if anyone came we would see them before they saw us in this hollow, so I quickly rolled over on top of her, placing one knee between her parted legs, and swooped in for those moist, inviting lips. Christina met me halfway and, placing her hand behind my neck, smothered my mouth with hungry kisses of desire. I put my hand behind her shoulder and pulled her close to me. She pressed tightly against my body and squirmed; she would know I was ready for love. Still kissing, my hand slipped round and flipped the top buttons on her blouse, then slid inside to caress the pink limpet that topped the lovely cream cone of her breast.

Chris responded with a little gasping moan. She may have been young, but she certainly knew how to enjoy herself. 'Ohh, Bob! I want you,' she muttered.

As my passion increased, I brought my hand down to the top edge of those white panties, which were still exposed, and slipped my fingers inside to explore the firm, downy swell of her pussy. At this stage our raging desire reached the point of no return. Trembling, I unbuttoned the front of my pants and pulling the leg of her panties to one side I entered her with a thrust. This time it was Christina's turn to gasp, followed by a series of moans. She was delicious. Wonderful sensations spread out from my groin and pulsed through my whole body, and with the sun warming my bare back I rode hungrily in a sort of delirium. I planted little kisses on her eyes, her cheeks and neck in a show of gratitude. She, in turn, rubbed her hands over my bare chest with her eyes closed as if to memorise every feature of our union.

Once sated, we clung to each other panting and basked in the afterglow of sex.

The clump of hooves and female voices told us that someone was using the bridle path at the other side of the hedge above us, and we quickly rearranged ourselves. Rex was laid stretched out on his tummy, panting. 'I hope he wasn't watching,' I remarked, 'he's too young.' Christina, still adjusting her skirt, giggled sheepishly. We set off back and as we walked on up the meadow I put my arm around her slim waist to reassure her. We were both happy in the thought that we had pleasured each other. As we walked hand in hand down the bridle path, still savouring the feeling of satisfaction, Christina told me that, as her dad wasn't sailing for two days, her parents were going to Grimsby the next day to spend the night with relatives and she had managed to opt out and stay at home studying.

Of course, she had to sleep overnight at an aunt's who lived locally; but she didn't have to do that till late and invited me to join her for a coffee in the afternoon.

This was news to me; I didn't know when we were sailing. But, of course, I hadn't been to see Gibby when I was last down the dock. No doubt he would ring me if I didn't check with him, or if Dad didn't pass on the information. Still, being bereft of friends, I couldn't think of a better way to spend the afternoon than being entertained by the lovely Christina in her home, especially if no parents were aware of it.

When we got back to the house, I retrieved Chris's bicycle from behind the garage. She suggested that she should pop in and visit my mother, but I didn't think this was a good idea. 'Too close to teatime,' I persuaded her. So, without more ado, she mounted her bike, gave me a meaningful glance, smiled and said, 'OK then, I'll see you tomorrow,' and rode off.

That evening, at tea, Dad told me that the ship would be sailing in a couple of days, and said I should get in touch with Gibby about signing on. He had also been told about my intentions to sit early for a bosun's ticket and wondered if I had enough experience yet. 'Well!' I said. 'Surely the thing to do is try and get the ticket first, then let the individual skippers decide when I'm good enough to go bosun.'

He appeared to agree. He just raised his eyebrows and shrugged, and then advised me how best to compose a letter for the company secretary.

The next morning, after contacting the ship's runner, I was advised to sign on the next day, the day before we sailed; most companies wouldn't let you sign on too early to save on wages. I spent the rest of the morning collecting together my freshly washed gear and made a start packing my kitbag myself, as I usually did.

That afternoon I went down to the Larsen's big house, making sure the big Rover that Leif Larsen drove wasn't in the drive before approaching the front door.

The melodious chimes brought a smiling Christina to the door. This time she was wearing a cotton-print summer dress, with a wide collar and white buttons right down the front.

She took me into the lounge with its large easy chairs and sat me down on the broad leather sofa. One or two reference books and a ruled notebook littered the floor, which showed she had made some attempt at studying. The room was filled with swinging music from Chris's portable autochange record player, which was running through some extended play discs. Guy Mitchell was belting out 'Roll a Silver Dollar' as I settled down to enjoy Christina's charms. She offered me a beer, which was a good start; I accepted gratefully and noted that she poured herself a shandy – a smart move if there was going to be any kissing.

After the ecstasies of the previous day, we both had the same thing at the back of our minds, and it didn't take long to get to the wrestling stage, where I tried to get a handful of breast and Chris was trying to rub up against me and arouse me once more. We both had some success, which left us hot, sweaty and excited. I had Christina's arms crossed in front of her, held from behind, and our cheeks were close together. I looked at her, hot and flushed, eyes sparkling, body aroused and I could not resist kissing her on her neck. Then, to explain myself, I said, 'There, you see, you're completely in my power. I could do anything I like to you?'

'Ooouwww!' crooned Chris. 'Promises, promises.'

That did it again. As far as I was concerned, that was a definite invitation. I threw my little Lolita down on her back on the sofa in a no-nonsense fashion and began to undo the buttons of her dress. She just laid there, offering no resistance as she squeaked in a tiny voice, 'Oh! No! No! What's happening?' in the style of an early-twenties film heroine. I peeled back both sides of her dress and revealed that sylph-like figure, wearing nothing but a pair of shaped panties. Christina laid with her knuckles pressed to her cheeks, her arms pushing out her breasts, and a quizzical look on her face.

I leaned forward and kissed her. Then hooking my fingers into the top of her panties, I pulled them down. Chris eased her bottom up to assist in the process and her bristling bush was revealed. I pulled the panties off and modestly stuffed them under a cushion.

My excitement was leg-trembling. I undid my trouser buttons, let them drop and kicked them off. Then I pulled down my underpants and my manhood sprang free. For the first time, Christina could observe what she was about to receive. She took a good look and let out an appreciative 'Wow.' Then she surprised me by taking hold and guiding me into her.

I sank into her gently and completely and as I did so Christina let out a long, low, satisfying moan. I was beginning to wonder just how much experience Christina had and who was seducing who.

We rolled around on the sofa and squirmed and humped vigorously. Then we finished up on the floor and Christina wrapped her legs around me. Her slim waist, flat stomach and fleshy thighs continued to motivate me until we collapsed in a heap, exhausted. Finally, Chris pushed herself away from me. Jumping up, she collected her dress and scampered up the stairs, calling for me to wait a few minutes as she disappeared.

Strangely my underpants were still around my ankles. I pulled them up and redonned my trousers. After a few minutes, Christina called me from upstairs and asked me to join her. Tentatively, I climbed the stairs and found her in the bathroom. She was submerged in a bathful of soap suds, with a big grin on her face. Gaily she called for me to strip off and join her in the tub. 'Come on, Bob. It'll be fun,' she begged me.

Guilt was already setting in and being caught naked in a bath with her, if some relative should come to the door, was a position that would be difficult to explain, so I declined.

'I think I'd better not, Chris,' I said. 'I've had a wonderful afternoon and you've been lovely. You're something special, but I think it's time for me to go today.'

'Oh no! Don't go just yet. We're just getting to know each other. Get in here with me and let me love you more. Don't worry, no one will come.'

'Chris, I really think we've got to know enough about each other for the time being, and I've got to go. But thanks, darl.'

I stepped forward and bent down and kissed her. She made a grab at me to try to pull me in, but I jumped back quickly and waved an admonishing finger at her.

'You see, I've already got to know you better than you think. Bye, darl. Maybe see you next trip.' And with that I left.

I met Charlie the next morning down at the company yard. 'Now then, this has been a smashing break, hasn't it,' he enthused. 'Me and mi brother had a great time with some birds we met at a club. We took them home and, although we didn't have it away, there was plenty of groping and a bit of stink finger. I wet mi pants a couple of times. How's it been for you. Did yer see any of the boys?'

'No, they're all away,' and I explained the situation. I wasn't going to tell him about me and Christina, in case he let it out on the ship. In fact, I wasn't going to tell anyone about Christina.

'To tell the truth,' continued Charlie, 'I wasn't going to sign back on with this bloke anymore, but I'm skint now, and I didn't fancy being at home without any cash while I look for another ship, so I'm going back for one more, but that's all.'

'Same here,' I agreed. 'I'm only doing one more, but better not let Gibby know.'

Surprisingly, most of the previous crew went back. Strange what a break at home can do.

One bit of good news that came out was that we were not going to Iceland this trip. Instead we were going to Bear Island, which was 1500 miles north, way past the north tip of Norway. Not so good in the winter, but in the summer not so bad. It meant that we were longer running off, which gave us more time to prepare the gear, and the grounds were much easier, being mostly soft mud. You rarely did damage to the trawl up there. In fact the deckies called it skipper learner's ground. There was plenty of fish reported at the moment, so we crossed our fingers for an easier trip.

Whoosh! 'There she blows again,' cried Charlie, as we stared out over the dipping rail into the swirling fog at the bulging bag of fish that leapt out of the water like a breaching whale and laid out on the surface of the bobbing, grey sea.'Another two hundred baskets by the look of it.' He grimaced as we pulled back on the quarter ropes that were winding off the whipping drums of the winch, lifting the bobbins to the ship's rail. We were into our third day's fishing, and we had been heaving this amount of fish on board with every haul since we started. With only two hours towing each time, it meant that we never cleared the previous haul's fish before we were hauling again. As a result, the fore-deck was plastered four-feet deep in fish from starboard to port.

Already I was tired out. We had picked up fish from our very first haul, so our illustrious skipper decided to give us a good start by working all hands for twenty-four hours before starting the watches. That meant that the first watch below had been up for twenty-four hours before they slept; and, by the time we completed the eighteen-hour cycle, the last watch, which included me, had been doing forty-two hours of hard labour before they squeezed in their five hours sleep. I had managed one nap in the last three days. Of course, I had experienced this sort of thing before as a decky learner, but a deck-hand has a greater work load, especially if he is being spot-balled by those in charge.

A lot of fish over a wide area usually meant a lot of ships, and there were hundreds of them, of all nationalities. Yet, because of the fog, we on deck were hardly aware of them, except when they slid silently into view at close quarters like great predators. With the advent of radar, ships' sirens were seldom heard. The man on the bridge had to pick and talk his way through the dozens of targets showing on his radar screen, and still make sure he put his gear down in the correct water where the fish were thickest.

For the men on deck, wallowing about in thigh boots and waterproofs in four feet of fish, trying to pull wires, bobbins and net around at the double was very exhausting. Usually we were glad to see the gear go back over the side, even though it meant there was more fish to gut.

'The trouble with this amount of fish around,' remarked Charlie, 'is that everyone is catching it and that means the markets will be down by the time we come to land.'

'That's always been the problem,' I agreed, as we watched the gear sinking back below the surface.

'I guess we'll just have to make sure we've got our share when the time comes.'

I was watching the clock at this time, just counting down the last couple of hours before watch time when I could rest my weary body.

With the gear lowered down into the water, the ship began to swing round and line up on its course to shoot. Once the skipper had picked his spot, he rang the engines on full speed and steered the ship as straight as possible while the warps were being paid away. To deviate too much from a straight course could result in foul gear, and with the warps streaming over the side towards aft, close to the starboard rail, to go to port was out of the question. Or was it?

I was among the gutting squad, making its way towards the fish mountain on the fore-deck, when the ship's whistle began to sound frantically. We looked up and looming out of the fog was a big German vessel, crossing our head from port to starboard. It must have started to come round at the same time as we started to shoot and was now too close for us to pull away to starboard and try to cross its bow. We just had to go to port or hit it.

I looked on in horror as the ship's head started to swing to the left, with the warps still streaming over the side, when suddenly there were two bangs in quick succession, and the thick wires slumped to the deck as the winch drums slowed to a stop.

'Oh no! Not both of them,' cried the third hand, jumping from behind the winch to look in disbelief over the rail towards aft. 'We've lost the lot.'

Ranting and raving could be heard from our bridge, as the German trawler slid harmlessly by down the starboard side and disappeared again into the fog.

The enormity of the disaster was hard to take in. By altering to port while shooting, the warps going over the starboard side had been forced under the ship, to be chopped by our flailing propellor. We were left with two bare ends.

The crew were dazed and numb, trying to assess the size of the task that now faced us. We had not only lost all the net but also all the ironwork, wires and working gear that went with it, including the two huge otter doors and half the warp. The cost of replacing a complete gear was enormous, not only in terms of money but also in time, man hours, effort and sweat. This was stuff that largely remained in place trip after trip.

When the skipper finally came to his senses and realised the amount of time it was going to cost us to put another gear in place while all this fish was available, he immediately stopped the watches again. Even with all hands it was going to take us from fourteen to eighteen hours to complete the job. I nearly died when they called the watch out again, and I knew that I would have to keep going for another eighteen hours without rest.

All the gear required would have to be taken across the fish from for'ard, or from the port side, and brought amidships on the starboard side to be reconstructed. All day we toiled, dragging the various items over the fish pounds, and saw all that lovely, fresh, firm, shiny fish deteriorate in to a soft, sloppy, rust-stained glop, which would still be put below.

But that was the least of our worries. In my case, it was staying on my feet and finding enough strength to compete and not show myself up by slacking in the heavy work – not that I would be allowed to do that. After about seven or eight hours, the bobbins and net were in place and the spare doors had been hove across. Now there was the heavy wireware, the hundreds of fathoms of warp and cables, to be pulled up out of the dill.

The dill, or lower hold, lies, of course, beneath the normal net-hold, right down in the bowels of the ship. It has a depth of only five feet and usually has water swilling about in the bottom, so it's only used for wires whose lead content tends to fend off rust. The problem is, it is fifteen feet below the deck hatch, which is a hell of a length for heavy wire to be pulled up by hand, as was the case here. There were only two bare, raggy ends dangling from the winch drums, so this could not be used to heave the wire out and it was a case of manual labour as usual. The trouble was I became the manual labour thanks, once again, to interference from our master.

As soon as the fog had lifted enough to see two miles, Lugs Larsen had started roaming around the deck, forcing the issue and pushing the men harder. When he saw the magnitude of this particular job, he selected two big lads, including me, to pull the cables and warp up on to the deck.

At first, my buddy and I worked side by side, bending over the hatch and pulling this heavy three-inch cable up from fifteen feet below, hand over hand. It was exhausting work; my shoulders were being pulled out of their sockets and the muscles in my forearms were numb. There was a man down in the hold reaching into the dill to flip the coils over, and a man behind us on deck coiling the awkward wire down. Eventually we managed to pull up two fifty-fathom cables which had been laying on top of the spare warp, a full 280 yards of wire. At this point, Lugs decided that my fellow labourer should be rested, and he changed places with the man behind us. I thought that I too would change with the man down below, who admittedly was a good deal older, but it didn't happen. Instead he passed me the end of the first 100-fathom warp and we laboured on.

My new companion did not share the load as well as my first partner, and he kept turning round to try and supervise the coiling down, in spite of my wisecracks about doing one job at a time. Gasping, I continued to pull up a few fathoms of warp on my own. Then I stopped to see what the pair of them were doing behind me, still holding the weight of the wire in one hand. The man down below was still trying to flip the coils over in the dill and must have wanted a bit of slack, but without saying so he just tugged at the warp I was holding. In my exhausted state, it was enough to topple me over into the hold below. I fell without uttering little more than a squawk at the back of my throat; the man working below made more noise when he saw me hurtling past him. Fortunately, I landed on some net that had been piled to one side, but I hit it with a thump which shook every bone in my body and sent shock waves right through a system which was too weak to resist them. I lay stunned while the pain resonated through me over again.

When my eyes focused, I could see a number of heads peering down at me over the edge of the hatch coaming, whether from curiosity or concern I wasn't sure. Then appeared a face that did show concern, but for all the wrong reasons. Annoyance showed in the face of Lugs Larsen; and, when he saw I was not seriously injured, there followed the taunt.

'Vell now, what have ve here? Has young Dash fallen down on der job?' He grinned at his own quip. 'If it's too much for him, maybe ve'd better find him an easier one.'

I looked up at the man who had undoubtedly been my tormentor for the last couple of trips.

OK, he'd been tough on all of us, but I had been singled out for special attention of the undesirable kind. I thought how funny it was that he, who had been the cause of so much misery and pain for me, had also indirectly been the source of some joy, in the shape of a beautiful daughter who seemed keen to repeat our recent experiences. The thought occurred to me that I might just let that happen and I couldn't stop a smirk creeping over my face. It was a smirk that Lugs certainly observed and it appeared to puzzle him before he turned away.

Charlie was one of the last to appear at the hatchway, having been working aft. He enquired if I was alright and helped me over the hatch coaming after I had struggled up the iron-rung ladder. 'I'm OK, Charlie,' I told him, 'but I can't wait for this trip to finish this time. Then I'm out o'here.'

'You and me both,' retorted Chas, 'and we're not the only ones.'

When we did finally set off for home, Larsen's luck proved to have held out again for we were not so far short of being full up. There would certainly be a number of other ships who were not so well off, but their crews would be in a better state than ours and that's for sure.

'Well! Looks like this jammy bastard'll do it again!' remarked Charlie.

A crowd of us were swilling seagull shit off the boat-deck and boat covers, the price of a fine run home. It was the day before docking and Larsen had called all hands again to clean the ship throughout.

'Did you see? The markets are picking up again just before he docks,' he continued.

'I – Uhuh! Uhuh!' I struggled to answer, as a persistent cough overtook me. I'd had it for all the later half of the trip, and it was obvious I was run down and needed the break. I tried again.

'Well, it doesn't bother me, Chas,' I replied. 'If he scores, we do, and I reckon we've earned a decent reward after the graft we've put in this trip.'

'You what!' continued my mate. 'Whatever we pick up, it won't compensate for the way we've suffered this trip. We're certainly going to celebrate with the girls when we dock, eh Bob? But we'd better hang on to enough cash to last us while we find another ship, heh!'

'We-ell,' I mused, as I scrubbed at a persistent bit of dirt. 'Actually, Charlie, I won't be looking for another ship. I'm going to school to study for my bosun's.'

Charlie looked up at me in surprise. 'How are you gunna do that? You haven't got enough sea time.'

'Yes, I have,' I retorted, 'Don't forget, I started before you. If you get a recommendation from the firm, you can sit for bosun's with just three years sea time, and I've got that. I've checked with the pool office.'

'My!' Charlie pondered. 'You kept that quiet, didn't yer, young Dash?' There was a bit of a sneer in his voice as he used my nickname instead of my normal name.

'Well, you know how it is, Chas?' I explained. 'You never know what's going to happen till the time comes; anyway, the lads would only have ribbed me about it if they'd known.'

"I don't know how you can afford it, to stay home all that time, unless your old man is helping yer?' mused Charlie.

'No, I'm doing it all under my own steam. I've been saving a long time for this and the day after tomorrow I'm signing off, no matter *what* we make. Then it's all systems go for bosun.'

Chapter 14

THE FINAL PAY-OFF

Charlie was right. Larsen's luck had held out again; the fact was we made a super trip when we landed. Well over £10,000, and with the amount of fish we landed it meant the cod liver oil money was good too. Both Charlie and I picked up just under £60 after stoppages, equivalent to the average shoreman's wage for three months.

After we had settled, Charlie wanted to meet up for a drink once we had cashed our cheques at the company bank in town, but I opted to call for him that evening because I had things I wanted to do.

I knew that once my shipmates all met up in one of the pubs near the bank with a pocketful of money there would be a celebration, and plenty of booze and dubious birds would be the order of the day. I had more important things to do. It was not necessary for me to go in to town to cash my cheque. I had an account in a bank on Hessle Road, where I deposited the cheque and withdrew a quarter of its value. That would let me have a good time for a week or maybe two, if I didn't use too many taxis. Then, as it was nearly lunchtime, I made a beeline for the Nautical School and some advice from my mentor.

Mr Glanville had just dismissed a class of decky learners when I arrived and was gathering up some pieces of net. He greeted me cordially, but carried on with what he was doing. When I explained that I had got my sea time in, and my letter of recommendation, and wanted to start now to study for my bosun's ticket, he became more enthusiastic. He would get more interest from taking someone through the many sections of a bosun's license, which extended from chart work to wire splicing, than from teaching a load of galley boys about deck work.

'So, you've got your reduced sea time now with a recommendation?'

'Yes,' I confirmed.

'Well, there are lots of things to do, but first we had better find the information in the rules that allows you to do it.'

'Where will I get that?' I enquired.

'I'm not sure,' pondered Glanville. 'It's not among my forms and papers; I checked when you were last in. Better go to the secretary's office in the main school building and see if she can find the sheet with it on. I know I've seen it somewhere.'

I visited the secretary and explained what Glanville had told me about special dispensation. She searched the rules regarding certification, but it only mentioned four years required for bosun and mate. Dejected, I returned to Mr Glanville and told him of the outcome. He was puzzled, he scratched his head. 'Well, I've seen it written down somewhere,' he insisted. 'Better leave it with me and I'll have a word with my colleagues. Come and see me tomorrow.'

I left the school completely deflated. If there was no rule that allowed me to sit for the ticket with only three years' sea time, I would have to do another year, which would seriously hamper my plan to be the youngest skipper. Surely I hadn't pushed myself all this time, only to find I couldn't sit. I didn't believe Mr Glanville could be wrong; he was too meticulous to make such a mistake. Unless, of course, the rules had changed.

That evening, I met up with Charlie and we elected to go to the theatre. The Tivoli had a variety show on with plenty of leggy chorus girls showing on the billboard. Of course, we visited the bar before the show started and only just managed to stagger out before the curtain went up.

The chorus line didn't disappoint us. There were some very pretty girls in the line-up and they gave the impression they were smiling straight at us, which was enough to keep us in our seats until the interval. Back in the bar, Charlie was lashing out on drinks and got chatting to four girls who were out on their own. After plying them with a couple of quick drinks, he offered to take them for a day out at the seaside the next day. This seemed to go down well, and one of the girls gave him her address, before the bell had them scampering out for the rest of the performance.

I tried to coax Charlie out too, but by this time he was chatting up the girls behind the bar, and as the room emptied he started buying champagne for them all. I wanted no part of this and left to take my seat, but Charlie didn't join me. It wasn't the same watching the show on my own; after fifteen minutes I went to look for him, but when I returned to the bar it was empty. There was no sign of Charlie; the night seemed to have fallen flat, and my persistent cough had come back, so I took a taxi home.

When I rose late the next day, I went to call for Charlie at his home. I was greeted at the back door by his mother, who was just leaving for the shops. She told me Charlie was still in bed.

'You can call him if you like, Bob. I've tried but it doesn't have much effect. I'm going out to do some shopping now, so I'll leave you to it.' She slammed the sticking back door as she left.

I meandered through to the bottom of the stairs and started shouting for Charlie to rouse himself. After two or three attempts there was finally a sleepy response and some sort of movement. Just then there was a knock at the front door, so I was obliged to answer it. When I opened the door, I saw a big Humber Hawk saloon parked outside; it would have held about six people in the back. The man on the step was telling me it was a taxi that had been ordered.

I passed this information on to Charlie and, shortly after, he came stumbling down the stairs in a vest, and the smart, silver-grey trousers from his suit, with their sharp creases, immaculate pleats and ticket pocket in the waistband. He was in his bare feet and his braces hung round his hips.

'What do you want?' he enquired of the taxi man.

'I'm here to pick you up, as ordered,' was the bright reply. 'You've ordered me for the day.'

'Well, you can sod off,' snapped Charlie. 'I've no money for a taxi.'

'It's already paid for,' the cabby reassured him. 'You paid me in advance.'

'Well, you can still sod off,' insisted Chas. 'I've no money at all and I'm not going to spend my day just cruising around in the back of a taxi. Go and have a day off on me.' With that he closed the door and slouched through to the living room, rubbing bleary eyes.

'NO MONEY AT ALL?' I reiterated. 'I hope that was an exaggeration for his benefit?'

'I'm afraid not,' said Charlie, clacking his tongue and looking around for something to drink. 'When I paid the other taxi off in the early hours of this morning, it only left me with some loose change.'

'But – but, you can't have spent all your settling in one day – surely,' I beseeched him.

'Must have – 'cos it's gone,' shrugged Charlie, settling for a swig out of the milk bottle.

'You won't have spent it,' I insisted. 'You must have given it away.'

'Dunno!' muttered Charlie in an uninterested fashion, as he grabbed two slices of bread for toasting. 'Can't remember.'

'Did you give any to your mother to look after?' I suggested hopefully.

'Oh aye!' Charlie assured me. 'I gave her ten quid as a backhander, but that was for herself to keep. I can't ask for any of that back.'

'So, what are you going to do?' I had to ask.

'Well, I've got enough money for a pint, so I'll go to the club this afternoon and have a game of snooker. Are you coming?'

I had agreed to see Glanville again at lunchtime, so I declined, but said I would join him some time in the afternoon. It was obvious that he didn't have enough to last that long, so I put my hand in my back pocket and threw him £5 on the table.

'Here,' I offered. 'You did all the spending last night and I hardly spent a thing, so this should see even you through the afternoon and tonight. I'm nipping off to Nautical School and I'll see you later.'

'Oh thanks, Bob,' Charlie shouted after me. 'I'll treat this as a loan and I'll pay you back when I can.'

I departed through the sticking back door.

My meeting with Glanville, when he broke off for lunch, didn't go any better than the day before. The other teachers didn't know where to find the information we were looking for, but his immediate colleague who taught the skippers and mates confirmed that he too had seen the clause Glanville referred to. Your best bet, he added, is to go to the people who set the examinations and issue the certificates, the Hull Trawler Owners' Insurance Company, and ask them.

It was pretty daunting for me to make my way up to those austere offices, housed in the Insurance Building at the entrance to the dock, where the men that controlled the whole of the sea-going personnel of the Hull trawling fleet resided.

I mounted the stairs to the first floor, where there was a reception area; two girls were typing at separate desks behind a raised counter. As I approached, one of them left her desk to attend to me. When I told her I required information about sitting for a bosun's ticket, she looked perplexed and asked her colleague who to refer me to.

The building was four stories high and contained all kinds of departments. The ground floor I was familiar with; it contained the medical centre and doctor's surgery, where the health of every trawler crew member was checked before signing on. Other departments included chart rooms and surveyors' offices, a radar and radio room, and various other departments needed for the control of a trawler fleet. All of this was headed by the managing director and chief examiner, Captain Beaumont, an ex-naval captain who had commanded a cruiser during the war. His assistant examiner was Commander Oswald, a pompous man, whose pedigree was less well-known. No wonder the girl was unsure who to turn to for such simple information. She opted to ask Oswald, as one of the examiners, and contacted him by intercom. After a brief conversation, during which she asked my name, I was instructed to go to his office, which was surprisingly close. I proceeded to the highly polished door she indicated to me and knocked, entering when instructed to do so.

I entered quite a large, fairly empty, room with a polished floor. Apart from some pictures of various modern ships on the walls, there were three high-backed easy chairs, one on each wall at either side, and one on the large rug in front of a substantial desk in the centre of the room. The only other item was a single filing cabinet to the left behind the desk. The man sitting behind the large desk was squat, of late middle age, and had greying hair which needed cutting, as it was hanging over his ears. His face was rough and weather-beaten, with piercing eyes. He was not exactly scruffy, but the suit was well worn and the collar on the striped shirt seemed a little too small; in fact, it stretched so tight around the neck that it drew wrinkles. He beckoned me towards him by flexing the fingers of one hand, rather like the Pharaohs or kings of old.

I advanced to within two or three feet of the desk.

'Now, what is it you want, young man?' The commander sat with his elbows on the desk, his hands pressed together at the fingertips, the forefingers tapping on his lower lip.

'Well, sir. I would like to sit for my bosun's ticket. I've been studying at every opportunity and I understand that, with a recommendation from the ship's company, it's possible to sit after only three years' sea time instead of the usual four.'

There was a pause while Oswald stared at me, then he spoke sharply. 'So you want preferential treatment, is that it?' The commander lifted his head for only five seconds, then continued to kiss the tips of his forefingers.

'No, sir!' It was obvious the commander knew who my father was, not surprising as he was well-known around the dock. 'It's just that I understood it was within the rules, but no one can tell me where it is written down.' Then as an afterthought, 'I figured if anyone knew the answer it had to be you.'

This did the trick. Without another word, Commander Oswald dived down into one of the drawers behind his desk, whipped out a sheet of paper and flourished it towards me on the desk. 'See this?' he asked, as I stepped nearer. 'This is an application form to test for a bosun's certificate.' Then again with a flourish he turned it over. 'And on the back is the clause which you seek.' He sat back in triumph.

I stooped and read the paragraph that stated exactly what I had been told. But what a place to put it, where it could be read only after the decision had been made to apply for examination.

Thank the Lord for Glanville's memory.

'Have you got what you wanted now?' boomed Oswald. It was difficult to think of him as a commander.

'Yes, sir. Thank you,' I beamed. 'Can I take this with me?'

'Well,' drawled Oswald, 'you shouldn't really. They're numbered and we're only supposed to give them out when you're actually applying.'

'Oh, I see,' I said hesitantly. 'Well, I'm going straight from here to school to study for this certificate. I hope it's not too long before I'm back.'

'Right,' snapped the commander. 'OK. Well, you'd better be especially good if you're trying to short-cut things because I'll be in charge of your exams when you return. Off you go.' And he dismissed me with a flap of the hand.

I danced down the stairs, out of the building and into the world beyond. I was so happy. My fears were groundless, I could sit for my ticket even at this early age, and I was confident I'd have all the answers when the time came. Don't you worry, Commander Os.

When I got back to the school and showed Glanville the sheet, he was delighted. 'I knew I'd seen it written somewhere,' he beamed, 'but I doubt if I've seen it there. I'm sure it used to be written elsewhere in the rules. They probably don't want to advertise the fact now. Anyway you've got the clearance you require, so get yourself off to the school secretary and pay your fee, then report back to me tomorrow and you can start.'

Later that afternoon, when I had completed the business, I went off to the local working men's club to meet Charlie, knowing I wouldn't be doing so anymore for a few weeks, not in an afternoon anyway. Charlie was following the horses being chalked up on a big board and listening to the commentary on the speaker. He was lucky enough to be £2 or £3 up with his gambling, but this didn't interest me in any shape or form, so I joined another ex-shipmate for a game of snooker. Eventually Chas came to inform me that the next race included a horse he had been following for some time, a dead cert that was going to clean up for him, and he tried to encourage me to join him in this chance of a lifetime.

He came over to the snooker table. 'Hey, Rob! Do you remember that horse I was telling you about all last trip?' Charlie paused while I confirmed that I did, without breaking my game. 'Well, at last it's running in this next race, so this is our chance. Give me your money and I'll put it on for yer.'

'It's OK, Chas. I'm not really bothered,' I tried to put him off.

'Not bothered! Are you kidding? This is the chance we've been waiting for. It can't lose. Give me your money and stop messing about.'

I realised that I'd have to placate him, so I broke off the game, dived my hand into my pocket and dug out two half-crowns. 'OK, here you are. Put half a dollar each way on it for me.' I offered it to him.

Charlie looked at me in dismay. 'You must be joking,' he sneered. 'I'm not going to fuck about with that. The price is only five to four on, that's how certain it is. Give me some paper money to put on for yer.'

To stop him pestering, I dug deep again and came up with a ten-bob note. 'OK,' I said, 'put this on any way you want to place it, but that's all I'm betting and that's final. Now let me finish the game.'

Charlie turned away in disgust. 'Well, if you want to miss out on a chance like this, that's your fault,' he muttered, as he moved off towards the bookie.

My snooker was looking good. I was making some good breaks and finished up beating Alfie, my opponent, who was no mug; and, as someone was waiting for the table, we sat down to finish our drinks. 'I wonder what's happened to the big pay-off?' I muttered to Alfie, who just grinned. Charlie was standing across the room with his back to us, staring up at the two or three blackboards where the results and prices were constantly being chalked up.

I studied him for a few moments. His broad, stocky figure, in his smart, double-breasted, silver-grey suit, with the twenty-two-inch trouser bottoms – the fashion of the day for fishermen – one hand in his pocket, the other clutching a half-empty pint glass.

Charlie had dark hair, combed straight back, and a rather square forehead, giving him an open, honest face, which was true to his character. He had a cheeky smile with strong teeth, spoilt only by his canines, which were larger than the norm and had the look of Dracula, or so the gang said. Yes, he may have had a weakness for gambling and squandering money, but that was because of his generous nature, and you couldn't have a more loyal or braver friend.

Once when we were at a dance at the notorious Scala ballroom, I was a little the worse for drink and made the mistake of chatting up the wrong bird. Before I realised what was happening, a great hefty brute had spun me round and cracked me on the jaw, putting me down in one. Charlie, who was close by, stepped in without hesitation and leaped on his massive back. Although barely half the muscle-man's size, he put a hammerlock across his throat while my adversary tried to throw him off. The delay was long enough for me to recover and extract some recompense from him, and from his little sidekick who had also joined in, before the stewards separated us and threw us out. We had always looked after each other at sea too, so there was a strong bond between us.

I returned from my reverie when Alfie offered me a cigarette. I lit it and then suggested that we go and find out how well our racing expert was doing.

'Come on, Alf,' I encouraged him. 'Let's go and see how much money I've got coming to me.' We strolled over to the betting area.

'Well, where's my winnings?' I enquired of my buddy.

Charlie looked sideways at me, then glanced down at his near-empty glass in an embarrassed fashion. 'Why, the cheating bastards!' he exploded. 'That race was a fiddle.'

'Huh, aren't they all?' I retorted. 'What went wrong this time?'

'The jockey must have held her back,' Charlie tried to placate me. 'She was going strong with the leaders, running easy, they reckon, but she didn't make much effort at the finish. The jockey must have been told to hold her back for a better price next time she runs. You keep an eye on her when you see her running again and get your money on her. You'll clean up next time.'

'You're kidding,' I burst out. 'Next time I'm in a club and I see that running, so will I.'

Alfie chipped in, 'Let's all sit down at a table and I'll buy you a drink.'

Charlie and I sat at a table, while Alfie went to the bar.

'I hope that's settled you for the afternoon,' I admonished him. 'No more backing the horses.'

'Oh, don't worry!' Charlie reassured me. 'I shan't be following them anymore. It's a mug's game, and besides I've no money left, but I fancy me chances in that domino school in the corner, if you'll lend me another quid.'

I started another fit of coughing. Whether it was the cigarette that Alfie had given me or Charlie's last remark, I'm not sure, but I chose to ignore it anyway. 'Listen buddy, you're going to have to go down the dock tomorrow and start looking for another ship. You can't draw any dole, you know, because you signed off yourself, you weren't sacked,' I reminded him.

'We'll all have to go down the dock,' chipped in Alfie, who had just returned with the beers.

'No, not this chap,' retorted Charlie, jerking a thumb at me. 'This guy is studying for his bosun's ticket tomorrow.'

'You what!' blurted Alfie. 'Already? You're not old enough, are yer?'

'Oh yes,' I smiled. 'I want to be the youngest skipper out of Hull if possible, and my dream starts tomorrow.'

'How long do you reckon, about five weeks?' asked Alf.

'Hmmm, well! Everything would have to fall into place just right to do it in that time,' I countered. 'Could be five or maybe six.'

'Anyway, it'll give you a chance to get rid of that shocking cough and stop you spreading germs all over the place.' I took that as a show of concern from Charlie but for whom I wasn't quite sure.

'Well, I'm going to sup up and slip home before tea. There's some things I want to do. Are you coming, Chuck? We can meet for a night out later.' I grabbed my glass and started to quaff it down.

'I'm not going just yet,' decided Charlie. 'I think I can nurse this drink a little bit longer.'

As I stood up, I took pity and threw a pound on the table in front of Charlie. 'Thanks, Bob. I'll add this to the fiver and pay you back later,' he called after me as I left the club.

After I'd sorted out a protractor, some compasses and other writing materials for school the next day, and enjoyed a lovely evening meal with the family, I smartened myself up, then went in search of Charlie. I found him at home, but he had only just arrived there and was grabbing himself a quick snack. While he was eating, he stuffed his hand in his back pocket, pulled out a wad of notes and threw six of them towards me on the table.

'There you are, Bob. That's what I owe you, and I can still have a night out and not worry about going down the dock tomorrer.' He gave me a big grin.

I looked closely at the wad as he put it back in his pocket. 'Don't tell me you won that lot gambling after I left you?' A bigger grin and a cackle gave me the answer. I was flabbergasted.

'How much is there?'

'About fifty quid.'

'Not all on the dominoes.'

'Well, that and the other.'

"So your vow didn't last very long then.'

'Ah well! There was a rank outsider called Big Time Bob, and after the way you'd lashed out on the nags earlier I couldn't ignore it, could I?' Charlie threw his head back and guffawed till he was red in the face, and in view of the result I had to grin too.

'So where do you intend to blow that lot tonight?' I asked.

'I thought we'd go to the St Andrew's Club for a start and see some of the lads. There's a group playing country and western on there tonight. Then later on I want to go to the Albert Hall.'

'*Where?*' My blurted query was in response to that last venue. The Albert Hall was a first-floor beer hall, as far removed in style from its grandiose name as it was possible to get. It was frequented in general by the rougher element and by loose ladies, plus maybe one or two curious deckies because some amusing antics were performed on the mike there by the clientele.

'You know,' continued Charlie, 'that concert place up some stairs down Midland Street. I understand there's a sexy blonde goes in there, that's red hot. I fancy me chances.'

'Oh great! And what am I supposed to do, if you score?' I asked.

'You'll be alright. We'll take a couple of the lads. You might spot some other crumpet while we're there,' Charlie reassured me.

The chances of that would be pretty remote, I fancied.

Our first call, the St Andrew's Club, was well-appointed, with a clean, smart interior and rather plush carpets. Due to its position in the dockland area, it was well frequented by fishermen and was often used as a meeting place, though the entertainment was also good if you wanted to remain. As usual, it was pretty full when we arrived, but we spotted a small table near the middle of the concert room, with three ex-shipmates sitting at it and a stool free, so we headed for that. Two of the guys I knew as Pete and Meggsy, the latter because his second name was Megginson or something; the other guy I knew only by sight, but his name turned out to be Colin.

'Now then, Pete,' Charlie greeted him as we approached the table. 'Do you mind if we join you?'

'Hiya, Charlie. Sure, if you grab a stool from somewhere, you and Bob come and sit down.'

Pete continued. 'What ship are you in at the moment?'

'Hardship,' quipped Charlie. 'We both signed off the *Apollo* after doing two or three trips with the Sea Beast.'

'The *Apollo*,' repeated Meggsy. 'Oh! You mean Larsen. Yeah, he is a bit of a beast in't eeh. So you're looking for a change, are yer?'

'Well *I am*,' responded Charlie, 'but Bob here is sitting for his bosun's ticket.'

'Good on yer, Bob,' chipped in Pete. 'I thought it wouldn't be long before you followed in your father's footsteps. So, another two or three years and maybe you'll be another sea beast screaming at us, eh!'

'Who? Not me, Pete,' I said, sitting down. 'You know me. I shall be an absolute daddy, with coffee-breaks every two hours, you'll see.' We all laughed at that one.

I looked around at the crowded room, mostly fishermen and their hangers-on, and a few groups of girls hoping for a free night out. If they could pick up a couple of young deckies who had just landed, then the town was theirs for the asking if they played their cards right. The fishermen were the ones with the money, as they nearly all earned two to three times as much as a shore guy; it's *time* they were always short of. This meant they had to move fast when meeting up with girls, and so were always regarded as being cheeky but generous; they would often buy whatever a girl wanted if they were drunk enough. Now, if a girl was lucky enough to pick up a share-man, that is a skipper or mate, then she was really in the big time.

As I looked around, I noticed a table with three girls sitting on their own, among them a very attractive, slightly-built, dark-haired, elfin-looking girl with cute almond eyes, rather like Brigitte Bardot. She had that bunny top lip that just showed the bottom of her two front teeth, but it was full and pouting, like she was halfway to giving you a kiss all the time.

This little doll might be slightly built, but she certainly swelled out in the right places and was very protruding up top. I rather fancied getting to know that little number and my eyes kept drifting in her direction. The country and western group came on, with drums, double bass and two guitars; and, as they went through their repertoire, elfin-face became aware that I was ogling her. Her head dropped down into a giggle, while she passed the information on to her friend. The lads at our table noticed I had my eye on someone. When I pointed out the little group that held my attention, Colin looked round and revealed, 'Oh, that's me sister and her friend, but I don't know who the little dark one is.'

'That's a pity,' I remarked, 'because that's the one whose name I'd like to know.'

'Well, we can find that out later,' Colin assured me.

As we continued to listen to the music and exchange fishing news we all bought a round of pints; only Charlie and I added rum chasers to the order as we were the last to settle. During this period Colin's sister came to the table to tell him she had spoken to his girlfriend earlier, who had said she was going to Dee Street Club with friends and would wait for him there. It was at this stage we learnt that his sister's name was Mary and her mate's name was Sylvia. The other girl was Jacqueline, or Jackie for short, and she had only recently moved into town.

I was still resolved to get to know Jackie, if the chance occurred.

When the country group stopped for a breather, the resident compere came on and started miming to 'Mule Train,' cracking a tiny whip from a little girl's whip-and-top game. It was at this point that we decided to move on.

'*We're* going on to the Albert Hall,' announced Charlie. 'Colin's going to meet his girl. What're you other two doing?'

'You're going *where?*' asked Pete.

'The Albert Hall,' repeated Charlie. 'Do you know it?'

'Yer, I know it,' said Pete with emphasis, 'a right dump.'

'He's heard there's a sexy blonde that get's in there,' I interrupted.

Then both together Pete and Meggsy chimed in. 'Oh, ho! You mean Marlene!'

'Oh yes, she's sexy alright,' continued Pete. 'She's red hot. If you can get into bed with her, she'll draw all the juices out o' yer, you can bet. But only if she fancies yer. She may be loose but she can take her pick.'

'Sounds like my type o' gal,' enthused Chas.

We broke up and Colin went across to talk to his sister while the rest of us left together.

The taxi dropped us outside a narrow open doorway that revealed a short, narrow passage, with a closed door to the right and a dingy stairway leading up. From above could be heard a keyboard and drums, trying to keep time with someone who appeared to be demonstrating the screech of a trapped cockerel to the tune of Johnny Ray's 'Cry.'

'This should be a laugh, if nothing else,' chuckled Charlie, as we mounted the stairs.

At the top, we passed through a door with a frosted-glass panel and entered a large, uncarpeted room with worn wooden floor boards. It looked as though in better days it might have been a dance studio, but there were no mirrored walls now; they were bare plaster painted with yellow distemper. The far right-hand corner was completely taken up with a foot-high dais, occupied by a cig-chewing bloke behind a set of drums, and a fairly tidy guy – except for his collar-length hair – playing an electric keyboard. At the front of the stage, there was an intoxicated, scruffy youth in a semi-comatose state, clinging to a mike.

He was dressed in a shabby, open mackintosh, but it was his body language that made you realise why the majority of the patrons were laughing and tittering. With body leaning back like a boomerang, and eyes closed, he endeavoured to take us with him from his apparently sad state, 'to the sunshine that can be found behind a cloudy sky.'

There was a bar along the wall to the right of the door, and the seating and tables – which were made up of all sorts – were set out in three groups around the room, leaving the centre free, presumably for dancing, if any of the clients were capable. One group of tables stood in front of the bar, which was where we sat along with the majority. Along the wall directly opposite were two long tables with chairs behind them and wooden forms in front. The other group of tables were arranged along the wall on the left of the room; only two of them were occupied.

We looked around to see if there was anyone of interest among the sparse occupants of the premises. The place was barely a quarter full, mostly fellas.

Most of the women were accompanied by men, except for a couple of little groups of fish-house lasses that had obviously come here for a laugh and some cheap booze.

'So much for the sexy talent,' I sighed, as two of the lads ordered drinks at the bar.

'Never mind. Enjoy the talent on stage, instead,' quipped Charlie, with a wry smirk.

When Pete and Meggsy came back to the table, they had the same grievance. 'Well, apart from cheaper beer, I can't see much point in wanting to come here,' moaned Meggsy.

'Hang on a minute,' interrupted Pete. 'I think the reason we're here just walked in.'

We all turned our heads towards the door to observe the two women clipping in on the new stiletto heels. The first to enter was a brunette, her hair long, straight and flicked up at the shoulder. She had a rosy complexion and no make-up, a stocky build and thick-ish, though shapely, legs, which were shown off with a thigh-hugging skirt to the knee, instead of the usual full or pleated skirt worn by most women. The second woman was the eye-catcher. It was not the fact that she was a natural blonde, the flowing hair was uncropped and ragged at the ends. Nor was it the lovely face with its creamy complexion – again with no make-up, except for a glossy lipstick – and the determined, well-sculptured jaw-line. Nor was it the superb figure, shown off again by a tight-fitting skirt with a slit up the side, and a fluffy shoulder jacket. It was the grey-blue flashing eyes, looking at you with amused confidence, and the way she moved that oozed sex and the love of it.

Both women were fairly tall, even without the high heels. They moved towards the tables on the left and sat down directly opposite us. As they took their place either side of the small table, each sideways on to us, the six-inch vent in Marlene's skirt (for that's obviously who it was), nearly reached up to her stocking tops when she crossed her legs.

The lads made it obvious they were interested with their blatant ogling, but Marlene just observed us quietly, with a little smile showing at the corner of her lips. I was having no part of this panting and slobbering, and decided to play it cool by relaxing back in my chair and displaying an air of nonchalance, which was not entirely false. There was no denying she was attractive and sexy, but I fancied she had far too much experience for my liking.

Pretty soon the barman came from behind the bar to serve the women personally with their drinks, proof if any were needed that they were regulars. All this time the entertainment went on, with a grey, bewhiskered old lag, wearing trousers two sizes too big, tied up round the waist with an old tie, trying to croak 'On Mother Kelly's Doorstep'. Although they were choking with laughter throughout, the fish-house lasses and some others threw a few coins on to the dais for his next beer when he finished.

The boys had been baiting Marlene and her friend, asking if they were going to give a turn on the stage, but they were not getting a lot in return. Then, during this lull in the music, Marlene suddenly pointed at me and blurted out, 'I fancy him. I think I'll have him tonight.'

This raised a surprised sort of cheer from my mates, as they looked to me for a response. I realised it required some saucy remark, so all I could do was to open my arms and say, 'Come on, help yourself,' knowing she wouldn't.

By this time a new artiste had taken the stage, in the shape of a very overweight little lass from one of the fish-house groups. She was obviously a regular performer, judging by the cheer she got from other members around the tables and the muttered remarks of 'It's daft Jean.'

Jean started singing 'If You Loved Me Half As Much As I Loved You'; but she kept adding the words 'If you do, if you do' and jumping up and down to the music. This caused her rather ample breasts to bounce up and down so much we were all transfixed, waiting to see if they were actually going to hit her in the face. Our attention was soon distracted, however, when three figures drifted past us and took up position behind the tables with the forms in front – well away from anyone else. We were startled to see it was the girls from the St Andrew's Club – Mary, Sylvia and Jackie. As they settled in and looked across at us, I automatically lifted my hand and gave a little wave to Mary, and right away she *and Jackie* responded. I was delighted at the wave from Jackie; this certainly proved she was interested.

I was determined to introduce myself to Jackie, so I thought I'd go across and offer to buy the girls a drink. If I was going to do it, I'd better do it now. Jumping up from my chair, I set off across the open floor, and as I did so Mary left the group and went to the bar.

Smiling as I approached the table, I swung one leg over the wooden form on my side of the table and straddled it as I asked Sylvia and Jackie if I could buy them a drink. Too late, it seemed, as Mary had gone to get them.

'What are you girls doing here?' I asked, as if scandalised. 'I wouldn't have thought sophisticated girls like you would risk being seen in a place like this.' I was looking directly at Jackie.

She giggled and blushed. 'Well, the girls thought I should see how the other half lived, to broaden the mind, sort o'speak. But what about you, what are you doing here?'

'Well, the same as you really. It's the first time I've been in here. Just came this once to see the antics on stage we've heard about.'

'Oh! So you don't know any of these people?' Jackie's eyes were flicking over my shoulder.

I knew where she was looking. 'No,' I grinned, 'I've never seen any of these people before.'

Just then I felt someone straddle the form behind me and put their arm around my waist. Marlene's chin was on my left shoulder. 'Now then!' she said. 'I think we had an agreement that I was to help myself, right?' With that she shot her hand down the front of my waistband and got a handful of all that is dear to me.

I shot up, along with my eyebrows. Then, clasping my hands in front of me, I quickly sat down again so as not to attract attention. While I grappled to restrain the hand within my clothing, I hissed over my shoulder at Marlene, *'What do you think you are doing? People are watching.'*

'I thought you said you didn't know anyone?' Sylvia's contemptuous voice cut in.

'I didn't, I don't,' I tried to assure her.

'Well, *she* certainly knows *you* now,' she snarled, as she stood up. 'Come on, Jackie. I think it's time we left.' They moved over to the bar and collected Mary, who glanced over at me with a look of pure distain as she cancelled the drinks and they clipped their way out in a huff.

My crestfallen eyes followed them out as they passed behind the guys, who were falling about in breath-choking mirth, witnesses to the complete destruction of my attempts at being a Don Juan.

Marlene withdrew her hand, having disposed of the competition. I swung round on her.

Her eyes sparkled at me, she flicked up her eyebrows and gave an approving nod and smirk.

'What's the idea?' I snorted indignantly.

'I wanna go to a party,' she replied promptly. 'Can any of your pals organise one?' She moved quickly across to them with me in tow.

Pete had already been chatting up Marlene's friend, Brenda, thinking, I guess, that there would be less competition, and he had been very encouraged. So when Marlene suggested a bit of a party he volunteered his house. 'My parents are out of town at a do themselves and won't be back until the early hours. There's only Gran at home and she'll be in bed by the time we get there.'

'Well, if we can get some booze from here to take out, we've cracked it,' said Charlie. 'It should be cheap enough. What can we get you to drink, darling?' he asked Marlene, sidling up to her and slipping his arm round her waist.

'We both like Babycham.' Marlene swept her face round close to his to give him a waft of her perfume. 'So if you can get six or eight of them that should be OK for a start.'

The silly, dreamy smile on Charlie's face assured her she would get what she wanted, so she disengaged herself and went across to Brenda for a confab.

We boys soon pooled some money to get a bag of booze to take out, and when the taxi arrived we enjoyed all squeezing in, much to the cabby's distress, for the short ride to Pete's house.

Pete lived in one of the large, old three-bedroomed houses down Constable Street, in the centre of the fishing area, just off Hessle Road. On the ground floor, apart from the main living room, it had a front room opening off the hall passageway, and a kitchen-cum-washhouse in a large lean-to extension at the back.

We followed Pete right out of the taxi, through the front door and straight into the living room, which contained a large table, a settee in a bay window behind it, an easy chair to one side of the fireplace, and the obligatory radiogram in the recess at the other side.

Pete and Brenda, having improved their acquaintance in the taxi, lost no time in getting to grips with each other and dived into a clinch on the sofa. Once the booze was unloaded on the table, both Charlie and Meggsy, having got no response from Pete, started to search a bureau for a bottle-opener.

Marlene slipped her little jacket off and threw it on the back of the easy chair; then, quickly weighing up the situation and seeing the boys preoccupied, she grabbed me by the hand and led me through the door out into the back scullery, taking the key out of the door as we passed. Once we were out in the darkened lean-to, she closed the door and gently turned the key in the lock. We did not search for the light switch. The only light we had was reflected from the living-room bay window into the yard and back through the scullery window, but it was enough for us to see what the room contained.

Marlene immediately swung round and flung her arms around my neck. Then, laying her body into mine, she pulled my head down and gave me a lovely juicy kiss. Her tongue played on my lips and teeth, forcing my mouth open so that her tongue could spar with mine. At the same time, she was grinding her pelvis into me, which quickly brought about the desired result. Then this brazen sex-bomb slid her hand down to my fly buttons; she knew she had to work quickly for it would not be long before we were interrupted. I glanced over her shoulder, looking for a place where we could recline. There was none, but there was a mangle with a wooden washboard protruding, so I backed Marlene up to that and sliding her skirt up, perched her bottom onto it.

At this point, someone started rattling at the doorknob that led to the living room; the boys had realised where we were. I continued where Marlene had left off and undid the rest of my fly buttons, and after a bit more fiddling about my erection sprang free. Now there was shouting and banging at the door; they were telling us to come out. Not likely, I thought, I haven't got in yet.

A voice said, 'We can get to them through the back yard. Quick, out the front door.' We heard feet scampering away. I was fumbling about with Marlene's knicker-leg, trying to pull it to one side; we were both breathing heavily, full of desire and desperate for me to enter. I wondered if the door into the yard was locked. We had never checked and now was not the time. Marlene was squirming into a better position for me to enter her, and I was probing – then there was a patter of feet down the side passageway and a rattling at the back gate.

'Someone's pushed the bolt in,' said Charlie's voice. He was right; both Marlene and I gasped as I slid into her.

Then Meggsy, who knew the house better, spoke. 'I think the bolt is near the top of the door, if you put your hand over.' We could here some scrabbling as they tried to reach it.

I was in seventh heaven, the ecstasy heightened by the excitement and danger. Could I bring myself to abort at a time like this? We knew we would be on view through the window as soon as the gate was opened.

'Let's nip back through the door and find somewhere else before they spot us,' Marlene whispered. Reluctantly I withdrew, and we unlocked the door and scampered through, relocking it behind us. Neither Pete nor Brenda even saw us, so busy were they with their own fumbling. I noticed Pete's coat was placed strategically across their middle, as we dashed right through and into the hall, intending to explore the front room.

We entered the darkened room with care, but the street light filtering through the net curtains showed it wasn't occupied. It also revealed a couch in the centre. Everything else escaped me. No time was lost as we dropped on to the sofa. We were both already aroused; Marlene prepared to speed things up by slipping her panties down over her heels, and I also gave myself more freedom. We knew our time was still limited. Briefly, I thought of Charlie and Meggsy; if they had managed to open the back gate, they would be peering through the scullery window, trying to identify us, or maybe they had come up against the locked living-room door again.

In moments I had re-entered her, and that exquisite feeling was pulsating through me again – enhanced by the expert gyrations of my partner's pelvis. Unfortunately, all too soon we were spent. I collapsed, gasping, on top of Marlene, cushioned by her well-padded breasts. She, too, was breathing heavily until she thrust me off unceremoniously and sat up to replace her pants.

Feet clattered into the hallway and the door was flung open; the boys had guessed right this time. They flicked on the light and strode into the room. Charlie was furious and glared at me. 'What sort of a caper's this, then?' he snarled. 'We all contributed to this so-called fucking party, you know.' Marlene stood up. 'I'm thirsty. I'm going to get a drink if that's OK with you,' she said, as she brushed past him. Charlie rounded on me again. 'You're a right pal. I'm going away tomorrow, but you'll be home. She should have been mine tonight. You'll have plenty of opportunity.'

'Well! She could still be yours,' I tried to calm him. 'Marlene is insatiable. By the time she's had a couple of drinks, she'll be radgy again and looking for a new conquest. If you play your cards right, it could be you.' This seemed to pacify him and he scampered after her.

The next morning I was supposed to register and start at Nautical School, but I had also agreed to meet Charlie during lunchbreak in the old Criterion pub.

When I reported to Glanville, he already had his little group of decky learners practising net-mending. The morning sessions concentrated on trawl and gear maintenance and these boys were studying and practising for their second-class net-mending certificate, which I had done when I sat for my decky learner's ticket. For a bosun's ticket I would be required to pass a first-class net-mending certificate. The boys would learn not only how to mend tears in the trawl, but also how to make fly meshes and backhanded fly meshes, which ran along the edge of the trawl wings.

Glanville knew I had done all this and asked me if I remembered it all and had used my knowledge. I assured him I had, so he wasted no time on that for me. He just pulled out a full top part, slashed out one of the two quarters (the most difficult part of a trawl) and told me to try and mend it correctly by studying the other quarter. If I couldn't, he would come and help me. I had observed many deck-hands struggle with this part of the net at sea, and occasionally some mates, but in the comfort of the classroom, with no rolling deck and no seas slopping over the rail, I knew I could take my time and figure it out.

Occasionally Glanville would come and look over my shoulder, and maybe point out a quicker way to do something, but on the whole he seemed happy with my progress. When I'd finished, he was more than satisfied, as I had only made a couple of minor mistakes.

'That's brilliant, Bob,' he enthused, 'considering you worked it out for yourself with no instruction. I don't think we need to waste much more time on net-mending. I'll move you on to wire splicing straight away.'

This was great. If I could continue to progress like this, it would be a doddle.

The Criterion was only a ten-minute walk away from the school and I ate my sandwich on the way. When I entered the bar, Charlie was nowhere to be seen. But, while I was getting served with a pint, I looked around and who should I see but Freddy Nott and Alfie, my snooker pal, both sitting at a small table rolling fags. They looked up when I approached.

'Hiya, Dasher,' beamed Freddy. 'What are you doing here? Someone said you were sitting for your ticket. Come and join us.'

'By 'eck,' I said, a little surprised, 'the word soon gets round. I am sitting for my ticket. I'm at school now, but it's lunch break and I'm supposed to be meeting my mate Charlie.' I sat down with them and Freddy offered me his pouch. 'Here, have a roll while you're waiting, I reckon he'll turn up soon.'

'Not if he has to pass a bookmaker's,' chipped in Alfie, grinning at me.

Criterion. [*Paul Gibson Collection*]

I rolled myself a cig; I didn't smoke a great deal, and when I did it was usually tailor-mades.

Fred gave me a light and I took a big drag, which was a mistake. The smoke seared the back of my throat and I started coughing.

'Oh ho! Can't handle the men's stuff, eh?' Freddy grinned and started to puff more on his own cig, as if to prove a point.

'No, it just went down the wrong way,' I insisted, clearing my throat. I took another drag with the same result – another bout of coughing. 'Bloody hell! What is this stuff?' I demanded.

'Wadda ya think? It's Old Friend, what everyone smokes,' jeered Freddy.

'Your old friend's socks more like, by the taste of it,' I replied.

'Hey up! Here's Charlie,' interrupted Alfie.

We turned to observe Charlie amble into the bar, with a glassy stare in his eyes. 'Looks like he's already had a few,' Alfie continued. 'Here, Chas. We're over here,' he sang out.

Charlie's head swung round; he focused on us and then swayed in our direction.

We pulled up a stool for him and he sat down to join us.

'Looks like you've started early,' I admonished him.

'I've had one or two,' said Charlie, purposely looking around the room to indicate his disdain for my remark, 'and as I'm going away tonight and won't be getting any for a while I might have one or two more.'

'In that case,' said Freddy, 'let *me* buy you a drink.' Fred didn't know Charlie particularly, but that's the way it was with fishermen; we were all buddies suffering for the same cause.

'What'll you have, Dash?' he continued. 'Same again?'

'No, not for me thanks, Fred. Not if I've to get back to college this afternoon.'

Fred took an order from the other two and moved off towards the bar.

I turned towards Charlie. 'Now, what's this about you going away tonight? A bit quick isn't it? What ship?'

'Well, if you're skint, there's no point in hanging about, so I've changed companies and signed on the *Loch Oskaig*.'

'The what!' I started coughing again. 'Why have you signed on that old rustbucket? She's always breaking down and seldom makes anything. Who kidded you to join her?'

'Well, I met up with some old friends who've signed on and they kidded me to go with them just for the laugh. They figure I'll be fishroom man, so that'll be more experience for me.'

'It'll be an experience alright. You might as well have stayed at home a bit longer, even without any cash.'

The irritation in my throat and the cough persisted, so I made my excuses. 'I'll have to get back,' I told Charlie, 'but I'll see you off tonight, OK.' I finished the dregs in my glass, acknowledged the lads and left.

Once outside the pub, the cool air seemed to hit my chest and prompted such a violent fit of coughing that I had to lean against the wall while I bent over and nearly brought the beer back up. I wasn't sick as such, but I must have done some damage because I started spewing out some blood. As I still leant over, catching my breath and looking at the splotch of blood that stained the pavement, I figured that I must have burst a little blood vessel in my throat. An elderly lady passing by stopped and asked if I was alright. As I was recovering I assured her I was, but she took a good look at the blood and said, 'I'd check that out with a doctor if I was you, luv.' Then she moved off on her way.

I was quite recovered by the time I got back to the school and that afternoon began with chart work, which I loved. As a youngster, I had messed about with my father's charts, and he had taught me the basics and some of the abbreviations, so I was well able to understand what Glanville was talking about. Of course, I was the only one doing chart work, as I was the only one sitting for bosun's at the time, so he was able to leave me with various tutorial books and papers, while he concentrated on his decky learners, though making himself available to me at all times. We finished the afternoon with flags and semaphore, which I had learnt as a boy scout, so I could sit back and take it easy for a time.

That night, when I got home, I told them of the day's events, how silly Charlie had been and how I intended to go and see him off. I also mentioned the coughing blood affair, which caused a bit of a flap with my mother, who insisted that I should see a doctor. I said I would do some time, but that didn't satisfy her, so she said she would make the appointment for me herself.

Charlie and I spent the evening at the St Andrew's Club, watching the entertainment and chatting to friends and their girlfriends; so, of course, there was plenty of ale flowing. Chas was due to sail on the midnight tide and was ordered aboard for eleven o'clock, so it was up to me to make sure he didn't go further astray when they called time. It was only with the help of a friendly taxi driver, and the support of our friends and a large fish bass of booze which had been donated by previous shipmates that I managed to get the now well-inebriated Charles away from the club and back home for his kitbag.

As happened far too often, when we arrived at the Fish Dock we found the *Oskaig* tied up outside a ship that was refitting. Any ship that is on survey or refitting is always well out of the water because she has no stores or fuel on board. Normally climbing on and over them is a problem, but in this case it didn't appear so. The ship was fended off to allow for painting the sides, so a gangway had been provided that reached up to the rail at an angle of forty degrees. It was very rare that a gangway was ever used on trawlers, and fishermen were not used to them, as Charlie was about to prove.

When the taxi dropped us on the quay opposite the ship Charlie managed to scramble out and hump his kitbag on to his shoulder, while I was left to collect his bass of booze and the new gear he had collected from the store. After I had made arrangements for the cabbie to come back later and collect me, I turned around to see Charlie taking his first tentative steps on the foot of the gangway; he was swaying about perilously. I called out for him to wait till I caught him up so that I could help, but Charles was deep in concentration, trying to focus on the ridged slope giving him access to the deck above. His left hand held the lanyard of the kitbag hanging from his left shoulder, while the right hand repeatedly clasped the rope handrail on the gangway as he hauled himself up.

Halfway up, he suddenly swayed much too far to his left, and the added weight of his kitbag had him toppling over. The strange thing was that he never relinquished his grip on either kitbag or handrope, with the result that the gangway turned over completely and left Charlie suspended upside down with his feet still on the gangway. This vision was both hilarious and incredible, as the cackle from the taxi driver confirmed. 'Well, I'm fucked if I've ever seen anything like that,' he howled.

I hadn't either, and I was puzzled to know how it had come about. Then I realised that the kitbag, still on Charlie's shoulder, had made contact with the edge of the quay and was in fact propping him up. Charlie wasn't moving – he was bemused as to where he was and how he was – but I could see that if he tried to extricate himself he was going to topple right into the dock. I dropped everything and dashed forward to grab hold of him and lower him to the ground.

'What the f-fuck happened there, huh? For a moment I thought I was in Australia,' he quipped. Good job I wasn't carrying the booze.'

'For a moment I thought you were in the dock,' I snapped. 'Let's take a bit more care and get you safely on board.'

With a struggle I did manage to get him and his gear on board and was able to guide him down the steep fo'c'sle ladder to the dingy dungeon below. There were three or four souls down there already, each squatting on the bunkside benches, with either a beer bottle or a dram glass in hand. The drink was inevitable when you looked around; all would be depressed without it, at the thought of living in this confined, stinking place. The *Loch Oskaig* was an old ship and the accommodation reflected that; it was smaller and grimier than most, and impregnated with the smell not only of fish and engine oil but of body odour as well.

As Charlie hailed a couple of the lads he knew and plonked himself down among them, searching in his bass for a beer, I looked around at the large oilskin bags containing the crew's waterproofs that filled every spare space. I noted the hatch cover in the centre of the room, which led down, no doubt, into a lower store or dill. This normally held spare bobbins and cables and other ironware that would constantly clatter when the ship was on the move, and would have to be brought up through the fo'c'sle whenever needed – regardless of who was watch below. I also noticed another covered hatchway in the forward bulkhead, which I knew would lead into the anchor cable locker next door; just something else to add to the cacophony when she got out to sea. I knew well what the pitching would be like at this end of the ship and I thanked my lucky stars that I had the chance to move aft from all this when I got my ticket.

By the time the call came to stand by on deck, they were all beyond feeling any pain, so I said my goodbyes and wished them all good luck, then skipped thankfully over the rail and back on to the quay. The old *Oskaig* was moving out through the lock before my taxi got back to pick me up, and I watched her in the murky light of the dockside floodlights as she slid silently by, except for an occasional tinkle on the telegraph. Charlie stood on the fore-deck, one hand in his pocket, the other still holding a half-consumed bottle of beer, which he raised to me in salute, a big grin on his face. 'Aye! You won't be grinning come watch time,' I thought, as I waved back. 'Good morning, Charlie. See you next trip.'

My studies at college were still going well, but Glanville warned me against getting over-confident and continued to double-check all that I did. I wasn't finding anything a problem and, although my cough persisted, I didn't have any recurrence of blood. Nevertheless, mother had booked an appointment with our doctor, so I was obliged to go and hope he could give me something for the cough. He knew about the blood, but I explained that it was a particularly heavy bout of coughing that had brought it on, and there had been no recurrence, so I figured it had been a burst blood vessel. Even so he insisted I had an X-ray and a sputum test. Quite unnecessary, I thought, but I had to go along with it, so that was another interruption to my studies.

Probably the most difficult part of the bosun's ticket was learning the articles and rules for preventing collisions at sea. There were thirty-two of these sailing rules, each containing an average of three or four paragraphs, and each had to be understood and learned word for word. Most evenings, then, would see me repeating these to any member of the family who would listen. Only occasionally would I have a night out with the lads when they came home, for time was of the essence for me.

All the other parts of the certificate were going well and, as I began to master most of the articles, Glanville and I began to discuss when I might apply to be examined.

'You're ahead of the time given, so unless you're tight for money why not wait a week or two and brush up on everything until you feel a hundred percent?' suggested my tutor.

'Well, I feel pretty confident on nearly everything. It's only the articles I'm not quite a hundred percent sure on, and I will be by the time I'm examined,' I assured him.

We decided that he would give me a mock exam over the next week, and I would put my papers in the following week.

When I got home that night it was the end of the week and I told my family of my intentions. It was all very exciting. They, in turn, had some good news; the doctor had been in touch and said nothing could be found on the X-ray to cause concern, though he was still waiting for the result from the lab. I wasn't sure what they were looking for, unless it was this so-called consumption I had heard about.

I don't know whether it was the thought of actually preparing to sit for my ticket that motivated me, but that weekend I spent little time on leisure in the pubs and clubs; instead I concentrated on studying at home.

Come Monday morning, Glanville had laid out a chart and various question papers for the first part of my test. He obviously intended to make this as real as possible.

Over the next couple of days, the tests continued on navigation, signals and ship construction. I appeared to come out with flying colours on each; so, over the next day or two, if Glanville decided to continue, I would be tested on the rule of the road at sea and anti-collision regulations. It was obvious that Glanville was going to test me on nearly all the thirty-two articles. At the beginning of the next day, I found several sheets of paper divided into boxes, each showing the navigation lights one would see during darkness; I then had to describe the vessel or craft and what it was doing. It was so easy to get this wrong if you didn't concentrate, so the morning passed quickly, but come lunchtime Glanville told me the office had received a message for me to go home or phone urgently.

I had no desire to go home in the middle of these mock exams, but I was struck with fear in case something had happened to Mum or there had been an accident. I found my way to a phone quickly. My sister answered in some consternation. It appeared the doctor had been in touch; he had received the results of my sputum tests and his orders were for me to go straight to bed.

'Why?' I enquired.

'We're not sure why, but that they were the doctor's orders,' she insisted, 'until he can get round to report in full.'

'Nonsense!' I responded. 'It's not as if I'm going to drop down dead this afternoon. Anyway, how long am I supposed to go to bed for? I'm not going to interfere with my work at school just now. We'll sort this out tonight, meantime calm down.' I finished the call at that.

That afternoon I warned Glanville that I might have to miss a day or two at school, if the doctor decided to do some tests. I could only be vague about it because I didn't know what was going to happen, but I was determined it would not delay things long.

I spent the following day in bed, impatiently waiting for the doctor. He didn't arrive till teatime.

'Where,' I asked him, 'was the need for me to be wasting my time lying in bed, when I had an important examination coming up?'

'Don't start worrying about the examination just now,' he warned. 'There are more important things to worry about.'

'Like what?' I insisted.

'Well, your results have come back and they're positive.' He spit the last word out and waited for my reaction.

'So what does that mean?' I shrugged.

'It means,' he said testily, 'that you've got it!'

'Got what?'

The doc was visibly taken aback at this question and looked at me suspiciously before replying with just one word. 'TB,' he said, standing at the bottom of the bed, with arms folded.

'OK, so what does that mean?' I pressed on.

The doctor expelled a long puff of air that suggested exasperation. 'Look, you've got TB, tuberculosis. It's a serious condition that's hard to cure. People have died of it.'

I was a bit taken aback at this. I had heard of tuberculosis, but I knew nothing about it. It was something that poor, deprived people got. I began to realise that I wouldn't be able to sit my exam the next week. I squared my shoulders and decided to face up to it. 'So! What do you recommend? What's the next step?' I challenged the doc.

'Well, as nothing showed up on that last X-ray we took, it suggests you may not be badly infected. But we must try to find out where it is, so I'll organise a series of X-rays at the hospital. Meantime you have to stay in bed and build yourself up so that with treatment your body can fight off the disease.'

'You mean I have to stay in bed all day? Every day?'

'Of course,' insisted the doctor. 'You have to give your lungs as little work as possible, if you want to get rid of this.'

I was crestfallen. This was beginning to look as if it might take a while. 'OK Doc, I'll work at it,' I promised. 'How many weeks do you think it might take?' I added hopefully.

The doctor took a step back and stood with a grim smile on his face as he studied me and assessed my naivety. 'Well – it could be a long time. It depends what we find in this series of X-rays. Just be patient till we find out what's what.'

'Don't worry, Doc,' I assured him. 'I'm a good healer. If there's going to be any records broken for curing this disease, I want to be the one to do it. I've a bosun's ticket to get through as soon as poss.'

Little did I realise that the doctor wasn't thinking in weeks, even if all went well. It was more like months, or even years. He wasn't going to tell me that at this stage, but he probably told the family. The X-rays did eventually reveal a spot at the very bottom of the left lung, and as time went on I was made to realise it was going to be a very long do. Then the family began to reveal that the doctor was recommending that I transfer to a sanatorium!! God! The very sound of the word sent a chill down my spine. Sanatoriums were a last resort, places where people were sent, usually with mental disorders, to be left and forgotten about. There was no way they were going to get me to go into one of those. My sister had been nursing me very well and had built me up to quite a size, putting flesh over the muscle my job had created, and every one of our family friends said I looked good, so I was OK where I was.

Then there was a setback. My mum's health took a turn for the worse and she too became bedridden. It became obvious that her illness was going to be long-term as well. I knew it wasn't fair to the rest of the family for me to remain at home, so I finally agreed to move to the hospital.

There was one consolation. The hospital was not far away, on the outskirts of town, surrounded by greenery and open countryside. Fresh air, it seemed, was a major part of the cure. Well, I'd had plenty of that in my time, so I elected to have my bed out in the open and even slept out there.

I was prepared to do anything I thought would speed my recovery, while they gave me various tests and took numerous X-rays from all directions. The latter were a bit of a bonus really because the girls in the X-ray department were very attractive and very flighty, so I made up my mind that I would find my way into their darkroom as soon as possible, and I told them so.

Among the many tests they performed was one for vital capacity, which tested the volume of your lungs. I did so well on this that the male nurse thought I was cheating; I was still expelling air when the machine had reached its limit. 'You're supposed to do it in one breath,' he insisted, but close observation over two or three attempts made him realise that was exactly what I was doing.

'Gosh!' he gasped. 'Yours are the largest lungs I've ever come across.'

That was encouraging and something worth knowing.

At the end of two months, the head surgeon, Mr Wilson, who was regarded as the top thoracic specialist in the north, and third in the entire country, came to see me to assess the situation.

After running through my file in detail he spoke. 'Good, you seem to be progressing very well. If you continue along at this rate, we could have you cured within the year,' he smiled.

My jaw dropped. 'A year,' I looked at him incredulously, 'you mean I'll have to remain in here a year?'

'Well, I think so. We want to make sure you're completely healed with little chance of it breaking out again.' He appeared firm.

For a moment I was stunned, then I composed myself. 'So after that do you think I will be able to go back to sea?' I asked hopefully.

'Go to sea!' Wilson was genuinely surprised. 'What as? Engine room or something like that?'

'No, I want to go back on deck and work my way up to skipper.'

'What! Go fishing? No, I'm afraid there's no chance of that. You'd better think of something else.'

Wilson certainly didn't beat about the bush.

I was devastated; all my dreams were shattered. I couldn't accept it; there had to be a way.

'Mr Wilson, I'm determined to go back to sea. There must be some chance,' I beseeched him.

Wilson stuck his hands in his white coat-pockets, pursed his lips and studied the bed wheel, which he was kicking about. 'Well-ll! If you're sensible and take great care, it might be possible to go back eventually, as say a steward or something like that, but nothing strenuous.'

'Ugh! A steward? But why? You can see I'm a big strong fella. Why shouldn't I go back?'

'Because the disease might break out again, and in confined spaces it could even infect someone else. That's the problem with this disease. In time to come they may bring out a drug that will completely eradicate it, but at the moment the drugs we have will only heal it enough to control it. All too often people have it break out again in later life.'

Around the ward, I had seen the horrific scars on patients whose lungs had been operated on, so I asked the question. 'What if you were to cut it out?'

'No, I don't think that's an option. You've only got a small infection at the bottom of the lung and to take it out would mean removing a complete lobe, that's half of it. That would be a waste of an otherwise healthy lung. No, we couldn't justify that.'

'But what if it was paid for privately?'

Wilson continued indulgently. 'Well, if a patient came to me and asked for a specific operation he was prepared to pay for, then I would have to consider it seriously. But an operation of this nature requires a lot of qualified people, and takes up quite a few theatre hours. It would cost many hundreds of pounds.' He tapped the covers over my feet. 'I think you would do better rethinking your future, you've plenty of time. Keep up the good work.' He smiled, nodded and moved on.

When each of the family came to visit, I told them Wilson's opinion. Of course, they all felt for me, but I thought my dad was particularly disappointed. He hadn't been very keen for me to follow in his footsteps at first; but, when he saw how hard I had worked at it and how quickly I had moved on, he became very keen for me to succeed. This was a blow for him too and one difficult to resolve. I decided to ask him for extra support.

'Dad,' I looked at him seriously, 'if I asked you to lend me a few hundred pounds for a worthy cause, you'd lend it to me, wouldn't you?'

He looked a little surprised. 'I suppose so, why?'

'Well, you know the surgeon said I should consider my future. I just thought it might take something like that. I just wondered if I could rely on you in that respect.'

He smiled, 'Of course you can.'

'I thought so,' I said, 'thanks.'

After over two months my mates eventually got round to the hospital to see me, though I wasn't surprised as there isn't much time between trips to cram everything in. Naturally the word had spread and they were up to date with my situation.

Both Charlie and Terry came to see me; they had waited until they were both at home before venturing so far off the beaten track. They seemed a little embarrassed about my illness and didn't discuss it very much. Charlie's grin was infectious as he told me about the latest trials and tribulations of his last couple of trips, including some of the pranks the crew had got up to.

'Gosh, I wish you'd been there, Bob,' he enthused. 'It doesn't bear thinking about that we won't be sailing together again.'

'No, I can't believe it either,' Terry agreed. 'I can't imagine you not being on the dock with us, talking the same language.'

'Well, don't be so sure,' I insisted. 'I have a plan, so we shall have to see. Don't you worry –

I'll be back.'

Deep-sea side-trawling, undoubtedly the
most arduous and dangerous profession
of the post-war years is, like the boxmen
of the 1900s, long gone now.
What Arctic fishing there is, is done by
stern-trawlers from sheltered decks,
where fish is gutted or processed below.
So different and risky was the job, often
unprofitable, that one wondered why men
went back to it time after time, except one
noted that the unity and cameraderie were
second to none.